19th Sett

# The Settler's Handbook
## for the U.S. Virgin Islands

### St. Croix, St. John, St. Thomas

## 19 th Edition

For those of you who are
considering settling in this
part of the tropics, or for
those already here,
this handbook provides
an objective look at living,
working, or investing in the
United States Virgin Islands.
For the visitor, this book
should help you get better
acquainted with these islands,
and explore them with a
greater awareness.

**On the cover:**

*"The U.S. Virgin Islands…
a piece of paradise for everyone!"*

Cover design by Pink Elephant Promotions
www.pinkelephantpromotions.com

Special thanks to Ivan Minarik, John Gutierrez
and other photo contributors to this edition.

Library of Congress Control Number
(reverts to Serial #)
ISSN 1554-9739

The Settler's Handbook
19th Edition
is published by
Chey'nanigans, Corp.
1524 Acorn Way, #1G
Solvang, Ca 93643
(888) 867-5979/ (340)277-6994
Publisher: Cheyenne Harty
Editor/Production Manager: Cheyenne Harty/Pink Elephant Promotions
Layout/Graphics/Video: Pink Elephant Promotions
Research Assistant/Asst Editor: Rhonda Roberts Jonas
Sales Manager/Reseach/ Asst Editor: Sandra Harty Gutierrez
info@cheynanigans.com/info@pinkelephantpromotions.com
www.visettlershandbook.com
© 2020 copyright Chey'nanigans Corp. All rights reserved.
Additional copies of this Handbook can be obtained from
Pink Elephant Promotions at P.O. Box 477, C'sted, St. Croix 00821
Quantity prices on request.
The current owner / publisher has revised the e-book in:
February 2020

Every effort has been made to ensure the accuracy and validity of the information contained in this book. We cannot be responsible for accidental errors, omissions or changes in facts or figures made, just prior to, or after, the publishing date. Reproduction in whole or in part of any original material in this book without express written permission of Chey'nanigans Corp. is prohibited.

### Acknowledgements

Much appreciation for the foresight of those who sowed the *VI Settler's Handbook's* first seeds during the early 1970s. That fine idea has continuously blossomed since, and this publisher hopes to continue the tradition. Special acknowledgements to previous publishers: Doug Burns, Gloria Bourne, Judy Megnin, and Linda Bruton for growing this book.

Consultation thanks to historian, William Cissell, various government agency personnel, as well as individuals, non-profits and businesses from the Virgin Islands too numerous to mention. Many thanks to all, past and present, who added a fact or clarification. Your assistance was a godsend.

19th settler's Handbook

# The Settler's Handbook for the U.S. Virgin Islands

# 19th Edition
# TABLE of CONTENTS

Introduction ........................................................................................... v
Chapter 1  **An Overview** ........................................................................ 1
Location, Population, Climate, Geography, History
Chapter 2  **Getting Acquainted** ............................................................ 15
A Look at St. Croix, St. John pg 23, St. Thomas pg 27
Sites, Hotels, Dining, Shopping
Chapter 3  **To Be A Virgin Islander** ...................................................... 32
Choices, Facts on Moving Your Home, Pet, Car
Chapter 4  **Settling In** .......................................................................... 48
Advice on Living in the Tropics —  Build? Rent? Taxes? Insurance?
Chapter 5  **The Infrastructure** .............................................................. 72
Services: Airlines, Banks, Transportation, Utilities
How to Get There
Chapter 6  **Your Basic Needs** ............................................................... 99
Daily Living Within the Framework of the Islands...
Hospitals, Schools, Churches
Chapter 7  **Community Life** ................................................................. 119
Folk Lore, Culture, Entertainment, Holidays, Events
Chapter 8  **The Great Outdoors** ........................................................... 131
Sports, Sporting Events, Diving, Swimming, Sailing
Chapter 9  **Business Climate** ............................................................... 153
Legal Requirements, Incentives, Taxes, Employment
Chapter 10  **You And The Government** ................................................ 171
Information on Local and Federal Government
**Services Directory** ............................................................................ 184
**Services Directory by Index** .............................................................. 211
**Index by Subject** ............................................................................... 214
**Colored Photos**
St. Croix ............................................................................................... 22
St. Thomas ........................................................................................... 47
St. John ................................................................................................ 152
**Cultural Tidbits** ................... 17, 46, 65, 67, 98, 120, 147, 151, 159
**Maps** ................................................................................................. 218

iii

11/19/2012 - "I used the Settler's Handbook to evaluate My move to Paradise and found the information provided to be both useful and accurate. My move to Paradise was a huge success, and it is now a distinct privilege for me to come full circle and advertise my business in this book. If you are looking to buy your own piece of America's Paradise come on down; the lifestyle and the water are both warm and inviting".
Scot F. McChain

11/13/12 - "The VI Settler's Handbook is a must-have for anyone interested in relocating to the Virgin Islands. It is an invaluable resource for how to ship your goods and offers choices of shipping companies. It also walks soon-to-be locals through the steps of moving, including car registration, insurance and any required documentation. The book educates the reader on local customs and holidays – something which could take years to learn without this handy resource. I highly recommend the VI Settler's Handbook!
Fran Geocaris,   Marketing Manager Divi Carina Bay Casino – 11 years, St. Croix Chamber of Commerce Board of Directors – 6 years

9/10 - "The Settlers Handbook" has been part of our relocation package for decades. We send it to all our buyers from off-island! It answers all those important questions like: How do I ship my car, personals. Will I be allowed to relocate my dog. How to build a home. What to expect.
Julie San Martin, Team San Martin, ReMax, St.Croix

9/10 - "We've watched this book grow in popularity since Linda's first revision in 2002. The SHB is a tremendous resource for anyone in the process of moving to the USVI, contemplating, or planning to. It contains extremely valuable information applicable to individuals, families or businesses.
Tom Yaegel, VisitTheVI.com

# The Settler's Handbook
## for the U.S. Virgin Islands

## *Introduction*

Yes, the Caribbean... visions of azure waters, swaying palm trees, pulsating rhythmns and rum punches. Sweet! Truly a dreamer's vacation, but can you imagine living here? Some people make those dreams a reality. The Settler's Handbook is for those who are vacationing here, contemplating moving here, investing here, or for those who have just moved here. It is for those who are lured to the tropics, and specifically to the Virgin Islands which charmed not only Christopher Columbus, but millions of others who have since landed on their shores.

How do you identify those who live here? For one thing, check out those bumper stickers that say, "Not all of us here are on vacation!" What's it like to live here? What can you expect? Read on.

The Settler's Handbook, 19th Edition, hopes to enlighten you on island living, whether you are a prospective settler, a vacationer, or a new business person. While each of the three islands, St. Croix, St. John and St. Thomas, has a unique style, they all share the charms and flavors of the Caribbean and the protection of the Stars and Stripes. In this up-dated 19th edition of The Handbook, we present the latest facts, figures, trends, pros and cons, about visiting, living and working in our islands.

It is virtually impossible for any one publication to incoporate every detail but we have given it a valiant attempt to consolidate relevant information here or at least direct you to a more detailed or practical source.

All information and contents of websites listed in this publication are for the convenience of the reader and are proprietary to their owners. Neither Chey'nanigans Corp. nor Pink Elephant Promotions is responsiible for errors, misinformation in or misuse of these websites. We do hope this book will make your transition smoother.

Welcome! Bienvenidos! Velkommen! Bles'sed Love!

19th Settler's Handbook

# Location
of the
## United States Virgin Islands

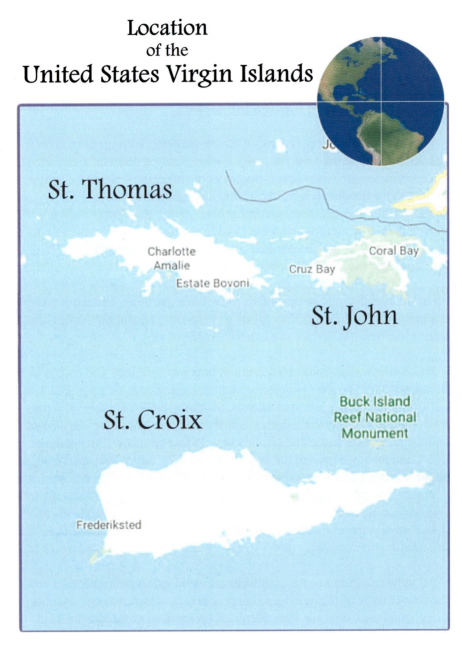

*The physical location and relationship of the United States Virgin Islands (inset) between North and South American continents. United States Mainland, the Atlantic Ocean and other islands of the Caribbean.*

# Settler's Handbook Chapter 1

## AN OVERVIEW...

The United States Virgin Islands, geologically formed of sedimentary rock and undersea lava flows, are located in the beautiful turquoise waters of the north eastern Caribbean, within the chain of all the Antilles, just west of the Atlantic Ocean. The Territory is more than one hundred and thirty-three (133.6) square miles and is almost twice the size of Washington, D.C. with territorial waters that stretch over six hundred and three (603.9) square miles into the Atlantic Ocean. Surrounding the three Virgin Islands of St. Croix, St. John, St. Thomas are 68 small, mostly uninhabited offshore islands and cays of which two are noteworthy as the other two inhabited Virgins – Water Island and Hassell Island.

St. Croix, St. John and St. Thomas lie approximately 1,075 miles southeast of Miami, Florida and 1,650 miles south and east of New York City. Puerto Rico, a U.S. Commonwealth, is west and a little north about ninety (90) miles away. The islands are in the Atlantic Time Zone, one hour ahead of New York and Florida, but on the same time during Daylight Savings Time.

St. Croix's latitude is a little over 17 degrees, while St. Thomas and St. John are at approximately 18 degrees. That means if you fly a direct path, east to west around the earth, you also fly over Mexico City, Hawaii and Bombay, India. The longitude at 64 degrees aligns with the Canadian province of Nova Scotia to the north, and the South American country of Venezuela to the south.

**St. Croix,** the southernmost island, is nearly forty miles south of St. Thomas and St. John. The "big island" is almost 84 square miles and has approximately two-thirds of the total land mass of the Virgins. It is almost twenty-four miles from end to end, with a width of just over five miles at its widest point. The highest point is Mount Eagle, which rises 1,165 feet above sea level. The two main towns are Christiansted, mid-island on the north shore, and Frederiksted, on the west end. Both retain their names from the Danish period on St. Croix. St. Croix sounds like St. Croy, and its residents refer to themselves as Crucians; pronounced Crew'-shuns. St. Croix, is the only one of the three Virgins completely surrounded by the

1

Caribbean Sea; St. Thomas and St. John are bounded by the Atlantic on the north.

**St. John**, the smallest of these three, is nine miles long and four miles wide, about twenty square miles of land. The highest point is Bordeaux Mountain at 1,277 feet. Cruz Bay at its west end is the main town and population center, and Coral Bay at the island's eastern end is a rapidly growing area. The island's residents are called St. Joe'-ne'ans. About two-thirds of St. John is a natural preservation, bequeathed by Laurance Rockefeller. Notable sites include historic ruins of Annaberg Plantation, a natural campsite at Maho Bay Campground and the famous Trunk Bay beach.

**St. Thomas**, thirteen miles long and three miles wide, has a total area of just over thirty-one square miles. Crown Mountain, at 1,550 feet and near the center of the island, is the highest point. Charlotte Amalie (pronounced (A'-mal-yah), the territorial capital of the U.S. Virgin Islands, is also the largest population center on St. Thomas. Growing population areas include the Tutu (mid-isle), and Red Hook sections (east end). Residents are called St. To'-me-ans.

**Water Island** is just off the south coast of St. Thomas and has under 250 residents.

**Hassel Island,** while inhabited by a dozen or so people, is part of the National Park system.

## A Brief History

One hundred and fifty million years ago, when reptiles ruled the earth, there was neither a Caribbean Sea nor an Atlantic Ocean. The world's dry land mass (Pangaea) gradually split and spread to form the continents as we know them today (Continental Drift Theory). Even now the geological spreading continues and, where the great blocks of the earth's crust meet or diverge, titanic forces construct mountain chains or open deep ocean trenches which lead to rumbling volcanoes or shifting earthquakes. Cuba, Hispaniola, Puerto Rico, St. Thomas, St. John and the British Virgin Islands share a single large submerged bank which is part of the North American Plate. St. Croix, separated from her northern sisters by a two-mile deep ocean trench called the Virgin Islands Trench, is aligned along the northern edge of the Caribbean Plate on a mass called the Aves Ridge. To the south of the Caribbean Plate is the landmass of the South American Plate. The only active area as far as geologists can see is located in the Cayman Trough which runs in a line east-west, north of St. Croix, including Puerto

Rico, St. Thomas, and other nearby islands. Other than minor tremors, no major activity has occurred in the area. Geologically, the islands are a conglomeration of ancient undersea lava flows, sedimentary and igneous rock formed under water from volcanic ash and layers of sand, and marine animals laid down by ocean currents. There was a major undersea earthquake along with tidal waves in 1867. Volcanic eruptions such as Montserrat in 1995 and the earthquake that submerged Port Royal, Jamaica three centuries ago, are reminders that the earth is in constant change.

The northern island chain in this part of the Caribbean, running east-west, is called the Greater Antilles. This includes: Hispaniola, Cuba and Puerto Rico. Southeast, including the Virgin Islands and extending in an arc toward the South American continent, are the Lesser Antilles. The island chains are the geophysical dividing line between the Atlantic and the Caribbean.

### The First Settlers

Archaeological finds on St. Croix reveal artifacts that proved man was present in the Virgin Islands around 2500 B.C. Discoveries on St. Thomas at the Krum Bay site, under the location of the Water and Power Authority, show that a pre-ceramic tribe dates back to 2050 B.C. Other than the pre-ceramic tribe, there have been three known pottery-making tribes who inhabited the islands: the Igneri or Ancient Ones from approximately A.D. 50 to A.D.650; the Taino or Arawak from A.D.650 to A.D.1425; and the Caribs from A.D. 1425 to the late 17th century. Scientists believe the original inhabitants of the islands migrated up the Lesser Antilles from the South American coast. A ceremonial ball court or religious cultural center from the Taino era was discovered in the Salt River Bay area on St. Croix. That ceremonial site is the only one of its kind that has been discovered in the Lesser Antilles.

### Explorers and Colonizers

Christopher Columbus and his crew were the first Europeans to visit the area known now as the Virgin Islands. While sailing north in 1493 along the Lesser Antilles chain, toward the community he'd established in Hispaniola (now Haiti and the Dominican Republic), Columbus sighted an island. The fleet decided to anchor near a bay (Salt River) in hopes of finding fresh water. The bay, called "AyAy" (The River) by the Tainos and "Cibuguiera" (Stony Land) by the Caribs, was to be named "Santa Cruz" by Columbus. The French would later keep the Holy Cross designation and call it "Ste. Croix."

Soldiers were dispatched in a longboat toward an Indian village for information. This landing party attacked some Caribs who approached in a canoe. A confrontation ensued, with at least one Spaniard and one Carib dying. Columbus, as a memorial to the dead Spaniard, named the site of the skirmish Cabo de las Flechas (Cape of the Arrows). Later, the Caribs would so harass the Spanish in Puerto Rico that they became a target for destruction and eventually retreated to other Carib communities on Dominica and Guadeloupe.

Columbus' fleet turned north to explore the islands on the horizon. They sailed past Anegada and Virgin Gorda (the eastern-most of what are now the British Virgin Islands), past St. Thomas and St. John. The explorer was so impressed by the number of islands that he named them in honor of St. Ursula and her legendary 11,000 martyred virgin companions. He resisted the temptation to anchor, continued westward and finally landed along Puerto Rico's west coast.

Though Spain claimed the Caribbean islands through Columbus' explorations, she made little effort to colonize the Lesser Antilles because they had no mineral wealth. During the two centuries that followed, the Greater and Lesser Antilles were the scenes of battles between English, Dutch and French admirals, pirates and privateers, all attracted first by rumor of Spanish treasure and later by the region's highly profitable products of cotton, sugar, rum, indigo and spices.

In the early 1640s, England and Holland were sparring over St. Croix. The English, farmers from the more settled island of St. Kitts, established a settlement around 1641 in the Salt River area of St. Croix. They would build a triangular earthwork structure to fortify their foothold. The structure, completed by the Dutch later, was called Fort Flamand (the Flemish fort) by the French. The Dutch West India Company also settled on the island around 1642. The English governor was killed and his settlers retaliated by killing the Dutch governor. The Dutch won, but allowed the English to remain. A few years later, the Dutch were forced out, leaving the English in control. In 1650, Spain would defeat and drive out the English. In 1650, the French surprised and defeated the Spanish garrison. The first French settlement was at Salt River; a later settlement was at the natural harbor on the north side of the island at present day Christiansted. They called it "Bassin." From 1655 to 1665, the French Crown leased the islands to the French Chapter of the Knights of Malta. During that time, the island continued to produce cotton, indigo, tobacco, sugar and tropical foods. In the late 17th century, the French were forced to abandon the island. Then, all but deserted, the island was occasionally visited by pirates and smugglers. French war ships arrived periodically to maintain title for the crown. When the French abandoned St. Croix, English woodcutters from Tortola moved in and engaged in lumbering.

France sold St. Croix to the Danish West India and Guinea Company in 1733. Denmark took over as a Crown Colony in 1755. This struggle for control of the islands, St. Croix in particular, demonstrates how the Caribbean would ebb and flow, matching the battles that existed in Europe in the 17th and 18th centuries. Blackbeard and other infamous pirates used St. Thomas to sell their plunder. St. Thomas continued to be the main port, and goods from the islands were shipped in and out by both legitimate companies and by smugglers and pirates. The coves and inlets of the islands proved to be havens for the smuggling of goods. By this period, sugar plantations and small farms had been established on St. John. With Charlotte Amalie's superb harbor, St. Thomas soon found its destiny as a trading center. In 1764 the island was proclaimed a free port. Many of the present-day Charlotte Amalie shops were once merchant warehouses with back doors facing the beaches and the harbor.

The Danes had become interested in sugar cultivation; the Danish West India and Guinea Company was chartered to expand the sugar plantations and control the African slave trade. Plantation agriculture began on St. Thomas, using Danish indentured servants as laborers. The first shipments of African slaves arrived in 1673. In 1717, the Danes added St. John to their territory. When the French sold the island of St. Croix, Danish settlers from the plantations on St. Thomas sailed to St. John to farm. In 1733, a violent slave rebellion on St. John dislodged the Europeans for six months.

**The Danish Era**

On St. Croix, the Danes established the towns of Christiansted (named for King Christian VI of Denmark) in 1735, and Frederiksted (named for King Frederik V) in 1752. Friederich Moth, governor of the West India Company, designed the town layout for Christiansted and had the island of St. Croix surveyed into 150-acre estates. Moth encouraged settlers, who came from throughout the Caribbean, by offering tax benefits and reasonable land prices. Danish tolerance of ethnicity and religion also helped make the Virgin islands a melting pot, in which English eventually became the common language and Danish the language of the courts.
Also spoken was a creole blend of Dutch, African, and later an English dialect, through which slaves and their owners communicated.
The rules and regulations put forth by the West India Company proved so

# 19th Settler's Handbook — Overview 1

*Fndr. Alexander Hamilton*

rigid that the monarchy had to dissolve the company before economic growth could begin. The Danish Crown purchased the charter from the West India Company in 1754 and moved the capital from Charlotte Amalie in St. Thomas to Christiansted in St. Croix. Prosperity peaked in the second half of the 18th century with exports of sugar and molasses, rum, hardwoods and cotton. At one point, due to its prodigious agricultural output, St. Croix was called the "Garden of the West Indies." Danish West Indian architecture is emulated in the territory's elegant, sturdy, neo-classical buildings that are customized for West Indian weather.

The second stories of these structures overhang sidewalks and create shady walkways called "galleries," which provide cover from both sun and rain. Windows, doors and open spacious rooms take advantage of the tradewinds, and Gutter systems on roofs help catch precious rainwater. The Danes established and rigidly enforced a strict building code for fire protection.

For building materials, Danes and black workers who had purchased their freedom made use of what was available. Yellow bricks from Danish ship ballasts were incorporated in much construction. And plantations were built mostly with coral quarried from the sea.

The islands of the West Indies played a significant role in the development of North America. Alexander Hamilton, the first Secretary of the U.S. Treasury, who wrote the *Federalist Papers*, began his career on St. Croix in a shipping firm owned by a New Yorker. The wealth and social status achieved by prominent island families appealed to colonial families in Philadelphia, New York and Charleston. Close family connections and trade would eventually help develop a natural friendship between the islands and the continent. And during the American Revolution the neutrality and freeport status of the Danish Virgins were important financial assets to the rebellious thirteen colonies. It is hence not surprising that the first salute from foreign soil to American independence was fired from Fort Frederik, St. Croix in 1776. Perhaps it is only fitting that the Virgin Islands now rest under America's Stars and Stripes.

## Decline of Prosperity

In the early 19th century, the bright economic picture in the Danish Virgins dimmed. In 1803, as newly invented processing of beet sugar cut into the cane sugar market, Denmark formally ended the slave trade. Though the slave trade was over, slavery was not until those in captivity took action decades later. In 1848, dissatisfied Crucian slaves marched in Frederiksted demanding emancipation, and on July 3 Governor General Peter von Scholten, a man sympathetic to their cause, emancipated them. The governor's actions were considered illegal by the Danish government, and von Scholten was tried in Denmark for dereliction of duty. Labor was hence regulated by a colonial labor law that was deemed oppressive; 30 years later, in 1878, it culminated in a riot that led to the burning and destruction of homes and plantations. Denmark attempted to remedy the problems, but never again would the island achieve the prosperity and glory of the "golden age of sugar."As a result of economic decline, the population of the islands fell from 32,000 in 1829 to 14,600 in 1917. The capital city of the Danish West Indies alternated every six months between Charlotte Amalie, St. Thomas and Christiansted, St. Croix, till 1917, when Charlotte Amalie was designated as the permanent capital. Heroes who were champions of the struggles for Freedom, Emanication and civil rights during those turbulent years sons and daughters include

*David Hamilton Jackson*

Moses "Buddhoe" Gottlieb, Queen Mary, David Hamilton Jackson, and Rothschild Francis. The territory was also home during his formative years to Alexander Hamilton, a USA founding father, as well as to modern day celebrities like basketball stars Tim Duncan and Raja Bell, professional boxers Emille Griffith and Julian Jackson, baseball players Joe Christopher and Calvin Pickering, plus actors Kelsey Grammer and Lisa Canning to name just a few.

## Government History

U.S. efforts to buy the islands began in 1871 but were not successful until World War I, when the United States became concerned about German threats to the Panama Canal. The threat brought diplomats back to the negotiating table, and on March 31, 1917, the United States purchased the Virgin Islands for $25 million. The free port status of the islands was retained and is still in effect.

19th Settler's Handbook            Overview 1

The islands were first administered by the U.S. Navy, with the Department of the Interior assuming jurisdiction in 1931. The Organic Act passed by the United States Congress, provided local government in 1936. A 1954 revision of the Organic Act established a three-branch territorial government: Legislative, Judicial and Executive.

The first popularly elected governor of the Virgin Islands, Dr. Melvin H. Evans, took office in 1970. In 1968, the position of Delegate to Congress for the Virgin Islands was approved, and in 1970 Ron de Lugo became the the Virgin Islands' first Delegate to Congress.

In 1982, the Judicial Branch was given more power to gradually create its own territorial court system. The U.S. Virgin Islands now is an organized, unincorporated Territory of the United States and a part of the United Nations list of Non-Self-Governing Territories.

## THE VI ECONOMY

**Tourism**

Tourism is the mainstay of the U.S. Virgin Islands economy. More than two million tourists visit annually via cruise ship or air arrivals. On September 6th, 2017 the Territory was struck by the category five Hurricane Irma. The St. Thomas-St. John district sustained severe infrastructure damage. Fourteen days later the US Virgin Islands was again impacted by another category five storm, Hurricane Maria on September 20th, 2017. Both districts experienced flooding and windstorm damages resulting in an estimated $10.76 billion in damages to the infrastructure and economy. Consequently, visitor arrivals were mixed in 2018.

- Cruise ship passenger arrivals for calendar year 2018 rebounded with a growth of 8.6% from 1,317,238 to 1,430,702 in 2018, while air visitor arrivals dropped by 25% to 477,840 from 636,812 in 2017 as a result of the loss of many hotels.
- Annual December 2019 cruise passenger arrivals was 1,433,212 an increase of 0.2%.
- Year-to-date November 2019 Territory-wide arrivals was 572,164 a healthy increase of 44.3% over the same coresponding period in 2018 that recorded 428,972
- St. Thomas and St. John reported 1,366,390 cruise ship visitors from 449 cruise ship calls while St. Croix, which has more shallow ports than St. Thomas and striving to increase cruise ship calls, reported 69,357 visitors.

The USVI Department of Tourism has partnered with Airbnb in developing a partnership that has resulted in the maintaining of flights to the Territory.

The Virgin Islands Port Authority and the West Indian Company continue to expand and improve docking facilities for maritime activities utilizing disaster-related Community Development Block Grant funding, to include the dredging of the West Indian Company Dock facility.

## Industry/Manufacturing

The last sugar factory on St. Croix closed in 1966. Since then, the island's economy has been based on light and heavy industry, services and tourism.

## Aluminum

St. Croix's industrial history is dynamic, and its changing nature is evidenced in the shining steel labyrinths dotting the south shore. On the western end of St.Croix's industrial landscape is the site of a former aluminum facility, which was first established in 1965 as Harvey Alumina. Over the years, the property has been owned by several aluminum companies, including Martin Marietta, Virgin Islands Alumina Corporation (VIALCO), and finally, Alcoa World Aluminum Corporation (ALCOA). Following a steady decline in the global aluminum market, ALCOA sold the site to St. Croix Renaissance Group, which has transformed the former Aluminum plant into an industrial plant. Renaissance Group touts the location's deep ports, desalinization plant and coal-fired power plant as amenities to attract tenants, which today includes Diageo, makers of Captain Morgan's rum.

## Oil

West of the Renaissance Park is the site of Limetree Bay Refining, LLC, formerly HOVENSA, the company that has had the most impact on the island's recent economic history.

Hess Oil Refinery of the Virgin Islands (HOVIC) had began operations in 1966 and gradually increased its production to 650,000, making it the largest oil refinery in the world until 1974. In 1998 Hess Oil entered into a partial merger with Venezuelan oil company Petroleos de Venezuela and became HOVENSA. In January 2012, citing hemorrhaging finances, a weak global economy, and anemic projections for the refinery industry, HOVENSA announced intentions to pull the plug on its refinery operations, a move that led to layoffs for most of the company's approximately 2,000 employees. The refinery was purchased by Limetree Bay Refining LLC, a subsidiary of ArcLight Capital Partners LLC, which restarted it mid 2018 and has recreated many lost jobs. It is anticipated that more jobs will come as this is just the beginning and they are still in the early stages of reopening.

The Limetree Bay companies operate out of the once shuttered refinery, the Terminal as an oil storage facility, and the Refinery slated to do do just that - refining.

The oil storage business started in 2015, three years after the refinery closed in 2012. A portion at least of the former Hovensa refinery is on schedule to resume refining oil some time by mid 2020 according to Limetree Bay Ventures, parent company of Limetree Bay Terminals and Limetree Bay Refining., LLC. The operation will have to respond to the changes to area fuel sulfur regulation by the International Maritime Oganization that took effect January 1, 2020 and will impact profitability of refining operations.

**Rum**

St. Croix's rum industry is also doing well. The U.S. Virgin Islands rum industry consists of two companies: Cruzan VIRIL, Ltd. and Diageo plc.

In June 2008, the US Virgin islands and Diageo, USVI began a public-private initiative for the construction and operation of a high capacity rum distillery on St. Croix.

This 30 year commitment is providing a major economic stimulus for the entire territory of the US Virgin Islands. In November 2011, the distillery began production supplying the rum used to make all Captain Morgan branded products for the United States. The Diageo distillery has the capacity to produce 20 million proof gallons annually. Today, all the rum used to make Captain Morgan branded products for the US Market comes from the U.S. Virgin Islands. Captain Morgan is a global leader among premium spirits and is the second leading rum in the world located in the St. Croix Renaissance park, the facility features state-of-the art eco-friendly visitor's center with a souvenir gift shop.

Cruzan VIRIL, Ltd., produces nearly 9 million proof gallons of rum per year. It has expanded its Cruzan brand by introducing new flavors and rum concepts to capitalize on the growth trend in dark and aged rums, and to accommodate shifts in consumer tastes.

Rum produced in the US Virgin Islands is exported to the US primarily in bulk, and sold to local and regional bottlers for sale under a variety of brands. The federal government imposes and collects federal excise taxes on rum produced in the Virgin Islands and exported to the United States. The current assessed excise tax rate is $13.50 price per proof gallon. The Department of the Interior's Office of Insular Affairs makes the "cover-over" payments to the USVI Government on behalf of the federal government.

For fiscal year 2019, the Department of Interior submitted $256,216,642 in cover-over payments to the local government.

Leatherback Brewing Company and Mutiny Island Vodka have recently thrown their hats into the ring as the newest alcohol manufacturers - beer and vodka respectively, both located on St. Croix.

## Recent Economic Development

**Gross Domestic Product**

In recent years, tourism spending contributed to the rise of the Territorial Real Gross Domestic Product (GDP) in 2015 to $3.09 billion, an increase of 0.3%. In 2016, the GDP grew by 1.2%. This growth was attributed to tourism and consumer spending and the Limetree Bay Terminals operating an oil storAge facility. In 2017, the Real Gross Domestic Product shrunk to by 0.6% and rose again by 1.5 percent in 2018.

In July 2017, the 32nd Legislature of the Virgin Islands ratified a landmark agreement signed between the Government of the Virgin Islands and and the aforementioned Limetree Bay Terminals, LLC. Limetree Bay will now operate two facilities; a storage terminal and a refinery with a combined estimated number of jobs at 1,400.

Since the storms, an average of 35,000 people are employed in non-agricultural positions and employment in construction has become the largest jobs sector due to rebuilding of the territory's infrastructure. Tourism-related employment fell by 5.6% in calendar year 2018. Prior to the 2017 storms, the tourism sector supported 8,000 direct jobs and contributed 20% of the USVI total wage and salary employment in four core tourism areas: accommodation, transportation, food and beverage, and other tourism industries. Tourism had a $1 billion impact on the USVI economy and contributed an estimated 30% to GDP. Its impact is substantially greater than the direct value because of its multiplier effect on related sectors and industries (e.g., retail, arts and entertainment, other services). Indirect economic impact is estimated at $1.2 billion for a total economic impact of $2.2 billion.

The Territory is making efforts to increase exposure and education of Information Technology and entrepreneurship at the K-12 level.
Virgin Islands Next Generation Network presents an important asset that can be leveraged for growth in the information technology, professional and financial services sector. This is not only due to the wholesale fiber optic infrastructure the Territory now enjoys, but also to the 33 public computer centers that were developed to provide basic digital literacy training to residents. Additionally, internet service providers (ISPs) can purchase high-speed bandwidth and sell to their customers at affordable rates. The Economic Develop-

ment Authority and the University of the Virgin Islands, Research Technology Park Offers marketing incentives to e-commerce or technology-based businesses.

Economic growth in the territory is in some aspects tied to the people it attracts. In this regard, there are some promising signs. In 2018 visitor arrivals to the three main islands totaled 1,926,845. The majority which totaled 435,747 were cruise ship tourists, but the territory also welcomed 491,098 air arrivals.

These statistics were supplied by the Office of Management and Budget. For further updates on visitor arrivals, visit the VI Bureau of Economic Research. *http://www.usviber.org*.

## Weather

The Virgin Islands proximity to the equator means that year-round, the length of the days are fairly consistent and the weather tropical. Residents lament the "cold" temperatures in January and February when the thermometer can dip in the evening or early morning hours to long-sleeved shirt or sweater weather for those who are acclimatized.

Winter Dec- February mid-day high    70s – mid 80s
Summer June- August   mid-day high 80s-mid 90s
The record low is 57 and the record high 99
Dry months –   February – March
Wet months –   May/June ; September-November
Annual Average Rainfall – 43 inches
Hurricane Season – June 1-November 30

St. John temperatures are usually a couple degrees cooler than its sisters'. The year round 80% humidity is mitigated by the near-constant tradewinds. While statistics show September- despite what are considered to be the rainiest months, downpours can occur anytime. One year may be extremely wet and the next very dry. The western end of the islands get the most rain.

One obvious indication is the scrub and cactus on the eastern end of St. Croix and the so-called rain forest near Frederiksted in the west. In 1994, only 26 inches of rain fell, 17 inches less than average and again in 2015 only 18 inches fell by September. The droughts caused hardships for all the the islands' residents who depend on rainfall to meet their agricultural, personal and household needs. A day-long downpour, however, can fill water-saving cisterns. One or two day's worth of such rain can turn the brown hillsides to an emerald green. Of the island weather it is often said "if you don't like the weather, wait 10 minutes and it will change!

# 19th Settler's Handbook  Overview 1

## Population

Historically, oil and aluminum have been a catalyst for immigration. Labor needs in the last four decades have been satisfied by heavy immigration from Puerto Rico (continuing a century-old trend), from the United States mainland, and other parts of the Caribbean. The territory's population was 32,099 in 1960, and nearly tripled that figure by the early 1970s due mainly to new settlers and slower emigration. Unfortunately, the '70s saw the same economic recession that affected the U.S. mainland and the population in the islands declined.

By 1977, when the territory's population was over 89,000, the portion of non-citizens had declined to less than a quarter of the population, with half of that number as permanent residents and the proportion of bonded workers or aliens dropping steadily. These figures don't necessarily represent the real number of people moving in or out, as categories change when residents become U.S. citizens and aliens achieve permanent status or return to home islands. Some bonded "temporary" workers have been in the Virgin Islands for two decades.

The U.S. census estimated the total population of the Virgin Islands in the '80s to be around 95,000 people. By 1990 it was 101,809. In 2018 reports, the population of the islands was 96,211, with about 45,980 on St. Croix, 3,910 on St. John and 46,321 on St. Thomas (what was available at press time December 2019). The drop is most likely due from the relocation of many families and individuals after the 2017 hurricanes.

In 1982, the Congress of the United States passed the Virgin Islands Non Immigrant Alien Adjustment Act in order "to eliminate the uncertainty and insecurity of aliens who: a) legally entered the Virgin Islands of the United States as non immigrants for employment under the temporary alien labor program; b) have continued to reside in the Virgin Islands for long periods and, as a result, c) have contributed to the economic, social and cultural development of the Virgin Islands and have become an integral part of the society of the Virgin Islands."

Those who fell in this category and had lived within the territory since June 30, 1975 were given one year to comply with residency prerequisites (inspection and admission to the Virgin Islands as non-immigrant alien workers, their spouses, or their minor children). In the late 1980s many illegal aliens who had complied with the earlier requirements were granted permanent status under a United States Immigration Service Amnesty program. This new status often brought access to healthcare, education, housing, and the opportunity to eventually apply for citizenship.

# 19th Settler's Handbook   Overview 1

A 1969 study estimated that nearly a third of the territory's population was born in the Virgin Islands. Another third was born in the United States mainland, Europe and Puerto Rico. The final third were residents, bonded, and/or illegal aliens, almost exclusively from other islands in the Caribbean. As a result of unofficial immigration, the hard figures on population breakdowns are nearly non-existent. The United States Coast Guard, and the United States Border Patrol continue to battle the illegal immigration problem.

**Ethnicity**

The inhabitants of the U.S. Virgin Islands are a unique collection of Natives and peoples from the United States, various islands of the Caribbean, as well as Europe, the Middle East and South America. This has created a diversity in culture, giving the islands an extraordinary quality and personality.

On St. Croix, possibly 45% of the population is Spanish speaking, traditionally of Puerto Rican descent and more recently, arrivals from the Dominican Republic.

St. Thomas has two French communities from St. Barths and Haiti. Settlers to the Virgin Islands have come from the British Virgin Islands, Denmark, Germany, Spain, Portugal, India, Philippines, the Lesser and Greater Antilles, the Caribbean in general, the Arab nations, and the Far East. The United States Virgin Islands is a mini-United Nations where the "melting pot" bubbles to quelbe, soca, reggae, country, zouk and mainstream top 40 beats. The traditional music of the US Virgin Islands is quelbe or 'scratch' music.

# Settler's Handbook Chapter 2

## *GETTING ACQUAINTED...*

### AROUND the UNITED STATES VIRGIN ISLANDS

Even though the three islands, St. Croix, St. John and St. Thomas, have many similarities with their neighbors in the Caribbean, their differences are considerable. St. Croix's terrain encouraged agricultural development and a general spreading of the population throughout the island. St. John's size and natural beauty led to preservation of a national park on the island. And St. Thomas, with her steep inclines and a natural deep harbor, became a world-class port. So each island is different due to terrain, beneficial intervention and surrounding water, developing delightful and individual personalities and styles. As a result, the three sister islands of the United States Virgin Islands are beautiful examples of life in the Caribbean. They share qualities of the quintessential American paradise, but, like sisters in many families, they are strikingly unique, fiercely independent, usually squabbling, yet quite loyal to each other should outsiders interfere.

### AROUND the ISLANDS - ST. CROIX

The island of St. Croix has two charming towns, Christiansted and Frederiksted, with other major shopping area such as Gallows Bay, Sunny Isle and Sunshine Mall, plus a rain forest, scenic drives, outstanding watersports activities, three golf courses, tennis courts all spread out across the island's approximate 84 sq. miles.

#### Christiansted

The **Buck Island Reef National Monument** features snorkeling, swimming, beautiful waters, sandy beaches, good hiking and is a frequent stop – not only for the day-charter boats, but also the locals on weekends. Note that signs on occasion may be posted closing some of the walking trails for nesting turtles and wild bird or endangered animal protection. Most boats stop at the sheltered sandy beach along the island's west shore, where you can practice snorkeling.

A few minutes sail to the east end puts you at the famed underwater trail.

Put your mask, fins and snorkle on, then splash into a dream world of beautiful coral and fish. Also note that there are only a few moorings placed at this end and you cannot drop anchor any other place here. These moorings were strategically placed to protect the coral and the underwater park. Only a few charter boats have their license to moor in this vicinity. If you can't swim, guides can tow you with a float. If you don't want to get wet, take a glass-bottomed boat for a glimpse of the island's superb marine life. The coral reef, lying just under the surface of the water, is a great mass of elkhorn coral extending like a horseshoe around the eastern side of the island. Within its protection are thousands of hard and soft coral formations in an astonishing range of sizes, shapes and colors identified by underwater markers and an equally dazzling array of fish. All this is at a depth of only about 13 ft.

There is no fishing or "take" whatsoever inside the park boundaries which extends 3 miles out from the coast of Buck Island. Possession of firearms, fishing, hunting gear, and spear guns are prohibited. You must stay off the fragile coral, and while on the shores and beaches, you must not collect any souvenirs. This is a nationally protected island on land and underwater. Also, before anchoring anywhere along the shores of St. Croix, look for mooring balls, put there for boats to tie up to and not drop their own anchor. Do not mistake fishermen's markers for fish pots or mooring balls.

**Christiansted Town**
Our round-the-island land tour begins with the historic city of Christiansted. Several blocks of the wharf area have been designated a National Historic Site by the National Park Service. The town features narrow Streets and sturdy architecture similar to the style of the 18th century neo-classical.
The strict requirements of the Danish building code, established in 1747 for fire and hurricane, spared the town from the dangers that have destroyed many historic areas elsewhere.

**Christiansted Boardwalk is** lined with restaurants, boutique hotels and Shops and at its furthest west point is the seaplane.
**Christiansted Harbor**, **Protestant Cay,** home to Hotel on the Cay, was once a burial ground for Protestants barred from the island cemetery by the French Catholic administration.

**Fort Christianvaern** is the most striking of these Danish structures and it currently serves as headquarters for the National Park Service, is a perfect place to begin architectural tours of the town. The fort is open seven days

# 19th Settler's Handbook  Getting Acquainted 2

a week 8:30 am - 4:30 pm except Thanksgiving and Christmas. A prime example of colonial military architecture, the fort contains posted descriptions of the town's historic buildings which all date from the earliest period of the 1700-1800's such as: **The Scalehouse w**here sugar and rum rum were weighed, **The Danish Customs House** where taxes for the good**s** weighed at the scalehouse were paid, **The Danish West India & Guinea Company Warehouse's** former administrative offices, and slave auction site;

**The Steeple Building -** the first Danish Lutheran church. At press time, the Steeple Building was closed for renovations.

**Government House,** residence of the governor when on island and the **Lieutenant Governor's** office building are both on King Street.

**St. Croix Archaelogy Museum** dedicated to preserving the historical artifacts, is a block over on Company Street and not far away around the corner is the quaint **Apothecary Hall and Museum**, one of two on island, the other being in Frederiksted.

**Point Udall**   While St. Croix offers many variations in topography, the East End with Point Udall, the easternmost point of land in the United States, offers breath-taking sea vistas, gentle hills dotted with cactus and an unobtructed view of Buck Island, just six miles away. To get to **Point Udall**, follow Route 82 past Cramer's Park, past the **National Radio Astronomy Observatory,** and east along a paved road to the very tip, where you will find a monument at this point. As you stare out on the vast ocean, remember that the next major piece of land is Africa!   This is a favorite spot for islanders and visitors to welcome the dawn of each New Year as the sun bursts radiantly up from the horizon.

*Cutural Tidbit*

*An author, folklorist and educator, Dr. George Franklin is well known for his witty and incisive look into Virgin Islands culture. Here are a few poignant pearls of local wisdom with Dr. Franklin's cachet.*

• Between the Sand, Sea and Shore, we all Share the Same Surf. In other words, there are no private beaches in the Virgin Islands. All beaches must be accessible to all visitors and residence alike. 'NJoy
• Dress for Success. Beach clothing is for the beach. It is against custom and civil law to walk the streets in your bikinis. Decorum dictates. We may be paradise but we've changed the rule since after the time of Adam and Eve with their Fig Leaves Fashion.
• Good Friday ain't so good if you are searching for a drink at a bar or restaurant between the hours of 9:00 am and 4:00 p.m. It is against the law to serve alcohol on that day. Yep, it sucks like sweet lime.

# 19th Settler's Handbook    Getting Acquainted 2

St. Croix's mid-island area has many special sites to visit. History comes alive at **Estate Whim Museum** (also on Rt. 70) as you walk among the historic 18th century buildings of this former sugar estate. The stately, Great House was severely damaged by Hurricane Maria in 2017 but gracious guides are waiting to tell you stories of past inhabtants and the reality of plantation life. Managed by the St.Croix Landmarks Society, this 12 acre site features a windmill in the sugar factory area, cookhouse and tropical trees. Cultural tradition bearers demonstrate music, food preparation, crafts & bush bath on Wednesdays and Saturdays! Revolving exhibits are displayed throughout the museum!

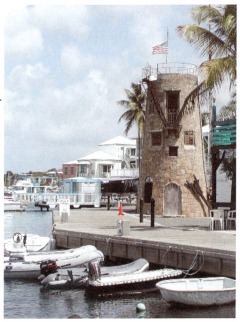

*Christiansted Boardwalk*

Nestled in the tranquil, tropical valley of Estate Little LaGrange (Rt. 76) is **Lawaetz Family Museum**, a traditional homestead museum. This Danish West Indian house, with its rambling gardens, orchards and authentic furnishings, was the home of the Lawaetz family for more than one hundred years. Self-guided tours now introduce visitors to the traditions and values of a farming family living and working on St. Croix now transforming to a 21st century farm. Call 220-0466 for information or csa@ridge2reef.org.

The **St. Croix Heritage Trail** which is nationally recognized is a 72-mile driving tour that connects St. Croix's historic sites, attractions and natural areas. Watch for the brown and white sugar mill symbol road signs and visit http://heritagetrails.stcroixlandmarks.org for more information.

**Friedensfeld Moravian Church**  Take Midland Road, Route 72 on the maps to this intricate structure prefabricated in Germany and carried to the islands in the mid-1800s. This is just one of the many historic churches on St. Croix.

**Cruzan Rum**   (Cruzan Viril Ltd.,) located in Estate Diamond, off Queen Mary Highway and left on Route 64, or West Airport Road, is home of the famous **Cruzan Rum**. The rum factory traces its origin back to 1760 symbolizes longevity in the rum category, and embodies the real "spirit" of of a hand-crafted, nurtured product. Produced by generations of the Nelthropp family, this distillery owes its legacy to hundreds of years of Crucian rum culture. Despite the termination of nearly 200+ sugar cane crushing mills on the island, the distillery has increased production capacity to serve a greater global demand for rum and has adapted its technology to remain current without sacrificing quality. The Cruzan credo is to produce superior rum, as exemplified by its Estate Diamond Collection. Popular Cruzan products include Cruzan Estate Light and Dark Rums and Single Barrel Rum which has earned the title of "World's Best Rum" and won Double Gold at the prestigious San Francisco World Spirit Competition in 2010.

The oak-aged Cruzan Rum was also voted best in a blind test conducted by The Washingtonian Magazine.

**Salt River**
Be sure to visit the west side of Salt River on the north shore on Rte. 80, just off of Route 75. It is here that Christopher Columbus and his fleet skirmished with Carib Indians on November 14, 1493. The Salt River Park also has the largest remaining mangrove forest left in the territory. The 1,015-acre Salt River Bay National Historical Park and Ecological Preserve is jointly managed by the National Park Service and the USVI Government. Within the Salt River Park, ownership is divided such that NPS has 212 acres and the V.I. Government has 653 acres.
Guided kayak tours can be accessed through Salt River Marina's office, as can diving the east and west Salt River Canyon Walls with Anchor Dive Shop at Salt River. There are bioluminescence (glow in the dark microorganisms) to be seen at the Salt River and Altona Lagoon. Guided ecological tours of the Salt River Mangrove shore and other breathtaking spots are available. Be sure to call Crucian Heritage and Nature Tourism (CHANT).

Golf buffs will love the world-class **Carambola Golf and Tennis Club**, located just off Route 69 and east of the Rain Forest. An outstanding course, designed by Robert Trent Jones, Senior, Carambola twists around a beautiful valley. **The Buccaneer Hotel** (18 holes), and **The Reef Condos** (9 holes), offer challenging courses for their guests and the general public.

For a spectacular view of the island, take Route 58 just outside of Frederiksted, the **Creque Dam Road**, and wind between the mountain tops and Through the **Rain Forest**. Because the roads go up hill and down dale, drive them only in the daylight, and with care, in a 4-wheel drive vehicle. The **Mahogany Road**, or Route 76, near Frederiksted, is another beautiful, peaceful drive through the lush Rain Forest.

At the **St. George Village Botanical Garden** sign, a right turn off Queen Mary Highway when you are heading west, you can spend as little as an hour or as long as a morning, wandering around its lush gardens, tropical rain forest and restored village buildings. The Garden is open dailyfrom 9-4 except for Christmas.

### Frederiksted

Our island tour continues with St. Croix's other major town, Frederiksted, also known as "Freedom City." If you should arrive by cruise ship, you will dock at the beautiful, Ann E. Abramson pier in Frederiksted where much of the town has been named an historic area. This turn-of-the- century town, and home of carnival, charms visitors with wide tree-shaded streets, a lovely waterfront, and several blocks of arcaded sidewalks. As a National Historic District, the city features such structures as the:

**Caribbean Museum Center of The Arts** houses a gallery, a community arts center and a gift shop that features the work and products of local artists.
**The Fleming Building** constructed of bricks from destroyed sugar mill Chimneys. **Victoria House** on Strand displays exquisite architecural details.
**The Old Customs House,** similarly to the one in Christiansted, was where goods were weighed and taxed
**Fort Frederik Museum** restored and located just to the left of the pier as you you disembark. Built in the mid 1700s, the Fort has been in continuous use for military and other government purposes. The Fort is now a venue for cultural events as well as a Museum specializing in the history and architecture of Frederiksted, with rotating exhibits of local artists and Crafts people.
**St. Paul's Anglican Church**, dating originally from 1812 with additions in 1848 and reconstruction in 1990s due to a fire. Holy Trintiy Lutheran and St. Patrick's Roman Catholic Churches are the other 2 historic churches in this Town. At St Patrick's is a monument dedicated to 14 crew who died when their ship was struck by a tidal wave in 1867.

Wherever you drive, you will find remnants of sugar mills in the landscape of the island. At the height of the plantation era, in the 1700s, St.Croix had 114 wind mills,14 ox-mills and was divided into 275 plantations, or estates. The island was once considered the premier sugar-producing area and the "bread basket" of the Caribbean. Most areas still carry the plantation or estate names that reflect the owner's thinking. Check a map, or, on your drive through the island, look for names like: Good Hope, Judith's Fancy, Lower and Upper Love, Barren Spot, Humbug, or William's Delight.

## STAYING ON THE ISLANDS...ST. CROIX

Since nothing on St. Croix is more than an hour away, stay at a hotel that best suits your fancy or your pocketbook. There are top-notch resorts located on beautiful beaches as well as charming small inns (bed and breakfast hospitality). If you prefer to rent a small condo or private home for the home away from home feeling a variety of these are also available. If you should choose to stay in Christiansted, you will find yourself near many of the island's finest restaurants and specialty duty-free shops. Located in town are a number of hotels that reflect the owner's personalities.

### Dining Out

Experience a little St. Croix history as you dine in a plantation greathouse, a restored Danish colonial townhouse, or simply sitting by the water enjoying a beautiful sunset. Watch yachts and sailing craft from your harbor-front table, or beachfront table, or enjoy the panoramic view of the Caribbean from a restaurant tucked into an island hillside.

There are a number of restaurants in downtown Christiansted offering upscale gastronomical delights and casual dining. There is a full variety of cuisines from West Indian, French, Danish, Continental, Cajun, Mexican, Thai,Latin and American, to fast food and deli specialties. In Frederiksted, not to be outdone, although since the hurricanes there are fewer restaurants the ones there offer great food, some with scheduled entertainment. There are also restaurants on the beach with a breathtaking view of the ocean and beautiful sunsets. Watch for the green flash as the sun dips below the horizon. Devotees of fast food will not be disappointed as you will find several franchises and a wealth of food trucks at various locations on island.

### Shopping Around

St. Croix is a duty-free port with much less hustle and bustle than St. Thomas, and that will make shopping easy. In Christiansted, a collection of galleries, mostly located on properties intersecting cross streets, displays the

19th Settler's Handbook    Getting Acquainted 2

# 19th Settler's Handbook  Getting Acquainted 2

best works of talented local artists. There are art galleries, mostly located on properties intersecting Company and Queen Cross Streets, displays the best works of talented local artists. There are art galleries located in Christiansted and Frederiksted. Don't forget the Caribbean Museum of Art in Frederiksted. One particularly fun way to take in the Crucian art scene is to attend one of Christiansted's Art Thursdays, a November-through-June art walk in which galleries stay open late and provide refreshment and conversation about their work to visitors. For more information, visit www.artthursday.com.

Christiansted also has several fabulous jewelry shops, offering hand-crafted original pieces. Visit Sonya's for the authentic 'hook' bracelet; Tropical Bracelet Factory for custom jewelry and gifts as well as Crucian Gold for the Crucian Knot bracelet. Duty-free liquor and cigars are available which means you can take up to $1600 in goods back with you. Unusual glass cut-pieces can be seen at the Mitchell-Larsen Studio on Company Street. Island fashions can be found at the stores in Christiansted.

If you are looking for Native crafts visit Many Hands, or The LEAP in the Rain Forest on route 76. LEAP specializes in locally carved wood artifacts ranging from custom furniture to smaller items made of mahogany, saman and Tibet. LEAP stands for Life and Environmental Arts Project, which is a special program established to train wood cutters/craftsmen in the utilization of the native woods of the island. There are boutiques, gift and souvenir shops in Frederiksted.

## AROUND THE ISLANDS….ST. JOHN

St. John is special. Lush mountains drop to white beaches and postcard bays. A getaway for the rich and famous and average Joes, this tiny island serves as a retreat for Crucians and St. Thomians. The Virgin Islands National Park, consisting of approximately two-thirds of the Island, is a major attraction for the more than one million people who visit yearly.

If you are in St. Thomas, you can ride a ferry to St. John by going to the Red Hook Visitor's Center a 15-minute ride. In St. John, see the Cruz Bay Visitors' Center for maps and tour information, and browse through the best collection of books you will find on the different islands. Taxis are available for island tours or you can rent a car. It can take a half day to see the island if you rush it, but you can relax and make it a full day, or plan to spend more time at one of St. John's inns, condos, or hotels. You can also take a ferry from downtown Charlotte Amalie on St. Thomas versus the taxi ride to Red Hook at east end.

Established in 1956 by the U.S. Congress, the seeds for the Park were sown by philanthropist Laurance Rockefeller who bought and donated 5,000 acres of land on the island. Over the years, the acreage has expanded to 7,200 acres of land with 5,650 acres offshore.

The Park offers gorgeous beaches, camping, prime cruising, snorkeling, and hiking trails. The underwater snorkel trail at **Trunk Bay**, on the northwestern shore of the island, is world famous. For a glimpse at the island's sugar legacy, visit **Annaberg Estate Plantation** on the northern shore near Route 20. Lovingly restored by park artisans, the Estate's stone mill dominates the skyline. The Park often has basket-makers, cooks and other crafts-people on hand to demonstrate and share their skills. On the Southern side, the trip through the Reef Bay valley past ancient ruins and stone carvings called petroglyphs dating back to the day when sugar was king, gives hikers a real chance to enjoy the natural beauty of the Virgin Islands.

Visitors can hike on well-maintained trails or through the bush, but keep in mind that some of the land within the Park boundaries is privately owned. The Park strictly enforces the laws that protect the Park's fragile environment. Take only pictures and leave only footprints.

Cruisers will find pristine anchorages and top-notch sailing when they wend their way through the Park. During the winter months, keep a lookout in Pillsbury Sound between St. John and St. Thomas for breaching whales.

To give everyone a chance to enjoy the Park's beautiful waters, sailors are limited to 14 nights per year in the Park. You might want to stop in Cruz Bay and pick up a box lunch before visiting the Park. However, most of the time lunch, restrooms and cool showers are available at Trunk Bay. Hawksnest Beach has restrooms. Francis Bay, Salt Pond and Lameshur Bay have natural rustic facilities.

The main town of **Cruz Bay** is now a bustling port. While it doesn't begin to rival St. Thomas for traffic, you will see cruise ships' tenders dropping off passengers nearly every day during winter season, sail boats clearing into the territory through the U.S. Customs facility, and barges hauling construction materials. If you want to absorb the local flavor, spend an hour sitting in Cruz Bay Park, just across from the ferry terminal, and watch an entire cross-section of humanity pass by.

Stop at the local Elaine Ione Sprauve Library just up from Cruz Bay center off Route 104, called South Shore, which after Fish Bay continues as Giftt Hill up to Centerline Road.
The library hours are 9 a.m. to 5 p.m., Monday through Friday. You can browse its collection of books on the Caribbean. Call the library at 776-6359 for more information.

To see more of the island, rent a car at any of the handful of agencies in Cruz Bay. You can take Centerline Road, which goes straight through the island, or the North Shore Road, which is winding and passes many National Park beaches and scenic lookouts. On Centerline you may encounter truck traffic, so it's slower, with no room to pass. Drive along Centerline Road, Route 10 from Cruz Bay, towards the east end, to the sleepy community of Coral Bay, which is ever expanding. Once out of Cruz Bay, the pace slows. Fill up on gas before you leave, since St. John has only two stations at this time,.

Once you leave the residential and commercial area of Cruz Bay, you will find green hills and spectacular views on the 20-minute drive. When you get to Coral Bay, turn right and head down Route 107 and see one breathtaking view after another. Watch for places to stop and take pictures. Also watch out for goats and donkeys that roam the roads. They will put quite a dent in your rental car if you hit one. Also drive slowly and on the left. It is very narrow. If you are truly intrepid, follow the up-hill and down-dale road past **Salt Pond** to **Lameshur Beach** for an afternoon of snorkeling, sunning or dozing in the shade. Explore the ruins of the old Lameshur plantation that hugs the western end of Lameshur Bay beach.

## STAYING ON THE ISLAND - ST. JOHN

St. John has a wide variety of accommodations to suit the visitor's taste and budget. There are luxury villas and also an assortment of budget guest houses in between.
(Movie stars such as: John Travolta, Kelly Preston, Kevin Bacon and Denzel Washington, have been known to frequent St. John in winter.) If you want a home away from home, there are more than 500 private homes for rent, with pools, hot tubs and spectacular views. Villas and condos are

available for rent. Call some realtors on St. John, such as Nick Bailey at John Foster Real Estate or Tammy Donnelly at 340 Real Estate.

### Dining Out

From native-style vegetarian to upscale dining, you can find it in St. John. Since the restaurant scene is ever-changing, ask the next person you see in the street for their favorite place for top-of-the line dining as well as moderately priced dinner.

### Shopping Around

From tee shirts to top locally designed jewelry, you are sure to finish your shopping list on St. John. There are dozens of boutiques to browse and make your purchases. Shopping is centered at Wharfside Village on the beach at Cruz Bay and at the two Mongoose Shopping Centers just past the Park Office. Don't miss the dozens of boutiques in between. As far as grocery shopping, there are several excellent grocery stores (prices are little higher than St. Thomas).

The shopping on St. John is a cultural extravaganza. Local crafts and art are available in small stores and galleries. Tropical clothing, hand made and locally designed jewelry, exotic clothing from around the world are tantalizingly displayed in the cute and colorful stores of Mongoose Junction. There you can mix a day of shopping with a delicious meal at any of the restaurants located there.

## AROUND THE ISLANDS - ST. THOMAS

**The Camille Pissaro** building on Main Street, once home of the Impressionist painter who went off to Paris to seek fame and fortune, is a great way to start your acquaintance with the downtown Charlotte Amalie area. This building now houses several of the stores that give St. Thomas its reputation as a shopping Mecca, as well as an art gallery named in his honor.

**Congregation of Blessing and Peace and Loving Deeds** on Crystal Gade is the Second oldest synagogue under continuous use in the western hemisphere. While this building went up in 1833 following a disastrous fire that wiped out much of Charlotte Amalie, the congregation dates back to 1796. A guide will point out the sand floor and the  19th century chandeliers. The Synagogue, is open from 9 a.m. to 4 p.m.

**Fort Christian** To glimpse the heart of the island's history, walk to this Fort and the museum located on the huge edifice's inland side. Built in 1671 by the Danes, the newly-refurbished museum has a changing series of exhibits on the island's culture and history. Explore the dozen plus cells that served as St. Thomas' only jail until the 1980s.
There is also a pay public parking lot adjacent to the Fort that is one of the best places to park your car while you explore old Charlotte Amalie. You will find public bathrooms on the north side of the parking lot.

Going inland across **Norre Gade** you will find the **99 Steps**, the site of the former **Hotel 1829** and **Blackbeards**, that lead up to **Government House**. Recent renovations to the 19th century building are complete, and escorted tours are usually available. One block over, you will find **Frederick Lutheran Church**, an 18th century building which is open to the public.

**Tillett Gardens** If you're interested in the local arts scene, visit cultural cluster of craft stores, visual art, music and theater. Patrons will find raku pottery, jewelry, candles, and a gallery displaying water colors, oils and acrylics by local and Caribbean artists. Tillet Gardens also hosts two music studios featuring lessons in piano, violin and voice. And an outdoor theatre accommodating 300 people is an annual home to four classical concerts and four non classical concerts, all performed by top international talent.

**The V.I. Legislature Building** is a must for a look at the art of Virgin Islands politics. Stroll eastward along the waterfront until you come to the VI Legislature Building. Built in the 19th century as a barracks for for the Danish militia and used by the U.S. Navy when it governed the island, it also served, at one point, as the island's only high school. The public is welcome to sit in when the 15 senators meet in full session, or in committee on the second- floor chambers (and no, you are not allowed to hurl tomatoes until you have lived here for at least 4 years and have paid all your taxes). Jest! We poke fun at politicians, lawyers, used car salesmen and insurance agents). The receptionist just inside the front door can tell you what is on the calendar for that particular Day.

For visitors who want to put some miles on their shoes and get closer to Mother Nature, **Hassel Island** sits in the middle of **Charlotte Amalie Harbor.** Visit the waterfront taxi services and find out how to get there. Once there, follow the trail up to the old fort on the ocean side of the 135- acre **Virgin Islands National Park**-owned island. There is also a trail to the signal tower used by the Danes to alert residents of approaching ships. It can be super hot at mid-day, so be sure to bring water.

While seeing the Charlotte Amalie sights can be fulfilling, there are still miles of island to explore.

Most visitors head to **Magen's Bay**, a gorgeous strand of white sand on the island's north side. A full-service beach with bathrooms, changing rooms, snack bar, covered picnic tables, sports equipment rental, and boutique await you. Magen's Bay also has an arboretum recently

*Magen's Bay*

restored by a local Rotary Club. Walk down the beach to the left and stroll through stands of palms and Norfolk pines included among the 200 varieties of exotic trees. The arboretum was established in 1948 by Philanthropist Arthur Fairchild when he donated Magens Bay to the people of the Virgin Islands.

If you have time to spare, plan a circular tour of the island. Head west along the waterfront from Charlotte Amalie to the left turn at the light by the **Veteran's Drive Post Office**. Or, stop for drinks or lunch at **Frenchtown**, an enclave settled by the French from St. Barths. Home to numerous restaurants and bars, the area seems to attract the island's movers and shakers.

Back on Veterans' Drive, continue past the Cyril E. King Airport and see the beautiful buildings of the **University of the Virgin Islands** nestled up in the hills to your right. The campus environs has an intimate feel reminiscent of a small New England college. Refresh yourself with a swim at Brewer's Bay or continue uphill. As you continue around the island, one panorama after another will unfold as you follow the narrow, twisting roads. Follow Route 30 through areas that still bear the names of Danish estates; Bonne Esperance, Perseverance, and Fortuna, are just a few.

Retrace your drive to Route 301 or West End Road for a trip along the island's northern side. Take northern Rte. 33 to head east. Make sure you have a good map, because the roads on this side of the island can easily confuse. Everybody stops at Drake's Seat because the view is stupendous. Drake's Seat is located at the intersection between Routes 40 and 35. For still more awesome views, continue along the north side, Route 42, until the land flattens out and you are on Smith Bay Road. Looking east, note the heart-stopping views of St. John and the British Virgin Islands.

Turn left at the signs for **Coral World**, a not-to-be missed attraction that features an under-sea viewing observatory. Watch Caribbean sea-dwellers swim by as divers feed them. You can stop for a swim at nearby **Coki Beach**. Head through Red Hook at the

29

very east end, along the south side on your return to Charlotte Amalie. For trendy night-life, Red Hook is it. The drive takes you past several hotels, groups of condos, local marinas and Havensight Mall before you get back to town.

### Dining Out ....

From food carts along the side of the road, to top-of-the line dining, you will find it on St. Thomas. If you are shopping in Charlotte Amalie, numerous restaurants are tucked away in alleys and up the hills. The island's hotels vie with each other to create the best in fine dining, creating through competition, a culinary experience bar none. You will find a mix of cuisnes on St. Thomas to include Italian, Mexican, Asian, American and other options. Be sure to try some of the local dishes. Of course there are always the usual fast food franchises so your kids won't feel like they are missing out.

### Staying on the Island

The 2017 hurricanes damaged several hotel structures and some are still being rebuilt as of press time however, from cozy guest houses to posh hotels and a coterie of vacation condominiums in between, St. Thomas still has the the accommodations you seek.

Strung along the south side of the island, visitors will find a chain of large hotels all individually owned. Along the north shore you will find a string of smaller, beachfront hotels.

Visitors who want all the comforts of home might want a condominium vacation. There are a variety of condominums and apartments as well.

In Charlotte Amalie, you will find a handful of guesthouses located in some of the historic buildings. You will also find a handful of less expensive guesthouses scattered in and around Charlotte Amalie.

### Shopping Around....

Like Rome, on St. Thomas, all roads or sea lanes leads to Charlotte Amalie, the seat of Government as well as a shopper's Mecca. The downtown district reflects the island's Danish heritage. While many of the streets now have English names; some still bear those given by the Danes, and some carry both names. For example, **Main Street** is also known as **Dronningen's Gade**.

A trading port almost since its beginning in the 1600s, Charlotte Amalie continues its merchant tradition, which is a hard act to follow.

A duty-free port, you will find prices below stateside. Housed in Historic warehouses, the city's brick buildings are filled to the rafters with a mind-boggling array of goods. Wind your way through narrow exotically named alleyways to find jewelry priced from a few dollars to the sky's the limit. Every kind of liquor imaginable, including made-in-St. Croix Cruzan Rum and Captain Morgan Rum, is there for the tasting. Fine linens, designer leather goods, tropical clothing, electronics, perfume and, of course, yards of tee shirts can be found in the shops of Charlotte Amalie. Over the years, the shopping district has sprawled northward, so don't forget to stroll the side streets to see what the merchants have to offer.

**Havensight Mall** adjacent to the cruise ship docks offers almost as wide a selection of comparable goods for your shopping pleasure **Red Hook** if you are on the East End of the island, is an area that boasts a growing select-ion of goods and small boutiques.

**Vendor's Plaza** at the east end of the downtown shopping district offers a chance to bargain bazaar style amongst an array of piles of tee shirts, African clothing and island-wraps, bathing suits, hats, bags and other access-ories and trivets.

**Yacht Haven Grande** another great shopping center is within walking distance to nearby Vendor's Plaza and downtown Charlotte Amalie

### Associations

Now that you have a modest acquaintance with St. Croix, St. John and St. Thomas, their similarities, differences and a little about their personalities, you will want information on associations and Clubs to get involved!

That's the best advice for anyone who wants to become a part of their new community. Like everywhere, many volunteer organizations fill in the gap where government stops. Others will help you discover a new hobby. All will help you to meet new friends. Everybody needs help. They will welcome you with open arms. See Chapter 7 for a list of organizations which has a wide scope of interests to meet your every need and if you can't find what you like - gather some like-minded people together and start a new one!

*Helping hands are available in abund-ance in the US Virgin Islands via a variety of ad hoc and organized, vol-unteer agencies.*

# Settler's Handbook Chapter 3

## *TO BE A VIRGIN ISLANDER...*

### Where Shall You Live?

So now that you agree with home grown reggae artiste, Pressure 'Buss Pipe', and the rest of us 'that Virgin Islands Nice, So Nice, So Nice', you have made up your mind to be a Virgin Islander. You are ready for the sun, sea and sand and goats and donkeys and well ...you already got the picture and you, fearless one, are determined to make a new start. Where shall you live? Which island? What kind of life or lifestyle are you seeking? Maybe you want a luxury estate, a condominium or a cozy cottage on the beach, an ocean-side cliff, a mountain top or a simple apartment. To help you make the decision, The Settler's Handbook has provided the following descriptions of the life and lifestyles on St. Croix, St. John and St. Thomas.

The real estate markets on all three Virgin Islands has been dramatically influenced in the last few years by the explosive growth of the EDC tax benefit program, although this has recently tapered off and leveled out. Almost overwhelming demand for luxury homes and condos had created a strong seller's market and in some cases almost doubled prices. The 2017 double hurricanes Ir-Maria along with the re-opening of the oil refinery on St. Croix, have changed the real estate landscape figuratively and literally. Construction costs and rental costs are quite a bit higher and not expected to taper off until another year. Many homes on the market have been fixer uppers.

### St. Croix

In its own inimitable style, St. Croix, known to locals as Twin City, combines all the best of the Virgin Islands. More laid back than St. Thomas, a few paces faster than St. John, the island called "the quiet Virgin" has amenities and beauty.

While St. Croix has its share of shopping centers, strip malls and local businesses, its slower pace has led to an atmosphere that's more town and country. It always seems to be feel less crowded and more roomy than the other two Virgin Islands. There is still plenty of room for development The island is large enough to go for an afternoon drive without traveling the same roads twice. It is blessed with abundant picturesque architecture from the sugar plantation days, and much of that architecture is incorporated into the newer buildings. The rural surroundings offer natural settings that can be breathtaking. There is a closeness to nature's treasures that strongly influences the visitor as well as the resident. The island does have cosmopolitan Christiansted, the uniqueness of Frederiksted, Island Center for the Performing Arts for concerts, superb restaurants and charming boutiques. The sparkling blue waters and white clean beaches make sailing, swimming, snorkeling, scuba diving and just enjoying the sunsets a Crucian pastime. St. Croix is an island of sports-minded people and family-oriented outdoor types, evident in the island's three golf courses, numerous tennis courts, rain forest hiking trails and active sports programs for adults and kids. The island also has many professional groups that will make it easy for you to meet others. With four Rotary Clubs, an active Chamber of Commerce, The American Legion, Whim Greathouse Plantation and Museum's Landmark Society, St. George Village Botanical Garden, youth groups, sports associations and

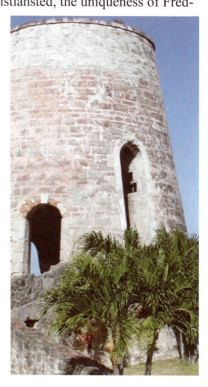

more. You will find sufficient volunteer work to help you learn about the people and the island.

## Real Estate

According to statsitics from Julie San Martin of ReMax, on St. Croix, the average house was sold at $403,914 in 2019. The past five years saw average prices ranging between $329,000-$403,000 with the lowest year Being 2018, after the huricanes. The average condo price was $220,498 with the average five year range being between $182,000 - $220,000. Residential lots averaged $64,821 - $79,000 over five years. Fixer upper houses from hurricanes can start at $125,000. Building costs have increased since the hurricanes. Perhaps more than any real estate market in the islands, **St. Croix is experiencing the biggest increase** primarily due to the reopening of the refinery. Bear in mind the priceswill depend on location.

### St. John

With two thirds owned by the Virgin Islands National Park, St. John a.k.a Love City, is the epitome of peace and serenity. Starting in 1950 with with 5,650 acres, the park now encompasses more than 27,000 land and underwater acres. Though it has a land mass of only 20 square miles, St. John is the purest of the Virgins, possessing steep and lush tropical forests, white sandy beaches unbelievable turquoise seas, and strikingly beautiful vistas. While positively placid by St. Croix and St. Thomas standards, Cruz

Bay does buzz, particularly during the winter months, when cruise ships drop off passengers in in the early morning hours. Connected to the commercial, educational and medical benefits of St. Thomas, St. John is for the settler who can put up with the short ferry or car barge rides and increasingly high cost of living. Rentals, if you can find them, average about $900.00 a month for a small apartment to $3,000 for larger accomodations. The grocery selection has vastly improved in recent years, but you may not find everything on your list in one of the island's handful of convenience stores, and the prices will be higher. Look for Chelsea Pharmacy and be sure to visit St. John Marketplace, with Star Fish Market and other stores. A visit will give you a feel for what it's like to live on an island with 3,700 people where everybody knows everybody else and news flies like wildfire on the "coconut telegraph."

Beach gatherings, the Friends of the Virgin Islands National Park, the Audubon Society, the Historical Society, the Lions Club, the St. John Yacht Club, the Business and Professional Women groups and a handful of committees of varying interests keep residents involved. While historically these organizations have mainly attracted flocks of retirees wintering in St. John, the make-up is changing, and younger St. Johnians are participating. Definitely feel free to attend these meetings. To find out who is meeting, read the Tradewinds Newspaper or the St. John Sun Times, or look for notices on the Cruz Bay bulletin boards. One is located at **Connections,** where locals get their mail and messages.

Another good way to meet islanders is the St. John School of the Arts, which offers various classes aimed at improving artistic ability and physical fitness.

**Real Estate**

As for homes, expect to pay around $300,000 for a handy man special or a cottage in the woods with no ocean view— if they can be found. At press time prices for houses on the market ranged as follows:

| | | |
|---|---|---|
| Houses | $399,000 to | $10,500,000 |
| Condos | $415,000 to | 2,100,000 |
| Land parcels | $ 50,000 to | $ 7,500,000 |

According to Tammy Donnelly of 340 Real Estate, for 2019, real property sales were going at up to 20-40% off of list price compared to 20-25% off of list in 2018. The trend at press time in 2020 was that prices were continuing to dome down. Land and homes price reductions were a bit more than for condos. Contractors have been busy with new construction and hurricane rebuilds for the past 2 years. Coral Bay was especially hard hit during the hurricanes therefore recovery on that side and tourism presence has been much slower than in Cruz Bay. The growth of St. John is related to construction of condos and villas. Parking and traffic are a problem, although there are now a few parking lots. If you have children, there is one public school on St. John, the Julius Sprauve nearer Cruz Bay is K-9 years. The Gifft Hill School and St. John Christian Academy are private. Children may also commute to school on St. Thomas.

## St. Thomas

St. Thomas - Rock City, is very mountainous, thus offers tropical mountain scenery from just about most locations and a coastline scalloped by picturesque bays fringed with inviting beaches. Homes tucked into mountainsides offer the owner views of numerous islands, reefs and coves of the Caribbean. The terraced hills on the north side, perfect for gardening spots, have a magnificent view of St. John and the British Virgins. The resorts and condos are primarily located on the east end. With style and energy, the thirty-two square mile St. Thomas juggles her dual role as the territorial capital and as the shopping center of the Caribbean. Her magnificent harbor at Charlotte Amalie receives about a thousand cruise ship visits a year; and, after three centuries as a trading center, the people and merchants know how to serve the passengers well. The stone warehouses from colonial days now glitter with an amazing array of products and goods from all over the world.

Many settlers have made St. Thomas home because of the career opportunities and a climate ripe for entrepreneurship. Membership in the island's numerous civic organizations will give you the opportunity to meet

other residents. There are several Rotary Clubs, a Chamber of Commerce, the St. Thomas Yacht Club and various associations and organizations devoted to special interests such as the Hibiscus and Orchid societies. with the airport, supermarkets and entertainment at your fingertips, stateside amenities with a Caribbean ambiance can be found. You can eat out at a different restaurant every day for months or try a different beach every weekend and not retrace retrace your steps. You will find the island is the perfect jumping off spot for short trips to St. John and points east. Compared to her sisters, St. Thomas is the island of energy and hustle.

Home prices on St. Thomas range from $200,000 for a three bedroom one bath to mansions that go for $20 million. A three bedroom, two-bath family-style home on a half acre will generally begin at about $350,000.

Houses are generally situated on a half-acre lot, though quarter-acre lots are common for densely developed locations.

Luxury homes with pools range upwards from $650,000. Condo prices from $75,000 to $325,000 for an efficiency or one bedroom, while three bedroom luxury models can range from $450,000 to $800,000, depending on condition and location. Fractional ownership in luxury condominiums has also become more popular with up to a month's occupancy available. Like anywhere, make an offer.

### Water Island

Often called "the last virgin", Water Island is the most recent addition to the USVIs. It consists of 491.5 acres, and offers a unique, informal, private vacation. There is a small full time / part time population of about 250 with private homes, one restaurant, and a great beach. You get there by private boat or water taxi. The taxis or ferries leave from **Crown Bay Marina** by Tickles restaurant and drop you off at **Phillips Landing**. Since it is largely undeveloped and non-commercial it is very peaceful. There are really no cars, so very little traffic other than bikes or golf carts. A restful vacation

# 19th Settler's Handbook    To Be A Virgin Islander 3

could consist of: hiking, biking, beaching, line-fishing, or snorkeling. For accommodations your choices are: private villas, cottages or apartments. You can visit the ruins of **Fort Segarra** and **Carolina Point Plantation**. However, Providence Point Plantation has been converted to a home. Fort Segarra was an underground fort from U.S. defense strategies in WWI.

## Your Decision…

Of the three islands, where you finally drop your hat will depend on your own expectations and challenges. There are those who recommend vacationing on each island before taking that leap to make the territory home. Some discover they really don't like living on a "rock" in the middle of the Caribbean, so "rock fever" becomes a reality. Keep in mind that cures come in the form of sail boat charters or airplane rides that can whisk you away for a day, weekend or week.

Aside from that, what these three wonderful islands have— sky blue waters, great beaches, a marvelous climate and people with a real love for their home— might help you to narrow your decision. With these brief descriptions and in the vernacular of the American lifestyle, you can just about determine that St. Croix is the sleepy, rural island with a small city charm; St. John, the small town with the edgy beach vibes and St. Thomas, is where all the big city slickers live work and play.

The following information will help you in your preparation for the Virgin Islands, no matter your decision, and no matter which island you should choose.

*"You know you have become a true islander when after having lived most of your adult life commuting, including park-and-ride, 90 minutes each way across state lines for work or play, but now attending an event waaay at the other end of one of these less than 80 sq miles 'continents' suddenly seems too far for you."*

## SHIPPING AND MOVING

While you are deciding on which island you prefer, unless you are one of those individuals who can move through life with nothing more than a toothbrush, you will find moving here a major expense.

### Household Goods and Personal Items

These items do have to be cleared. This should be easier to clear. There might be a "customs duty" but it is not an excise tax. If they are used items, and not of a foreign make, there should be no customs duty. Cars can be moved separate from a trailer of personal items. It is easier for the inspector to find and would clear faster so you have your car and drive it away, while your other items may not be delivered till a moving truck picks them up. It could all be same day.

### By Ship

The cheapest way to move your entire household is by ship under $5 per cubic foot of household goods, and/or personal effects port-to-port. The items must be delivered by yourself, or a moving company, in crates to shippers located in port cities. Most national moving companies have agents in the U.S. Virgin Islands to facilitate your move. Shipping from Florida to either their St. Thomas or St. Croix office will take one to two weeks. Going door-to-door back to states, about four weeks due to customs. You must hire a trucker to move your goods to your house. St. John residents must hire a trucker to pick up their goods at the shipping company in St. Thomas for the barge trip to St John. Best to call around since prices vary greatly. Do-it-yourself movers once used the major airlines to airfreight their household goods; however, that has all changed since 9/11. Prior to that, one would ship from a major airport because feeder planes are too small to carry large-sized freight. (Boxes or crates couldn't exceed "height or 126" in width.) Prices also may be high, if it is available at all. It was also on a space available basis. Since the rules and regulations have changed, you need to check with your local airport, and with the airlines to find out who flies here. Since this may not be a possible venue anymore, it is best to employ a professional moving company to place your belongings on containers for boat shipment. It does pay to shop around, compare and let the specialists handle it.

Some freight handlers make a specialty of consolidating less-than-trailer

# 19th Settler's Handbook   To Be A Virgin Islander 3

load shipments into full trailers for a single destination. By sharing a trailer, you save money. A freight forwarder where you live can advise on how to get your car, trailerable boat, or almost anything else on wheels, into these ships. A freight forwarder's services are required except when using a national moving company or a consolidator.

Hiring one of the big nationwide movers to pack, ship, and unpack your island home is the easiest, but most expensive way to move. You will prepay the entire cost in the States after your shipment has been packed into huge sealed containers and an accurate weight determined. Check with movers listed in this section (and in the directory) as they may represent a nation-wide mover. The whole moving process will take several weeks. Furniture, or fragile and precious things should be handled by professionals. Other goods that can survive amateur packing will probably be alright if they arrive via USPS. You can also bring some items as excess baggage on the airline in conjunction with your trip. Check with your air carrier on prices and how many pieces are allowed. Compare shipping times, insurance coverage while in transit, handling costs on the ground at both ends, storage if needed and ulti-  mately, the speed of delivery- new items should always have an invoice accompanying them.

However your goods travel, except via the USPS, U.S., customs will check them when they arrive, for firearms, or any resaleable goods. Used personal effects enter duty free. For door-to-door help in shipping contact the numbers listed in this section.

## US POST OFFICE

If you only have boxes to move, consider the USPS. Boxes shipped this way will not have to go through U.S. Customs and can arrive at your general delivery address if you do not have a post office box. Delivery can take several weeks. Boxes shipped priority mail cannot weigh more than 70 pounds, while the combined length and girth must be less than 108 inches. Since rates vary from where you are shipping, check with the USPS where you live.

## Household Movers (all area code 340)

|  | St. Croix | St. Thomas |
|---|---|---|
| Bob Lynch Moving/Storage | 778-1813 | 774-5872 |
| Ferrol Trucking | 778-9602 | |
| Flemings' Transport | 778-9160 | |
| O'Neale's Transport | 778-1111 | |

## Shipping Companies and Agents

| | | |
|---|---|---|
| Blue Ocean Transport | | 305-428-2735 |
| Bob Lynch Moving and Storage | 778-1813, | 774-5872 |
| Ferrol Trucking | 778-9602 | |
| Flemings' Transport | 778-9160 | |
| O'Neale's Transport | 778-1111 | |
| Paradise Freight | 713-0033 | |
| St. Thomas Cargo | | 776-8660 |

## Bringing in Your Animals

If your pet is moving with you, you must obtain a health certificate from your local veterinarian stating the animal has not been exposed to any communicable diseases and is not sick. The certificate must state that the animal is not coming from an area under quarantine for rabies. Your pet must be vaccinated against rabies. This **must** be done within ten days in advance of arrival. Since most veterinarians are reluctant to give new puppies rabies shots before they are three to six months old, it is not necessary to have your puppy vaccinated. The veterinarian should indicate this on the health certificate. Check with your vet regarding status of your pet's parvo-virus shots. In Chapter 6 of this book you will find more information on helping your pet adjust to living in the tropics. Note the list of vets to call in Chapter 6, if you have specific questions, especially regarding exotic pets. Also, be sure to check with the airlines about any restriction on animal moving, especially May 15 — Sept. 15 because of heat considerations if they must travel in baggage.

## Bringing Your Vehicle

**Choice of Vehicle**

Before importing a stateside car or buying one here, it pays to discover what the car is up against: many short trips, very steep hills, narrow twisting roads, and downtown streets that, while picturesque, are often hot and crowded. What about parts? Arrival time for automobile parts can take longer than you like. Many residents rely on backyard mechanics (get referrals or license) or knowledgeable residents whose skill in scavenging parts from other cars can get you driving again.

You will need a car with a sturdy engine, high-capacity cooling system and an axle ratio designed for mountains, with good brakes, a tough suspension and tight steering. With those constraints in mind, many people opt for four-wheel drive vehicles. Depending on where you live and where you will drive the most, residents can get along with a non-four-wheel drive.

If you have dirt roads to travel, particularly in rainy weather, a four-wheel -drive vehicle with a lot of ground clearance is a wise choice. Some locals rely on a "solid" running vehicle rather than a good-looking one, for the roads and salt air can play havoc on "good" vehicles.

**Shipping It**

To import a vehicle from the U.S. mainland, you must arrange to have it shipped on one of the carriers that call in the islands. You should arrange transit insurance with the carrier. Note you will need original title.

- When it rolls off the ship, collect the bill of lading from the shipper and and take it to the Internal Revenue Bureau to pay the 16 cents per pound road tax. You must pay in cash, certified check or money order.
- Once that is done, go to the Police Department's Motor Vehicle Bureau for a permit to move your car. It's located off Melvin Evans Highway, close to airport on St. Croix- 713-4268;   St. John in the Cruz Bay government complex 776-6262;   On St. Thomas in Sub-Base. -774-4268.

Next, clear U.S. Customs at an office near your shipper. If the car is made totally in the U.S., that means its serial number starts with a one or four, it may come into the Virgin Islands duty free. You will pay a six percent duty on cars made in Canada or Mexico or with foreign-made parts (fees may change since printing). None on U.S. Cars. U.S. Customs takes cash, certified check or money order. Fax 778-2257.

- Next, get insurance through a local agent, then go back to the Motor Vehicle Bureau to get your vehicle inspected and registered. Bring your road tax receipt and the title or bill of sale and a lot of patience to get your new island license plates and title. Renewals will be a lot easier and can be on-line.

   St. John residents can ship their car on the barge that leaves from Red Hook (St. Thomas), but plan on spending all day at this since the various offices are located hither and yon around the islands. Check ahead for their hours of business both at Customs and Motor Vehicle.

## Buying a New or Used Vehicle

If you have decided against shipping and plan to buy locally. Instead, there are dealers in the islands for most makes of domestic and foreign cars

While prices may seem high, they do include U.S. Customs duty, and if it's a foreign car, local road tax, and freight charges. The territory has a lemon law, so do not hesitate to complain if the car has problems. Be cautious when buying a used car. Take a test drive and have your mechanic check it out. To find a used car, check the classified sections in the daily newspapers, weekly free shopper guides or online at the increasingly popular VI craigslist: *http://virgin.craigslist.org/cta/* or on Facebook.

Ask your friends if they know of anyone leaving the islands, or have referrals. You often can get a good deal from people leaving the islands. Car rental agencies will often sell off their older models.

### Automobile Insurance

Auto Liability insurance is mandatory in the V.I. The minimum limit for private Third Party Liability is $10,000/20,000/10,000, for commercial vehicles $10,000/25,000/10,000, (Taxis depends on number of passengers) but of course you can opt for higher limits to ensure your assets are properly protected. All other coverages apart from third party liability are optional. You will need to provide proof of liability insurance to move your car from the dock so be sure to get insurance prior to shipping it. It will help if you get a traffic report from your home state to present to the insurance carrier here. If you are over 70 years old you might require a physician's report. Except for certain programs such as USAA, no mainland companies write Personal policies here. The companies based here, or in Puerto Rico, are fully licensed. As on the manlaind, it pays to shop around.

### Vehicle Titles

All automobiles need titles, and the fee is $30.00. If you have moved here from the U.S. mainland, apply for the title at the Bureau of Motor Vehicles with your current title attached to the application.

### Vehicle Registration and Inspection

You must get your vehicle re-registered yearly and for vehicles over 6 yrs. old, inspected annually at the Bureau of Motor Vehicles (Public Safety). See your registration paper for expiration date. This applies to private cars. St. Croix 713-4268 (Motor Vehicles); 718-2211 (Public Safety) and St. Thomas 774-4268 (Motor Vehicles); 774-5765 (Public Safety).

You must bring your current registration and a valid driver's license to register your automobile, as well as your proof of car insurance certificate. Inspectors will check the low and high beams on your headlights, parking, side and back-up lights, turn signals, windshield wipers, horn, emergency brakes, tinted windows and brakes. They also may check to see if you have a spare tire and a jack. If they find an overly rusty spot on your car or a piece of loose metal, your car may be rejected. If you fail any test, you will have until the end of that month to institute repairs and then have your vehicle re-inspected.

Once the inspection is finished, you will be handed a typed registration and a dated sticker for your windshield and, in certain years, a set of new plates. Cash, credit cards, and certified checks are accepted in payment for vehicle registration. No personal checks are accepted.

### Annual Registration Fees - As of Press Time
(all rates subject to change)

| Vehicles | Weight | Seniors | Registration Fee |
|---|---|---|---|
| All Types (Cars, Jeeps, SUVs) | 0-2500 | 21.50 | 41.00 |
| | 2501-3500 | 26.00 | 50.00 |
| | 3501-4500 | 32.00 | 62.00 |
| | 4501-5500 | 38.00 | 74.00 |
| | 5501-6500 | 44.00 | 86.00 |
| | 6501-7500 | 50.00 | 98.00 |
| Motorcycles | 250cc | 12.00 | 22.00 |
| | 250cc-750cc | 13.50 | 25.00 |
| | Over 750cc | 15.00 | 28.00 |
| Vehicles for Hires Taxi, Limos, Safari buses and such | 0-3000 | | 60.00 |
| | 3001-4000 | | 81.00 |
| | 4001-5000 | | 103.00 |
| | 5001-6000 | | 125.00 |
| | 6001-7000 | | 147.00 |

# DRIVER'S LICENSE

**Valid Drivers License**

If you already have a valid driver's license from the U.S. mainland, it is good here for 90 days. If your license comes from somewhere other than the U.S., you must immediately get a temporary V.I. license, which will be good for 30 days (small fee). In both instances you must obtain a valid Virgin Islands license by the end of your 90-day grace period.

Driver's licenses are good for five years and to become permanently "licensed" you must pass a simple vision exam, written exam and road test. Return the physical exam form and two, two-inch square, passport-size head-and shoulder photographs of yourself to the Motor Vehicle Bureau. Photos must be taken wearing clothing with sleeves.

You may call ahead or reserve an appointment online at http://usvibmv.org to take the written test. Bring your social security card, birth certificate or passport to prove your age. Be sure to study the learner manual supplied by the Bureau of Motor Vehicles at Public Safety, located in the Golden Grove area just off Melvin Evans Highway opposite the Industrial Park. On St. Thomas the BMV is near to the shipping center at Subbase in Charlotte Amalie. On St. John it is in the government complex in Cruz Bay. If you do not have a valid driver's license, you will need to take a road test. Schedule once you pass your written test. If the road test is not necessary, the Motor Vehicle Bureau will snap your photo and issue your photo-laminated license on the spot. The license will cost $35, seniors $17.50 with card, and is good for five years and will expire on your birthday. To renew, simply visit the Motor Vehicle Bureau just before your birthday. You must be 18 to be licensed, but those graduating driver's school, may get a license at 16.

The driving age for rentals is 25. If you get a ticket you can pay tickets for parking or minor violations by mail or in person at the Superior Court's cashier where personal checks are accepted.

If you wish to contest your ticket, A personal appearance is required. Tickets for more serious violations require a court appearance. All tickets that Are paid late will incur a delinquency fee of $75. For more information visit *http://www.visuperiorcourt.org/clerk/Traffic.aspx.*

## Note:

The BMV is also no longer accepting Puerto Rico birth certificates issued prior to July 2010 as documentation. This is because earlier forms of the Puerto Rican document were deemed easily forgeable, and the Puerto Rican Government has recently issued more security sensitive alternatives for other documents that are admissible contact the BMV.

## Driver's License Requirements

Also, to meet Congress' REAL ID Act of 2005, applicants for a VI driver's license must provide originals (not photo-copy) of the following:

### One of These

- Certified U.S. Birth Certificate
- Naturalization Certificate
- Certificate of Citizenship
- Valid unexpired US passport
- Alien Registration Card
- Consular proof of birth abroad
- Work Authorization permit
- If Name Change, original document
- Social Security Number

- Social Security Card
- DD214
- SSA 1099
- SSA Non 1099
- Stamped IRB Income Tax Return
- Proof of residential address

### Two of These

- Utility bill
- Phone bill
- Cable/satellite TV bill
- W-2/other filed tax forms
- Homeowner insurance

- Local property deed, mortgage or rental agreement
- Property tax statement
- Notarized statement from person you live with plus one of above

### If You Have An Accident

Remain on the scene and do not move the vehicles. Ask a passerby or, if you have a cell phone, call police and ambulance, if necessary, or 911. When police arrive they will fill out the forms on the spot. If an extreme emergency should make you leave the scene before the officers arrive, exchange driver's license plate numbers and names and addresses with the other driver. Report the accident to the police later yourself.

# 19th Settler's Handbook    To Be A Virgin Islander 3

## Cutural Tidbit

One of the hardest adjustments for newcomers to the Virgin Islands to make is learning how to drive on the left side of the road. Indeed, the territory is a curious case because we use vehicles made for stateside, right-hand driving. Why then is it, one may ask, that Virgin Islanders have insisted on this tradition? Crucian cultural aficiando. Dr. George Franklin says he has the answer: "Back in the days donkey was king. We used the donkey for everything especially for transportation. Well sir, when cars came they started right-hand drive but the vehicles kept bumping into the donkeys who were trained to walk on the left. So, to make things run smoothly, because you know donkey stubborn, the cars had to follow the way of the donkey. And donkey still run things up to this day.

The Democratic party symbol is the donkey. So you know, the donkeys will always win out in the end."

### Virgin Island Traffic Hints

• Drive on the left

• Carry a valid driver's license which creates new authentication;

• Watch and obey traffic signs

• Even if a school bus' red flashers, do not work, following and on-coming cars must stop for loading and unloading;

• Make sure the road ahead is clear before passing traffic;

• Put low-beam headlights on a half-hour before sunset and a half-hour before sunrise;

• Use hand signals or blinker signals for turns and stops;

• To help others see you in the rain turn on headlights; and use emergency flashers when your car is disabled;

• Obey speed limits. They are low due to the islands' sharp curves, steep grades; narrow shoulders, and poor visibility. In St. Croix and St. Thomas, it is 20 miles per hour in town and 35 miles per hour outside of town. On St. Croix's Melvin H. Evans Highway, the speed limit is 55 mph.

In St. John, the speed limit is 10 mph in Cruz Bay and 20 mph elsewhere.

Before visiting the BMV, visit *http://usvibmv.org* for more information or call: Customs STX/STT Bureau of Motor Vehicles STX/STT: 713-4268 or 774-4268; Public Safety STX/STT: 718- 2211/774-5765

# 19th Settler's Handbook    To Be A Virgin Islander 3

# Settler's Handbook Chapter 4

## SETTLING IN...

### Local Architecture and Your Home

The climate of the Virgin Islands has inspired a style of architecture quite different from that in the states. Most mainland homes, even in Florida, are heavily built, insulated and designated for heating and air conditioning efficiency. Most contemporary Virgin Islands homes are designed to take advantage of the cooling trade winds, offer shade from the brilliant sunlight and protect the interiors from heavy rains. They feature open floor plans to maximize air flow and are often only one room wide for optimum cross ventilation. They may well be designed in long, narrow arrangements or surrounding a large open patio or pool. A wide spreading roof with large overhangs to keep out sun and rain and wide gutters to capture the rain, may float on columns with just enough wall space to give some privacy. Other outside walls are either glass, for enjoying the beautiful views, or louvers, jalousies or concrete grill work for ventilation and semi-privacy.

High, open ceilings are best for coolness while ceiling fans are a must to keep air moving when breezes are light. Roofs are sometimes made of concrete, but more often they are constructed with heavy wooden beams, topped with a waterproofed plywood, or in some cases, galvanized metal to reflect the heat. Floors are cooler and most practical when made of ceramic tile or terrazzo. Area rugs may be used to define special areas, but wall-to-wall carpeting is not appropriate for the tropical climate, since they may harbor dust, mildew or insects. Throw rugs are a nice touch, and easily cleaned.

Lush greenery and area landscaping well placed around the outside and the inside of the dwelling add to the coolness of the home. The brilliant colors and scents of blossoms abound, especially following heavy rainfall, and add to the beauty of your dream home.

### Rent First

Try before you buy is good advice. Don't begrudge the time and money you spend under a rented roof, for what you are really after is a period of adjustment. Can you adapt your mainland habits to the realities of living, working and housekeeping on a tropical island? Better to discover how you feel about living in the tropics before you burn your bridges back home. If you own a mainland home, try to find a renter. If you live in an apartment try to sublease it if you can. Be sure to bring a few of your favorite things to make your temporary island house feel like home. The Islands have a variety of furnished, semi-furnished and unfurnished rentals in all price ranges. Several years ago it was almost impossible to find housing if you arrived in winter months, but that has changed. The choice is even greater in the summer low season. If you plan to stay only a few months, you will pay more than if you sign a longer term lease. And, don't be afraid to bargain. You may be able to keep the rent down by offering to garden, for example. Some winter residents will occasionally rent out their homes or condominiums for a part of the year. Once you are an established island resident, you may be able to luck into an occasional house-sitting arrangement with an absentee owner.

Persistence pays off. Start with the classified sections of the daily newspapers, check with real estate agents, and ask everyone you meet if they or anyone they know has a rental unit. The best deals often come through unconventional methods.

| Size of Rental | Monthly Home Rentals for Long Term Rentals (Utilities not included) | | |
|---|---|---|---|
| | St. Croix | St. John | St. Thomas |
| Efficiency/Studio | $700 - $900 | $850 - $1000 | $775 - $1000 |
| Cottage | $1200 - $1800 | $1200 - $2000 | $1200 - $2000 |
| 1 bedroom Apt. | $750 - $1500 | $950 - $1800 | $850 - $1800 |
| 2 bedroom Apt. | $1200 - $2500 | $1200 - $3000 | $1300 - $2500 |
| 2-3 Bedrm Condo | $1200 - $3500 | $1400 - $4000 | $1500 - $3500 |
| 2-4 Bedrm House | $1800 - $4500 | $2250 - $5000 | $1800 - $4500 |

## Buying a House or Condominium

Prices are high by most stateside standards. While you can buy a house or a condominium directly from its owner, your best bet is to start with a real estate agent. They know more about its realistic value and can help you locate financing. Many homes are bought for use as short-term rentals, and to keep for retirement. While federal tax laws are no longer as generous as they once were, it provides an income as well as an island getaway several weeks a year. Homes often include a rental apartment, normally under the main house or in an adjacent cottage. The presence of renters adds to the security of your house and will add income.

Because of moving costs, a lot of homes change hands fully furnished. If you buy a furnished home, the sellers may ask you to pay separately for the furnishings so they can save on the capital gains tax. It also keeps property taxes lower for you.

You may be asked to pay yearly dues to a homeowner's association. Because the government is not responsible for privately-owned subdivision roads, the homeowner's associations frequently control road improvements. Be sure and check with the homeowner's association, for they may have rules prohibiting hanging laundry outside, limiting pets and other constraints.

People who do not live here year-round usually buy a condo. They try to combine the tax advantages of home ownership with the reduced responsibilities of apartment living. However, the monthly fees often run in the $400 to $2100 range, due to the high cost of windstorm insurance, and, like other condo associations, the owners share the responsibility of upkeep for the common areas such as the pool, tennis courts, walkways and also for the management and maintenance costs.

**Is Your Dream House Historically Significant?**

The ruins of old sugar plantations are strewn across much of St. Croix's landscape. While some of the plantations are restored to serve as the landscaping centerpiece of elegant homes, other plantation ruins may need the loving touch of a creative architect and a sensitive builder to find their former glory. If you decide to undertake such a project, ask your local real estate agent to show you the market. Count on paying double for a lot that may contain such historical ruins.

Christiansted, Frederiksted and Charlotte Amalie are designated historic districts by the local government and the National Register of Historic Places. If you would like to register your 50-yr. old-or-older house, call the Planning and Natural Resources Department for an application. If the house is so designated, you will receive a plaque with the information. If you restore your Historic District house, you will receive a 20 percent tax credit on your income tax. Houses in Christiansted can date to the 18th century and many of the houses in Frederiksted are Victorian in style and era. Devastating fires over the years have wiped out many of the older homes in Charlotte Amalie. The remaining ones date back to the mid-1800s.

Any changes to houses in those areas are governed by rules set down by the Planning and Natural Resources' Historic Preservation Commission. While you can demolish a building in those districts, you have to explain in great detail to the Historic Preservation Commission why it is necessary.

The Commission works to maintain the historic aspects of those districts. Citizens groups, such as the St. Croix Landmarks Society, The St. Croix Foundation, the St. Thomas Historical Trust, Our Town Frederiksted, and St. John Historical Society encourage local residents to restore their houses with the island's history in mind.

## Buying a Homesite

Want to build your own home? Before you buy your dream lot, take the advice of your real estate agent, friends who know or the experts at the building permit office in the Government's Planning and Natural Resources Department (DPNR).

Are the access roads drained and passable in the rainiest weather? Who is responsible for road maintenance? It is usually left to the sub-divider, association of owners or the homeowner to build and maintain the roads. Most homesites are half-acre lots with quarter-acre lots available in denser areas. However, lots zoned before the 1972 ordinances went into effect could be irregularly-sized or shaped. While the Planning and Natural Resources Department has been working on a comprehensive land and water use plan that will restructure all zoning in the U.S. Virgin Islands, as of now it has not been reported or implemented. There are numerous caveats when buying a lot. If it is on a hillside, check the impact of extra structural requirements and site preparation to make sure your budget can meet these demands. Orientation to the wind, grade, salt spray, road access and availability of utility connections will affect the desirability, cost and the home you will build.

## Getting Ready to Build

While you could do it all yourself, settlers should depend on the experts when it comes to building here. Building here is a horse of a different color than building a home on the mainland. Your architect, builder or designer can shepherd your plans and permits through the government red tape process.

While you will be getting involved with much of the same types of building codes and permits as elsewhere, the Virgin Islands Building Code, based on: the Universal Plumbing Code 2009, National Electrical Code 2008 (which changes every 3 years), Fire Codes and the Uniform Building Code, all have special provisions to ensure all structures are hurricane and earthquake resistant.

If you are a do-it-yourselfer, do your research and find out if the land you like is zoned correctly for your use. Check the zoning maps at the Planning and Natural Resources Department for their regulations. Copies of zoning ordinances and plot layouts are for sale in the cadastral, or registration section in the Lieutenant Governor's office. (773-6449 St. Croix, 774-2991 St.Thomas).

Your plans must be prepared by a licensed architect, engineer or draftsman. You can pick up the requirements for a properly detailed set of plans from the Planning and Natural Resources Department and with that information, if the home will be your own, draw the structure. At this point, meet with the building inspector to insure that you are on the right track. After all, he is the one who will Put the final stamp of approval on your house. Next, submit three copies of the working drawings and the site location for an earth-change permit from the Planning and Natural Resources Department's building permits section.

After you have secured your earth-change permit from CZM, then bring the three final sets of working drawings to the Planning and Natural Resources building permits section for building, electrical and plumbing permits. This also puts your job on the building inspector's schedule.

Before you start to build it is best to visit DPNR to learn about, and review, all permits etc. required. For example permits for plumbing, power, central air, demolition, flood. Currently they run $20 for residential application fees and $40 each for commercial applications. Rates are subject to change. There are review plan fees. Those fees are 35% for residential and 65% for commercial of the cost of the building. Please note these are rated with the International Building Code of 2009. (See V.I. Code Title 29, Chapter 5, Section 296 (b) (1). The plumbing and electrical permit fees, obtainable only by licensed plumbers and electricians, are also based on the cost of the job. Driveway permits from the Public Works Department will cost you about ten dollars. To connect to the potable water line, if you are building in an area where it is available, apply at the Virgin Islands Water & Power Authority office. It costs around $120 for a single-family residence. Any construction along the shore or offshore up to the three mile limit, or up to the British Virgin Islands sea boundary, if you are on the north side of St. John, needs a Coastal Zone Management Permit from the Planning and Natural Resources Department. You must plead your case before the Coastal Zone Management Commission and the local Legislature. Projects in navigable waters also need a U.S.

Army Corps of Engineers permit. This includes dredging, removing piers, seawalls, sand mining, filling and just about every kind of alteration to the fragile and precious coastal zone. It pays to ask before you invest.

In St. John The IGLA, (Island Green Living Association, formerly (IGBA)was established in 2004 by a group of concerned construction industry professionals and island residents to promote responsible and sustainable development there. They suggest thinking about greening up the house you own, are buying, or consider building a green home. Current home owners can start by making a few enhancements / changes a few at a time. Incorporate some of these thoughts into your building plans. It isn't only a matter of economics but environmental impact too. Homes can be certified with an IBLA logo designation. Green certified homes seem to sell faster. For information on going green and building green go to: www.igla-stjohn.org

*Contessa's "Castle" - St. Croix*

The site suggests that attention can be given to reduce erosion pollution and destruction of marine and terrestrial communities. Retain native / natural vegetation; use setbacks as green belt area. A tropical architectural design can take advantage of trade winds and sun paths. Use renewable, recyclable, local, sustainable, non-toxic materials. Build for protection against hurricanes and earthquakes. Develop rain water and gray water collection systems. Design an energy system to maximize the use of renewable energy. Solar panels and wind generators play a key role. To start your search on St. Croix call DPNR 773-1082 ext.2295. On St. Thomas call 774-3320. The website for DPNR is steadily improving: *http://www.dpnr.gov.vi.*

## Construction Cost in the VI

The Virgin Islands, and all Caribbean island locations, require a more stringent construction technique. First, the structures need to be built to withstand hurricanes and flooding. Secondly, homes will typically require a water collection system and a cistern to store the collected water for both drinking and sanitation. Thirdly, an on-site septic or waste water treatment plant must be constructed. For remote islands, electricity generation may be the only way to have power. So all of these issues conspire to impact the cost of home construction. The costs are varied and not fixed. Luxury features and extravagant materials tend to raise prices disproportionately and cause average per square foot prices to escalate. Following is a list of average construction cost per island.

As these figures plainly show building in the VI is more expensive. But the positive aspect is that homes built today are far more energy efficient and habitable then in the past.

Most houses have a septic tank with septic pit or drain field rather than

| | St. Croix | St. Thomas | St. John |
|---|---|---|---|
| *All prices are dollars per sf* | | | |
| Affordable Housing | 150-200 | 200-220 | 250-275 |
| Moderate | 200-275 | 225-300 | 275-350 |
| Hi end/ Luxury | 300 + | 325 + | 375 + |

a sewer. In your new home, make sure they are not installed in a place where roots could clog the openings. Some houses have graywater systems in order to reuse household water for gardening or landscape areas. Try to design your home to maximize on tropical breezes, and sunlight to save on utility bills.

Houses with **cisterns** for water storage require an intricate system of gutters and drain pipes. This water may be used for drinking and other personal household purposes. Ten gallons of cistern capacity are required for every square foot of roof on a single story residence. This includes roofs over porches and decks. For a two-story residence, it is 15 gallons for every square foot of roof. Commercial buildings must have five gallons per square foot of roof. The cistern may account for almost 10 % of your final building costs. The roof surface that catches the precious water must not degrade in any way. To make your hot water supply efficient, buy a well-insulated hot-water tank and insulate the supply pipes. Using solar collectors mounted on your roof for heating the water, can save you 20-40% of your electric bill. Check with the Virgin Islands Energy office to see if they might be offering one of their periodic rebates for energy saving devices.

### Security

As elsewhere, crime is also a problem in the U.S. Virgin Islands. Prevention is the key to keep your house from becoming a statistic on the police blotter. If you are going to be away for more than a day or two, consider finding a reliable house sitter and tell your neighbors when you will be off-island. If you live in a high crime area, install decorative wrought iron grills on your windows and doors and consider a high-tech alarm system. If you are a fulltime resident, there is no better deterrent than a good watchdog.

Since it only takes a minute for burglars to be in and out, do not go out and leave windows or doors open. As in the states, make your house look occupied to deter burglars. Invest in a timer that will turn lights and radio on and off. Forget those wimpy door locks that turn with a flick of the finger. Instead buy solid deadbolts that need a key to open. Invest in a locking device for your sliding doors that pushes a strong pin right through the frame into the sliding panel and cannot be opened if the regular lock is broken.

Again, as in the states, police recommend that you engrave some identifying information (NOT your social security number ) in a plainly visible spot on your television set, CD player, home office equipment, cameras and other appliances. This will make it harder for burglars to fence your property and will serve as a deterrent. Record the serial numbers so you can claim them if they are stolen and keep an inventory of those possessions for insurance purposes. Use good judgment when you are out and about. Do not pick up hitchhikers and avoid questionable, unfamiliar areas and keep your car doors locked, especially at night. In case of emergency, call 911 to reach the Police Department, Fire Department or an ambulance from your landline or cellphone.

### Financing

Financing in the Virgin Islands is similar to the States except the available programs are somewhat limited. Conventional loans are offered and FHA, VA and Rural Development loans are available for primary residences. Schaffer Mortgage offers offers a variety of mortgage products to suit your needs. The borrower will normally apply and qualify for one of these loans through a local bank or mortgage broker. Since we are located in what is called an ultra high cost area, our loan limits are somewhat higher than Stateside.

Conventional loan limits start at $765,600 for a one unit property and go up from there depending on the number of units. The VA has lifted loan limits for qualified veterans. FHA limits vary by island and the number of units. The FHA single family lending limit for St. Croix is $331,760, St. Thomas $446,200 and St. John $623,300 says Alexandria of Schaffer Mortgage. These limits are influenced and adjusted by the median housing price. The FHA "Rescue Bill" which was passed and signed in the summer of 2008 may have additional impact on lending limits. Check with a local bank or mortgage broker to see which program is best for you. As in the

States, normal closing costs apply and excellent real estate attorneys are available.

## Property Insurance

Whether you rent, buy or build, you need coverage. Most banks, stateside or local will require fire, earthquake and windstorm insurance with a mortgage; and depending on the location, you may need flood. Your agent can help you select what is best for your particular needs and location. Property insurance rates might be a bit higher than most of the other Caribbean islands and Puerto Rico, and post hurricance of the past 2 years they have actually hardened. Stateside companies do not write Homeowner insurance here but several local carriers plus carriers from Europe and other islands do, plus if you are a member of AARP you could be eligible for insurance under the AARP homeowners program. Businesses might have a bit more flexibility in carriers. Be sure you are insuring based on the cost to rebuild at going constructon prices, and also that you are insuring all of your various options such as fences and your contents. Your insurance agent will guide you.

## Property Taxes

Residential property taxes are .377 percent of the market value of the property. Property owners can qualify for certain discounts, including a homestead tax credit ($400), a veteran's tax credit ($650), a senior tax credit ($500), and a disabled tax credit ($500). The tax year runs from January 1 to December 31. Tax bills for the previous year are mailed June 15 and are delinquent by September l. The interest charge is 1 per cent each month up to 25% until paid.

Other forms of property incur separate tax rates. Commercial property is taxed at .71 percent of market value; unimproved commercial property is taxed at .49 percent of market value; and time share real property is taxed at 1.4 percent of market value. Tax bills are issued on or before June 30th of each year. Tax bills are mailed to the last known mailing address on file in the Tax Assessor's Office. Property owners are responsible for notifying the Tax Assessor of their correct mailing address.

Property taxes are payable at the Office of the Tax Collector, a division under The Office of the Lieutenant Governor. Taxes become delinquent if not paid within sixty (60) days of issue. If taxes are paid after ninety days, they become delinquent, and an interest rate of one percent (1%) is added per month to the amount of tax that is due. For more information contact the VI Tax Assessors Office at http://ltg.gov.vi/office-of-the-tax-assessor-cadastral.html, or by phone at the following numbers: St.Croix(340-773-4052), St. Thomas (340-774-2991), or St, John (340-693-9916 - Fax).

## Problems and Solutions to Your Décor

How to furnish your house depends on your taste, your environment and your pocketbook. Most residents favor colors that reflect the tropics so you will discover that fabrics the color of rainbows with bold, splashy prints, stripes or solids, may predominate. If you want spot color, try throw rugs you can dunk in the washer instead of carpeting. Wall-to-wall carpeting is an option only for dust, mildew and bugs. Colorful sheets will also brighten up a bedroom and with the warm, tropical climate, bedspreads are often not necessary.

When deciding whether to move, store or sell your furniture, keep in mind that the tropical climate can take its toll. The sun will fade fabrics, while termites and humidity can ravage some wooden furniture. What is cozy in the cool north will feel heavy and hot in the Caribbean. Mahogany and pitch pine resist termites while fruitwood, pine and oak do not. Humidity can cause stuck drawers, splitting veneers and loose joints. There are ways to protect your fine furniture. Coat all unfinished parts, bottoms of legs, inside cabinets, and under drawers, etc., with pentachlorophenol, which will prevent the onslaught of termites, fungus, and wood rot, while minimizing humidity-induced swelling. To protect your baby grand piano against humidity, purchase an electric heater rod. Should you discover a pile of termite droppings under your furniture, (a small, round pile that looks like dark sand) call a professional exterminator who will spray the piece for termites and look for other insect infestations.

Furniture with a minimum amount of upholstery is the coolest and the most practical, hence the great popularity of rattan and cane. However, after several years of living with cushion-only furniture, some folks long for the deep comfort of fully upholstered furniture. In this case, occasional airing and sunning are helpful in dispelling any musty odors that might develop during a damp spell. Choose all cotton or a cotton polyester blend simply because they are washable and cooler.

If you like the look of metal, try aluminum with a baked enamel finish, for rust happens quickly in any tropical climate. For your outdoor furniture, look for aluminum frames with vinyl straps to hold the cushions. If you buy woven mesh cushions made of Tixtaline, you can leave them out in the weather since the rain drains through. Know, however, that the sun will take its toll on the padding as well as the color. New breathable vinyl, which has minute holes or an open mesh, is much cooler than regular vinyl or plastic that sticks to the skin. The new vinyl will also stand up better to spilled food and wet bathing suits. Always use plastic hangers, not metal. Keep bedspreads up off floors, just so floor creatures don't stray!

## House Maintenance

The tropics are tough on the contents of your home. Chances are it will fall prey to salt, dust, bugs and a myriad of other problems that need a watchful eye. If a full-time housekeeper is not in your budget, learn to adjust and accept the fact that cobwebs will grow in the corners, fuzzies will appear under your bed and the clothes in the closet and drawers will grow mysterious small brown spots. As for those mysterious brown spots, they appear to come from insects. There's no cure, but bleach or spot remover will take most of them out of clothes or linens. Try drawer deodorizers in the drawer and closet. If you keep up with the outside maintenance, you won't be in a pinch during our tropical storms or hurricane season. Check all joints for caulking and give your home a frequent freshening with paint or caulking or with paint or preservative stains to protect it. Remember that all finishes should be fungus resistant. The local paint stores will have additives that you can mix with your paint for non-treated finishes. Fungus appears as a dark discoloration on the surface, under the eaves or in other shaded areas. Inspect exterior woodwork periodically to make sure dry-rot hasn't appeared in joints that are slow to dry after rains; a problem that won't exist if you use redwood or pressure treated lumber.

While the briny breezes keep you cool, they also eat away at your house and its contents. Salt destroys because it holds moisture, causing corrosion and mildew in the darndest places. Rust can eat through car bodies, belt and shoe buckles, turning them black, create a soggy smell even in line dried linens and your cranky electronics. It's all the work of salt.

To clean your metal objects, sand and scrape to remove rust then scrub clean with fresh water. Dry quickly, prime with rust inhibitor, and paint. Waxes and oils help keep salt from reaching the surface and prolonging the life of painted or plated metals. Rust spots won't go away so try to treat them before they become a real problem.

Refrigerators are particularly vulnerable to rust due to condensation forming on cold spots on the cabinet. Make sure doors and gaskets fit properly and have a service contractor check the insulation. Those cute magnets cause rust spots that spread. You can wax your appliances with car wax to protect from those attacks of rust.

If you live on a dirt road, a film of sand will cover your window sills and screens on the road side of the house. The best solution? Vacuum regularly. To keep things smelling fresh, install louver doors on your closet so the air can circulate. To prevent mildew, never store anything in a drawer or closest that is not clean or dry and be sure to rotate your linens and clothes as you use them. Avoid rust stains on your clothes by using only plastic hangers.

## Gardening

Is gardening a labor of love for you or just another phase of home maintenance? If it's the former, the pleasures in store in the Virgin Islands will last a lifetime. If the latter, welcome to the majority! You will never have it easier than in the islands where pests are minimal and hardy tropical plants are abundant. For most who garden, tropical gardening is mainly a matter of no muss, no fuss. While you can grow orchids, strawberries or other exotic species, most gardeners are content to grow native. Your best bets are  flowers and fruits that also grow in the wild. With a little bit of pampering, these native plants and trees will flourish in your garden or around your home. To make this appropriate setting for your home, first begin with an evaluation of the soil, slope, rain, sun and wind on your own lot. One thing to know, Virgin Islands soils are usually quite alkaline (high pH) so most plants will need extra nitrogen.

While there's a widespread assumption that anything will grow here, it just isn't so. Plants, like all living things, tend to do best in the environment where they first evolved. Drought, sudden downpours, high temperatures in the air and soil all influence the successful growth patterns of your favorite stateside plants. Rats, mongoose or birds will make a meal out of your favorite papayas or other fruit. In some areas, goats, donkeys and horses regularly have lunch on what you have just invested time and money to plant. But don't give up, because there are ways around the problem. Do-it-yourselfers should start with a good how-to book that specializes In warm-weather gardening. In St. Croix, the St. George Village Botanical Garden has frequent classes on tropical gardening. The University of the Virgin Islands extension service on all three islands has a myriad of pamphlets on the subject, and the local government's Agriculture Department will not only give advice but also sell low cost plants. You might consider joining the hibiscus, orchid, or other plant societies, in either St. Croix or St. Thomas and meet residents who will love to share their hard-won knowledge with you.

Now comes the fun! As you read through the plant books to develop your landscape, remember to check how tall the plants will grow and how wide they will spread. Plant shade trees first, so you can protect plants that need partial sun. Think two years down the road to prevent your plants from overrunning each other. Make sure the roots won't invade the plumbing pipes or its leaves, or overhead power lines. Be sure to talk to your builder. Stress to him the importance of not only keeping the construction materials and waste water away from your potential garden site, but also from the roots of your already established trees.

One of the most important things to remember before you decide to become a landscaper or gardener is to watch out for hazardous plants. Toxic or thorny plants are far more common in the tropics than in the north, so be careful not to plant them near your walkways or doors. Even some of the more common plants, Poinsettias for one, may irritate the skin of those who are sensitive. The sap of Poinsettia and its cousins, Monkey Puzzle and Christmas Candle, are the troublemakers. Wear gloves, but if you should get some on your skin while pruning, scrub well afterward. Another one of those problem plants, Pencil Cactus, can cause blindness if you get the sap in your eye. Oleander, another poisonous variety, is a beautiful large garden shrub bearing clusters of deep pink or white blossoms among long straight branches. While it is one of the few plants not devoured by goats (perhaps they are smarter than what we think), those who would use those handy looking branches as barbecue skewers could, just possibly, get sick or die. Something else to watch for is the Century Plant, or Yucca, which has sharp, sword-like points. Protect your eyes. The Lucky Nut Tree is full of a deadly white latex. Eating the fruit is not a good idea for to do so may cause hearing failure, or death. While few people plant Manchineel in their yards, it is more common near the shore, watch out for this spreading tree with a fruit resembling a crabapple for it is highly poisonous. The sap or rain drippings from this tree or even the smoke from its burning wood can cause a nasty rash. Ackees, commonly eaten as the national dish in Jamaica, grow here, but the use of these yellow colored, fleshy arils in red pods are highly toxic and must be picked and prepared only _after_ the pods mature and open _on_ _their_ _own_. It's best to consult with the University or someone local who knows how to prepare them. Trees in the Virgin Islands National Park in St. John and the Buck Island National Monument in St. Croix are often marked with "red skull and crossbones" to indicate their danger to you.

If allergy sensitive members of your family react to some plant pollens and spores, have them be careful around Cassia and Mango trees or Bermuda and Guinea grasses, since these plants are known to cause problems. But, all these problems will be addressed through your reading materials or through conversations with your neighbors or friends. To see what does well in your neighborhood, drive around to observe what your neighbors have planted. Try asking those neighbors for cuttings of plants you like. In the true island spirit, most people will even root them for you, plant several in a pot and, six weeks later, plant the survivors in their own pots. When they look hale and hearty, move them to a ground area you have chosen. Water them regularly until it looks like they are established.

While some home gardeners say they never water unless they have new plants,even during droughts,the pros suggest that you drip irrigate. A little bit of water every day is better than a whole lot once a week. Sprinklers waste water due to evaporation in the tropical climate. Instead try using your washing machine or kitchen sink water to moisten your plants. While some plants do not do well with soapy water (check with neighbors or friends here, or a local nursery), others will do just fine. Due to the tropical sun most soil is compact with a hard crust so, for a few days before you plant, soak the soil to soften it. When it comes right down to planting, start with a big hole, put peat moss around the roots and fertilize regularly because of the alkaline soil. Mulch around the plant to keep water in and pests out then use a non-toxic brand pesticide like Sunoil or Dipel to keep down the pest population. Consider using potted plants as part of your landscape. Requiring less water, these plants can be sheltered during storms or put out of sight when they are not blooming. To save back strain use large pots with casters or wheels.

Last, but not least, do not clear more land than you are ready to plant immediately. Without plant cover to hold it, the few inches of topsoil that covers the rocks will vanish with the first wind or rain. If you need to, a mulch of tall Guinea grass cut from the roadside will hold your soil in place. Now that you have done your reading on the botany of the tropics from books and pamphlets, have talked to friends and neighbors and have planted your special choices, enjoy the fruits of your labor for in the tropics the results can be delicious and the colors spectacular.

### Insects

Let's face it, insects are a fact of tropical life. Some creep, some crawl and some fly, but unless you are a maniac with the bug spray, they are always with you. Learn to love your lizards or geckos. Besides providing hours of entertainment, they eat mosquitoes, probably the number one pest during the rainy season. To combat mosquitoes, dispose of standing water and close open doors at sundown and sunup. Some types of mosquitoes can carry the dengue virus. It may pay to invest in a mosquito net for your bed. Of course you can always spray or fog, as you can for any pest, but prevention is kinder to you and the environment.

The heavier gauge mosquito nets also keep out the gnats, sand flies, or "no see-ems", as they are known by some. They make themselves known, particularly around your ankles, at sundown. If you are really bothered, try Avon Skin-So-Soft diluted with water as a repellent. It's been proven to work by some. It's been rumored that sheets of "Bounce" placed by you, by the bed and in closets helps with that, as well as keeping the air fresh.

From time to time, every house suffers with ants in sizes that range from minuscule to downright huge. Wipe up crumbs quickly and set traps to prevent them from overrunning your house. To keep out flies, cover your food and take garbage to the dumpsters promptly. Despite your best efforts, big brown cockroaches will make their appearance, usually when your most fastidious aunt makes her annual visit. Sprinkle boric acid tablets in every nook and cranny of your house to keep them under control. You can also call one of the local pest control companies and get a yearly contract for a quick easy monthly maintenance spray. Check occasionally for hives hanging around your eaves or yard trees. They often have hives in the old sugar mill ruins too.

Watch out for Jack Spaniards if you are out hiking. Members of the wasp family, they will sting if you disturb them. Try ammonia, baking soda or a chunk of papaya to stop the stinging. Creatures that look somewhat like a caterpillar with many pairs of legs, are centipedes and their toxic bites can hurt your toddler. Be on the lookout for them. While they hunt roaches and crickets, they have a nasty bite/sting. Take a shoe to them instantly. Some adults can have a very bad allergic reaction to them. Scorpions are poisonous and their sting hurts. While it is rare to find one lurking about, every once in a while one appears. Termites can eat the wooden parts of your house quicker than your kids can down a pizza. Dozens of tropical varieties live in subterranean nests, building a mud tube up the walls or making big globular nests in trees. Others live entirely within dead lumber like your furniture or rafters with no clue to their presence except an occasional mysterious pile of sawdust or tiny pellets. Prevention is imperative. Use masonry construction over treated soil, pressure treated or naturally resistant lumber. You may be able to knock out an infestation in a single piece of furniture with a drenching of wood preservative, but if they are munching on the building, call the exterminator. In fact, monthly calls by the exterminator does keep down the pests. Many residents would not live without this visit.

If you are bitten by any island creepy crawlies, you may experience some redness, swelling and itching. If it grows, call your doctor. Allergic reactions to insect bites can be serious. Another little crawler found regularly in these parts, as well as worldwide, is the Gongolo, or millipede.

They are about 2" long, red, yellow or dark brown and skinny. Normally they dwell outdoors, but often times after heavy rains, tend to meander indoors. If they are kicked, they usually curl into a hard ball. If threatened, they exude a yucky odor and brown substance to deter enemies, which can burn or rash the skin. They enter through door, window, and wall cracks, so be sure to check these spaces. While regular pesticides treatment might kill them, the most common pest control is the swift whip of a broom. Also, if you come across leeches, it has been said that salt dries them out. Do watch out for centipedes.

### Clothing

Boutiques on all three islands carry chic tropical wear for men, women and children for almost every occasion. For those who like bargains, Kmart is available. Savvy shoppers and locals wait for end-of-the-season sales to stock up. Since some items are a little harder to find, many residents depend on trips to the mainland or mail-order. Yes, you need a sweater for those cool winter nights and you probably need more bathing suits than you did in the north, but your clothes budget should shrink. For those who must go north, it is common practice to borrow an overcoat from a neighbor.

What you will wear for the day depends on where you work. Government workers and bank employees tend to wear uniforms. Other agencies such as law firms and insurance companies will favour business casual. Those in more casual offices dress down with colorful cottons for regular office jobs. Island wrap skirts can be dressed up or down. As far as shorts and tee shirts, you can't go wrong with cotton. It breathes, is lightweight, and you can throw it in the washer.

Look for loose-fitting styles that allow air to circulate. Sandals help to keep your feet cool. Unless you are familiar with your surroundings, never go barefoot, you will leave your feet unprotected against insects, plants, and hot surfaces.

While it does appear that "anything" goes in the islands and nothing is "in" or "out" keep in mind that the law requires you to cover up, even if you are on your way to the beach. The U.S. Virgin Islands is neither Miami Beach nor Cape Cod, and islanders frown when they see a tourist on the street wearing only a bathing suit. In fact, they may just tell you to cover up. A long tee shirt does just fine. Men must wear shirts.

At night, some crowds dress up and others down. If you are invited to a special local event, know that Virgin Islanders like to dress up. Only a few hotel dining rooms require jackets for men; you can ask when you make your dinner reservations.

## Cooking

Cooking in the islands elevates the art of compromise to new levels. Pueblo, Plaza Extra and Cost-U-Less in St. Croix and St. Thomas are all stocked to the rafters with goodies. But the truth of the matter is, if you have set your heart and your menu on mint jelly with your lamb chops, it could be the week that the Miami or Puerto Rico supplier didn't send any. Should you depend on St. John's small grocery stores to fill your pantry, you may never find all you want. You may want to plan a shopping day to St. Thomas and combine it with other business.

You could spend half a day visiting stores to complete your menu or you can adjust and serve what is available. Sometimes you may want to spend the time on the hunt and other times you may decide to keep it simple. You will also find roadside fresh fruit and vegetable stands (in season), or specialized seafood markets and delis. When not in season, you can usually find them frozen or canned. Normally there will be varieties of lettuce, peppers, mushrooms, potatoes, and scallions in stock. Stateside fruits like peaches, pears and plums are sometimes mealy and tasteless due to early harvesting for shipping. Citrus fruits, bananas, papayas and pineapples are always a good bet. For a real treat, try grafted mango. While the smaller ones are usually stringy, the larger ones melt in your mouth. You can depend on the fact that you will find just about anything here you see in the mainland stores, although there may fewer brands to choose from and the package size may not be adequate for a desired recipe. The new products you see advertised on cable television will probably take several months to arrive in the islands.

Retailers blame the price on shipping and costs may run as much as 25 percent higher than expensive Washington, D.C. or nearly 20 percent higher than in nearby San Juan, Puerto Rico. Local food, a little cheaper, does add a new dimension to your menu. For the freshest local and some stateside style produce, try the farmer's market and the roadside stands. The proprietors are usually happy to give you a sample of some unfamiliar fruit or vegetable to try on the spot, and their advice on how to cook it is always free. Native foods reflect the varied local history. Caribs, Arawaks, Tainos, transported Africans, Caribbean immigrants and U.S. mainlanders have all left their mark on the cuisine. The Spaniards left a legacy of red beans and rice. Recipes Often reflect a European tradition cooked up with what was available here. Those odd-looking roots and tubers you see in the veggie departments date to antiquity. Dasheen, cassava breadfruit, taro and genuine white yam are cook-Ed as side dishes or served as the basis for breads and meat dishes. Banana's not-so-sweet cousin, the plantain, appears as a vegetable baked or fried.

# 19th Settler's Handbook — Settling In 4

Local tangy greens and okra are used mostly for their seasoning qualities rather than served alone.

Chefs are masters at creating tasty stews and entrees from fish, chicken, pork, goat or conch which is harvested locally. Lechon (roast pork) is a big favorite. The entrees are accompanied by a seasoned rice or a cornmeal dish called fungi. For a taste of native cuisine try kallaloo, a stew of seasoned meat, crab and fish boiled with greens and okra, Roti and conch fritters, as a Taste suggestion, are wonderful samples of local fare. The Roti, similar to a floured tortilla, can be stuffed with a combination of potatoes, in a spicy curry sauce with chicken, beef or conch added to it. The Conch fritters, similar in appearance to a hush puppy, are often served as appetizers at restaurants and cocktail parties and again, taste will depend upon the individual chef. Gundi, another unusual dish, is a cold, molded salad made from salted fish (red herring or cod) or lobster with potatoes, onion or beets.

A Johnny cake, (a fried dumpling), is served up wherever West Indians gather whether it be at political rallies, festivals or roadside food carts.

Pates, another finger food staple, are spicy fried turnovers filled with fish, chicken or ground beef. Popular desserts are Vienna cake and fruit tart to sample West Indian food at its best, be sure to attend the food fairs that are held on all three islands' festive holidays. To learn about local cuisine, look for the numerous books cookbooks at local bookstores or call the extension service at the UVI for their "Native Recipes" booklet. Andrew Zimmern of Bizarre Foods did an episode here. CBS ran a special for several weeks called 'Best Bites' which featured local restaurants such as Dashi and Singh's, with hostess Jessica

---

## Cultural Tidbit

"White, grey, purple, green, brown, and sable, are all the colors that bundle themselves tightly up in this juicy, pulpy, fruit. Sugar Apple is a staple treat on the island. Entire calypso songs have been sung celebrating this fruit!

The first thing that greets you when you open a sugar apple is the scent. It is such a mild, peppery-clean, and sugary-warm aroma. I would honestly buy anyone's perfume that was made entirely from this fruit. The first taste you get is a very subtle mellowed sweetness. Smooth caramel undertones that suspend the fruit's seeds in a soft, edible, cotton-like sac. Sugar Apple really defies description. This is one you will simply have to come down to the island and taste for yourself.

Are you packing yet?!"

— Taisha Bailey-Roka, local food blogger and attorney. Visit her blog at http://www.cruciancontessa.com

# 19th SETTLER's Handbook    Settling In 4

Cuyler. The Annual "Taste of St. Croix" food and wine experience is a smash and in 2015 The Dept. Of Tourism launched its first annual Taste of the Islands.

While most local foods won't cause any problems, on rare occasions the **ciguatera toxin** in fish can cause trouble. Despite what you may hear, ciguatera is not fish poisoning. It is caused by a toxin produced by a single-celled animal that lives on algae. Ingested by algae-eating fish, the toxin heads up the fish chain when those fish are eaten by other fish. Since the toxin is cumulative, the bigger the fish, the more likely the problem. Barracuda, some jacks, some snappers, the larger kingfish and groupers may have the problem. Some claim that the toxin only affects fish caught in certain waters, but there is no scientific proof of that. If you eat a fish with ciguatera, you will ache all over. And what is hot will feel cold and vice versa. You may also suffer nausea and diarrhea. If you suffer these symptoms, head for the hospital where a drug called Mannitol is available. While there is no known cure, the Federal Drug Administration is working on a test kit to help doctors determine if what you have is really ciguatera.

If a stomach upset is your only symptom, you probably have eaten a fish with scrombrid toxin which is found in larger fish with red meat. Those fish should be iced immediately after catching to prevent development of the toxin.

### Drinks

Hot sun plus warm temperatures equals a big thirst in the tropics. It is always wise to carry some bottled water with you on long planned errands around the island. While water is the best thirst quencher, there is also a big variety of fruit juices from which to choose. In addition to the mango, tamarind, guava, soursop and coconut nectars on the local supermarket shelves, you will also find the usual orange, cranberry and apple juices. Look for Vita Malt, a non-alcoholic drink produced throughout the Caribbean. Try coconut water right from the coconut at roadside stands. You will also find Locally-brewed maubi, ginger beer, sorrel and sea moss, an alleged aphrodisiac, at native restaurants. Also try the Schnapps (i.e. Akvavit), the Danish drink served right from the freezer. It is often chased with beer. Most stateside beers can be found here, but of course the most popular island drinks Are anything made with rum. That special Cruzan Rum and Captain Morgan are distilled right on the island of St. Croix.

St. John brews St. John beer and there is a brewery in St. Thomas called Frenchtown Brewing Company. St. Croix has Leatherback Brewery and Mutiny Isand Vodka Distillery, the only vodka made from breadfruit was recently opened on St. Croix. Local bars all have their favorite special rum cocktails.

# 19th Settler's Handbook — Settling In 4

## Cultural Tidbit

Though the seasons in the Virgin Island's are not as visually dramatic as in the northern U.S. mainland, when summer time comes you will feel the change. It will show in the form of damp, sticky shirts and often oppressive humidity. To help ease the transition to summer, here is a cooling elixir created by the Crucian Contessa, **Tanisha Bailey-Roka**

Ingredients:

- About 50 Ounces of Water
- 1 1/4 Cups (Organic Evaporated Cane Juice)
- Sugar • 1/4 Cup of Local Honey
- 2-3 drops of Banana essence (to taste)
- 6 Bags of Orange Pekoe Black Tea (Lipton)   • 2-3 Limes
- 2 Cups Passion Fruit Pulp

### Directions:

- In a large heat-resistant pitcher, pour gently boiled water over six tea bags and allow to steep for no more than 4-5 minutes. If you let the tea steep longer it will turn bitter. While the water is still warm, add the passion fruit pulp, the sugar and the honey. Stir until the sugar and honey dissolves.

- Add the juice of the limes and the banana essence. Be careful with the banana essence.

- It is very powerful and can add a bitter-ish taste to your drink if too much is used.

- Let the drink cool to room temperature, and then refrigerate.

### Suggestions:

You can leave it overnight to ensure that all the flavors properly marry. You can also strain prior to serving. However, I prefer to let the passion fruit seeds show themselves off, as a great visual contrast. I also add ice to the cups instead of to the pitcher, since it tends to dilute the flavors. It is to your own taste and preference. It literally looks and tastes like SUNSHINE in a cup! Enjoy!!

Tanisha Bailey-Roka.

## WEATHER IN THE TROPICS

Most of the weather patterns come from the East, out of the Atlantic Ocean and, in some cases, all the way from the shores of Africa. The haze seen at times during the year is the "Sahara dust" floating across the Atlantic Ocean from the African continent. Some of the most beautiful sunsets seen in the Virgins are created by these "imported" dust particles.

On the U.S. mainland, high and low-pressure systems bring well-defined weather changes to a region before moving eastward. While these air masses rarely penetrate as far southeast as the Virgin Islands, when they do, the warm seas warm their passage. Occurring in the winter months, the result could be strong northerly winds, rough seas, rain, a temperature drop and what the locals call the cooling, refreshing "Christmas breeze," which usually start in December. Seasonal changes are subtle, but they are there with temperatures 10 degrees cooler in winter than summer — around 70 low / 80 high winter and 80 low / 90 high in summer months. Trade winds help to cool. For those who are acclimatized, it can feel cooler in winter months, especially at night.

The trade-winds, drifting across the Atlantic and into the Caribbean with their accompanying ocean waves, always move west. While these are not as well defined as the Lows and Highs of the northern air masses, they can cause cloudiness, rain and a predictable wind-shift pattern and therefore changes in the weather.

When an easterly wave forms just north of the equator in the Atlantic, as often happens during the late spring and late summer, a tropical wave may appear. Should this wave intensify, the weather system grows in magnitude, with wind speed rising over 34 miles per hour, it will become a tropical storm. Once the wind speed reaches higher than 74 mph, the tropical storm is then designated as a full-fledged hurricane.

### Earthquakes

While we haven't had to contend with any major earthquake in decades and it is not normally perceived as an imminent peril for the USVI, the fact is that the territory is in an earthquake zone and one should not underestimate the unpredictability and devastation that can be caused in a few seconds by one of these. Minor tremors can be felt from time to time and repeated ones can and have caused damage to your real property. Tsunamis can be a by product of seaquakes. There were tsunamis in the

US Virgin Islands in 1867 and 1967. Several earthquakes were experienced in neighbouring Puerto Rico over several days in January 2020 causing moderate damage and the loss of at least one life.

### Flood

Because of our size, proximity to the seas, low lying areas and run off from hills, we are subject to flooding which can happen with or without a named storm. Enough rainfall in a short period can result in flash flooding. As a matter of fact, rain can start very suddenly without any warning and blow over just as quickly so it is best to keep car windows and openings where you have vulnerable property closed if you will not be around to close them fast in the event of these rapid downpours. It is highly recommended that you consider flood insurance (which is not normally covered under your homeonwer or tenant's policy, even if you are not within ta designated flood zone.

### Hurricanes

When an easterly wave forms just north of the equator in the Atlantic, as often happens during the late spring and late summer, a tropical wave may appear. Should this wave intensify, the weather system grows in magnitude, with wind speed rising over 34 miles per hour, it will become a tropical storm. Once the wind speed reaches higher than 74 mph, the tropical storm is then designated as a full-fledged hurricane.

During the years from 1928 to 1989, there were no major storms in the Virgin Islands. In September 1989, Hurricane Hugo roared through the Caribbean and stalled over St. Croix for almost 18 hours on September 17 and 18. The island suffered massive destruction. St. John and St. Thomas were hard hit by Hugo, but one comment about the island of St. Croix "of the trees still standing there wasn't a leaf left." When Hurricane Hugo hit the islands in 1989 some areas clocked the wind speed at over 200 miles per hour and one anemometer on St. Croix broke at 217 mph. Heavy rainfall in West Africa may create major storms in these areas but, research has uncovered the coincidence that when Africa is dry, as has been the case up until 1995, the threat of hurricanes appear to diminish. Tropical weather systems are also affected by conditions referred to as La Nina (more favorable to development), and El Nino, some-what opposite.

In early September 1995, Hurricane Luis, while devastating St. Maarten and Antigua and the other islands in the Eastern Caribbean, was kinder to the U.S. Virgin Islands. Mainly causing waterfront destruction by its high tides and wave surges, Luis did not affect the infrastructure of the Virgin Islands. However, Hurricane Marilyn, ten days later, was a different story.

St. Croix suffered moderate damage to its structures, utilities and landscape. St. Thomas and St. John received the brunt of Marilyn with 90% of its homes, hotels and utilities severely damaged. An extensive reconstruction program was conducted. Building codes have been revised since, resulting in more stringent codes and more reinforcement to all structures being built.

St. Croix's new pier in Frederiksted was not damaged by Hurricane Marilyn, and cruise ship lines re-routed some of their ships from St.Maarten and St.Thomas to St. Croix. After a few years of visiting the same port, and because of repeat customers, cruise ship operators often change ports for a few years. St. Croix saw an increase in cruise ship visits in 2009 with more in ensuing years. St. Thomas has always been a port of call because of its natural deep water port, and now two docks, one at Havensight and one at Crown Bay.

While residents have always observed Hurricane Supplication Day around the end of July, and Hurricane Thanksgiving Day in the month of October, the observance of Thanksgiving Day took on a deeper meaning following Hurricane Hugo in September of 1989, Hurricane Marilyn in September of 1995 and Lenny in November of 1999 and a brush with hurricane Omar in 2008.

The Virgin Islands made history in 2017 with the battering of all its islands by double hurricanes Irma and Maria, two category 5 systems that occurred within two weeks of each other on September 6 and on September 17. The devastation caused by these had long lasting effects on the infrastructure of the territory including hospitals, utilities, schools, real and personal property and widespread damage to crops, vegetation and livestock.

The Virgin Islanders have pulled together along with insurance carriers, FEMA and other Federal assistance, and by most accounts have recovered and regrouped from the force of these two major hurricanes.

As a result of these two Hurricanes, buildings have been rebuilt with the new and updated hurricane specification codes.

### Disaster Preparedness

Since Hurricane Hugo 1989, the U.S. Virgin Islands government tuned up its hurricane response system and was prepared for Hurricanes Luis and Marilyn and have once again upgraded their responses from the lessons learned from Ir-Maria. Communication systems have been improved, shelters identified and fortified and emergency personnel trained. Thanks to up-to-the-minute weather forecasting, residents get fair warning when a hurricane threatens. And since then, the Hurricane Hunters have made their summer home base in St. Croix and are here from June till October yearly. They fly in the storm and send data back to the Hurricane Center in Miami. Don't wait until a storm threatens, instead, be prepared. Long before there is any storm on the horizon, make sure you have enough plywood to protect windows and doors. In the last few years, companies here have specialized in supplying secure hurricane shutters. Keep a supply of large plastic bags to store your small appliances, books and other valuables. A battery-operated emergency radio that receives weather and forecast alerts from NOAA for example, is a necessity. Radios and newspapers give plenty of warning a few days prior to help you prepare.

    Virgin Islands Territorial Emergency Management (VITEMA) does an excellent job in preparing us for these potential disasters by giving frequent updates, warnings and alerts via current technology. They also give out sandbags to shore up against flooding.

    Tarps are handy to have if your roof blows off. Invest in a generator to insure you have enough power to run your refrigerator. Of course, you will need to keep an adequate supply of gasoline in a proper container on hand. If you live in an all-electric house, buy a camp stove that runs on sterno or white gas to make sure you can warm up a can of soup, make coffee or tea. Buy several battery-operated flashlights and lanterns and enough batteries to last until the power comes on again. Since you could be without electricity for days, don't depend on the rechargeable kind. Battery operated lanterns work best, since wind can blow out kerosene oil lamps or candles, possibly increasing the danger of fire.

    At the start of hurricane season in June, stock up on non-perishables. Keep bottled water, an assortment of basic canned goods, and a manual can opener on hand. Store dry goods such as powdered milk, cereals, pasta products, sugar and crackers in plastic bags to keep them moisture free. Don't forget food for your pets, too. Make sure you have enough toilet paper, bleach to purify contaminated water, your basic tools, a fully-stocked first aid kit, and adequate supplies of any drug prescriptions you feel are necessary. Also, store your important documents in plastic bags.

    There is a wealth of information available from VITEMA, community organizations and not least of all, your insurance agent.

# Settler's Handbook Chapter 5

## *THE INFRASTRUCTURE...SERVICES...UTILITIES AIRLINES..MEDICAL...*

The infrastructure within the Virgin Islands has vastly improved in the last decade. Electrical power failures, which used to be a way of life, are now the exception. The city water, through desalination, is safe to drink. All major streets, though they still have the proverbial pothole here and there, are paved and considered some of the best in the Caribbean. The telecommunications system is better than in some areas in the United States. But, like all structural systems, problems do exist and it is considered part and parcel of living in the islands and the tropics.

### BANKING AND CREDIT

When relocating to the Virgin Islands there are a few things that may be helpful to know about banking and credit before you arrive. There are five brands of banks in the U.S. Virgin Islands with different locations on each island. Banking hours are usually from 9 a.m. to 2:30-3 p.m. Monday through Thursday, Fridays 9 a.m. to 4:30-5 p.m., with some having Saturday hours of 9 a.m. to noon. Usually deposits made after 3 p.m. on Fridays won't be credited to your account until the next regular banking day. Banks are closed for all Federal and some local holidays including Carnival and Three King's Day. Most of these banks offer online services or telephone banking where you can bank anytime.

Your ATM Card is the best way to insure you have cash on hand when you arrive. You can use any stateside bankcard that carries the NYCE or PLUS logo at any of the local banks free of charge. The figure for maximum withdrawals may vary so you need to check before making any major purchases. Traveler's checks are an expensive way to move your money. Do not however, count on cashiers or bank drafts as some banks will treat them as personal checks and may not allow you to draw against them right away.

Most banks may cash off-island checks, but due to slow transit time to clearing houses often force the banks to be very careful. Allow a minimum of one week for a check drawn on a U.S. mainland to clear, five days for one drawn on a Puerto Rico bank or on a different island in the Virgin

Islands and three days for a bank on the same island. Cashiers checks will not be any quicker unless drawn on a mainland branch of an island bank or one of its affiliates.

When here to scout, it may be a good idea to open a savings or checking account, for which you will need 2 types of identification, at least one being a picture ID with your physical address or proof of residence (like a phone bill, electricity bill, etc). As the moving day nears, have your mainland bank transfer funds you want available upon your arrival.

### St. Croix Banks (all are area code 340)

**Bank of St. Croix** (has ATMs)
| | |
|---|---|
| Anchor Way, Gallows Bay | 773-8500 |
| Peter's Rest | 713-8500 |

**Banco Popular de Puerto Rico**
| | |
|---|---|
| All branches | 693-2777 |
| Orange Grove | 693-2902 |
| Sunny Isle Shopping Center | 693-2935 |
| Sunshine Mall | 693-2972 |

**First Bank** (has ATMs) www.firstbankvi.com  866-811-2700
| | |
|---|---|
| FirstLine Telebanking | 775-8899 |
| Orange Grove Branch | 775-7777 |
| Sunny Isle Branch | 719-8686 |
| Strand St., Frederiksted | 712-1020 |
| King St., Christiansted | 773-0440 |

**Oriental Bank** (safe, secure 24/7 ATMs)
| | |
|---|---|
| Estate Diamond (near Sunny Isle) | 778-5350 |

### St. John Banks

**First Bank** (has ATMs) www.firstbankvi.com  866-695-2511
| | |
|---|---|
| FirstLine Telebanking | 775-8899 |
| Cruz Bay | 776-6881 |

**Merchants Commercial Bank**
| | |
|---|---|
| 18-23 Estate Enighed | 779-2265 |

### St. Thomas Banks

**Banco Popular de Puerto Rico**
| | | | |
|---|---|---|---|
| Veteran's Drive 693-2777 | | Hibiscus Alley | 693-2823 |
| Altona | 693-2704 | Lockhart Shpg Ctr | 693-2880 |
| Fort Mylner | 693-2860 | Red Hook | 693-2873 |

| St. Thomas Banks (cont'd) | |
|---|---:|
| **First Bank** (has ATMs)  www.firstbankvi.com | 866-695-2511 |
| FirstLine Telebanking | 775-8899 |
| First Bank Plaza | 775-8502 |
| Crown Bay Branch | 775-7777 |
| Waterfront Branch | 775-7777 |
| East End Plaza Branch | 775-5650 |
| Port of Sale Branch | 774-4800 |
| **Merchants Commercial Bank** Tutu Park Mall | 779-2265 |
| **Scotiabank** | |
| 214C Altona & Welgunst, Altona | 774-0037 |

### Communications

Viya is the largest telecommunications provider in the U.S. Virgin Islands (USVI), providing a full suite of telecommunications and entertainment services. Viya's family of services, for both the business and residential markets, include wireline and wireless voice service, fixed and mobile broadband and cable television service offered over a fiber core network and a state-of-the-art 4G LTE wireless network serving St. Croix, St. Thomas, and St. John.   (www.viya.vi)

Viya, formerly Choice and Innovative, was rebranded in 2017 as the Company morphed into more than a provider of service by offering solutions for residential and business customers. The Company delivers exceptional benefits to their customers, including multi-service bundle discounts, custom solutions for many of their business and government clients; convenient, one stop customer service through their integrated billing and service centers. Viya has conveniently located Customer Experience Centers in locations in St. Thomas at Tutu Park, St. John at The Marketplace and St. Croix at Estate Diamond. Viya also offers multiple convenient payment methods. Customers have the online, pay by phone, pay at the bank, pay by mail, use auto-pay or at one of the Customer Experience Centers. Viya's website is www.viya.vi. and the contact number is 340-777-VIYA (8492).

## Viya Telephone

The U.S. Virgin Islands has a state-of-the-art communications system provided and operated by Viya. The company was the first in the Caribbean and one of the first in the continental United States to have a fully digital switching network. All central offices are connected by fiber-optic cable allowing for significantly higher transfer speeds.

Viya provides residential and business landlines, including local and International long-distance with popular features like three-way calling, speed dialing and call waiting.

The USVI consists of one calling area which makes it easy for residents to call between all islands in the territory for one flat fee with no limit on intra-island calls. Tolls are only charged when calling outside of the territory.

The Area Code for the USVI is (340). To make a long distance call to the continental U.S. or Canada, customers must dial 1+ Area Code + Phone Number. Toll Free (800) numbers are available for both incoming and outgoing calls.

## Viya TV

Viya offers Basic and Expanded Cable packages with more than 295 channels of the highest quality digital programming. Premium offerings include: High Definition (HD) channels, premium movie channels, Pay-Per-View, Digital Video Recording (DVR), TV Everywhere, local and mainland programming, Channel Guide and digital music.

## Viya Internet

The Viya network delivers the fastest, most reliable Internet service in the USVI, with speeds in excess of 100 Mbps over a Hybrid- Fiber Coax network. Customers can download pictures, social media sharing, Skype with Family and friends and stream video. Customers have the capability to work in real time with speeds comparable to regional and national standards supported by the most advanced technology services, including anti-virus protection and 24/7 technical support. Viya is consistently broadening its product/service portfolio to provide the best Internet service available in the territory.

## Viya Mobile

Viya's 4GLTE Mobile service takes into account that Virgin Islands residents travel extensively throughout the region and the United States for business and pleasure. Viya's plans include local calling, calling to the U.S. and Puerto Rico, special rates for calling other Caribbean and international countries and unlimited voice and data that can be used in the caribbean and in the continental US. Viya also offers a wide selection of the newest mobile phones and accessories on the market.

## Business/ Enterprise Solutions

Viya's Business Solutions provide customized services for any size of business. Account Managers provide individual attention to small business, large corporations and local government agencies. Local businesses choose Viya to provide a reliable network of multi-line and hosted PBX calling systems, wireless plans, Mi-Fi, Ethernet, High Speed Data, DIA, SIP/VOIP, Managed services and 24/7 technical support.

## Television and Radio Stations

The territory benefits from local and stateside channels allowing residents on all three islands to enjoy current cable and radio programming. TV stations range from CNN to the Disney channel plus specialty stations to keep you in-tune with the latest information from around the world. Radio offerings include a full breadth of genres – Top 40, Rock, Jazz, Oldies, Religious, and Spanish to name a few. All available 24 hours a day, 7 days a week.

New settlers should make a point to watch WSVI, the local ABC affiliate in St. Croix and Public TV station WTJX in St. Thomas, and St. Croix, Channel 12, to get in touch with events and locally-based programming. Also, TV-2 (Cable Ch.2) has local news and produces local commercials and production for industry and non-TV use.

In St. Croix, 97.5 AM, 95 FM and 99.5 FM are the major news radio stations. In St. Thomas, listen to WVWI at 1000 AM and WSTA at 1340 AM for news. 99.5 also reaches St. Thomas and St. John. Numerous other AM and FM stations air many types of music (for different demographics), headline news, sports and community programming.

### Broadcast Television Stations
**Channel 8** (ABC Affiliate) **WSVI**, Box 8 ABC, Christiansted, 00823, 778-5008
**Channel 12 (PBS) WTJX**, Box 7879, St. Thomas, 00801, 774-6255 St. Croix, 718-3339, recently acquired four digital channels.
**VIYA Cable TV-St. Croix**, Box 5968, Sunny Isle, 00823, 779-9999
**VIYA Cable TV-St. Thomas/St. John Cable TV** (774-6655 (Fax), Tutu Park Mall, St. Thomas, 00802, 776-2150
**TV-2 7** Estate Diamond, St. Croix, 00820, 774-8492 / 779-9999
Tutu Park Mall, St. Thomas, 00802, 774-2200
**WVXF (CBS)**. St. Thomas, 00802, 774-2013

### Cellular Phone Company Providers
**AT&T Mobility** (340)778-6400 St. Croix / (340)774-0005 St. Thomas
**VIYA** (340)779-9999 St. Croix / (340) 777-8899 St. Thomas
**Sprint PCS** (340) 713-0055 St. Croix

### Internet Service Providers (From Dial-up to Wireless)
**Broadband VI Wireless** 340-719-2943 - St. Croix 340-774-0024 St. Thomas, www.BroadbandVI.com
**SmartNet** 340-715-4819 St. Thomas/St. Croix
**VIYA** 340-714-3700/340-779-9999, www.viyavi.com

### Radio Stations
**WVVI-FM Caribbean Country 93.5 FM**, Box 25868, Christiansted VI 00824, (news, country music, talk shows M-F)
**WJKC/Isle 95, 95 FM**, Box 25680, Christiansted, VI 00824, 773-0995 (urban/reggae)
**WMNG, Mongoose 104.9 FM**, Box 25680 Christiansted VI 00824 (adult contemporary, some news, local, regional, national)
**WVIQ Sunny 99.5 FM**, Box 25680, Christiansted, VI 00824, 773-0995 (some news, adult contemporary)
**Latino 98.3** (Spanish) Christiansted, St. Croix VI 00824
**WVWI-AM 1000**, St. Thomas, 776-1000
**WVJZ-FM 105.3 JAMZ**, St. Thomas
**WWKS-FM 101.3 KISS**, St. Thomas
**WSTA Lucky 1340 AM**, St. Thomas
**WSTX Ft. Louise Augusta**, St. Croix, 773-0390

## MAIL AND PARCEL SERVICE

Since this is the good old U.S.of A, the USPS first class rates from the U.S. Virgin Islands are the same as in the states. Those rates are subject to increase at any time. Parcel post and priority mail rates depend on where the package goes. Keep in mind that anything that does not go by air must go by ship. This means you have to allow four to six weeks extra when you are shipping your Christmas packages. Most islanders send items by parcel post and priority.

All mail is flown in and out several times a day from Puerto Rico with the mail going directly to either St. Croix or St. Thomas. First class mail up to 13 ounces and priority mail over 11 ounces will automatically go by air. Priority mail, with a top weight limit of 70 pounds, cannot exceed 108 inches of combined length and girth. Fourth class mail, used primarily for books and parcels will go by ship. Express Mail is available to all areas on the U.S. mainland with service to major cities usually about one day, two days elsewhere.

St. Croix has post offices or branches at Richmond, downtown Christiansted, Gallows Bay, Sunny Isle, Kingshill and Frederiksted. Post offices box availability changes as people move off-island and new people move in. Home delivery is available across the island and if you live in a hard-to-reach location, you can have a mail box on the nearest main road.

St. John has a post office, but you may have to wait for a post office box. If you do, you can pick up your mail at General Delivery until then. The windows are open as posted. Carriers will deliver twice a day to boxes placed along a route on Centerline Road from Cruz Bay to Coral Bay.

St. Thomas has post offices in downtown Charlotte Amalie, Sugar Estate, Veterans' Drive near Frenchtown, Havensight Mall, and at Tutu Park Mall. While you wait for a box at a post office more convenient to your house, again you can receive your mail through general delivery. Hours are as posted.

### By Boat

Important envelopes or packages, with prices starting around $5.00 can be sent to and from St. John, Red Hook and Charlotte Amalie, St. Thomas via the St. John ferry. You can give your parcel to the ticket seller or to the captain. You must, however, have someone meet the envelope or package island ferry service or the Seaplane will carry small packages for a fee.

## Zip Codes and phone numbers for USPS (area code 340)
### Postmaster of the Virgin Islands

| | | |
|---|---|---|
| Sugar Estate Post Office, St. Thomas | 00801 | 774-1950 |

### St. Croix

| | | |
|---|---|---|
| All Christiansted street delivery | 00820 | |
| Company St. (Downtown) Post Office boxes | 00822 | 773-3586 |
| Gallows Bay Post Office boxes | 00824 | 773-4538 |
| Kingshill Post Office boxes | 00851 | 778-0199 |
| All Kingshill street delivery | 00850 | 778-0199 |
| Frederiksted street delivery | 00840 | 772-0040 |
| Frederiksted Post Office boxes | 00841 | 772-0040 |
| Richmond | 00821 | 718-1500 |
| Sunny Isle Post Offices boxes | 00823 | 778-6805 |
| Express Mail | | 1-800-222-1811 |

### St. John

| | | |
|---|---|---|
| All street delivery | 00830 | |
| Cruz Bay Post Office boxes | 00831 | 779-4227 |

### St. Thomas

| | | |
|---|---|---|
| All St. Thomas street delivery | 00802 | 774-1950 |
| Havensight Mall | 00801 | 776-9897 |
| 5046 Norre Gade | 00804 | 774-3750 |
| Sugar Estate Post Office boxes | 00801 | 774-1950 |
| Tutu Park Mall | 00805 | 775-7354 |
| Veterans' Dr. P.O. Boxes, Frenchtown | 00803 | 774-6980 |

    The zip codes ending in '0' are for street addresses and the others with a number such as 00821, 00822, 00841 are for post office boxes.
The island is full of areas with rural delivery. There are cluster boxes in those areas which sometimes have availability. If a homeowner goes with a copy of their lease or deed and if there is availability they issue a USPS mailing format which normally begins with 4 digits. If there is no availability, then the home-owners in that area may erect a centralized unit for receipt of deliveries.
    Homeowner Associations who install their own postmaster general approved centralized mail Delivery units will receive delivery services once the USPS issue them a proper postal mailing address format.

To avoid return of improperly addressed mail being returned for insufficient address, please adhere to the following rules:

- Do not abbreviate the words "Christiansted" or "Frederiksted"
- Do not write US before the VI abbreviation
- Do not spell out the word "Virgin Islands" or they might go the British Virgin Islands
- The number in the address shown on your physical street map might not be the number for mailing purposes

Be sure to check with your area post office for a proper physical or postal box mailing address format before shipping items or printing documents or mailing labels for your personal use.

Retail Ground and Parcel Select Mail takes 3 to 5 weeks in average to arrive whereas the Priority mail currently averages 3 days.

### Courier Companies

*Several courier companies offer service to and from St. Thomas and St. Croix. Some companies have drop off, pickup and delivery service on all three islands. Prices vary.*

**American Airlines** Cyril E. King Airport Cargo Hangar, St. Thomas  774-6550

| | |
|---|---|
| **DHL Worldwide Express** | 1-800-225-5345 |
| **Nisky Center**, St. Thomas | 774-4066 |
| **St. Croix** | 778-8553 |

| | |
|---|---|
| **Federal Express** Peter's Rest, St. Croix | 1-800-GOFEDEX |
| (pick-ups in St. Croix call by 3:30 p.m.) | 1-877-838-7834 |
| **Cyril E. King Airport** cargo hangar | 776-8887 |
| **St. Thomas** | 1-800-463-3339 |
| Drop-off box: business accounts, First Bank, waterfront, St. Thomas | |

| | |
|---|---|
| **UPS** Airport, St. Croix | 778-7100 |
| **Raphune Hill**, St. Thomas | 776-1700 |
| **Seaborne Airlines** | (787) 946-7800 |

# 19th Settler's Handbook  Infrastructure 5

> **Sending a Telegram**
> To send a telegram? Call 1–800-3472 or go online to the website *https://americantelegram.com* to send. Telegrams can also be delivered to these islands via this same provider.

## TRANSPORTATION
### Streets and Roads

Finding your way around can be a major hassle. Residents often give directions that begin with "turn right at the big tree" or "left just after that paved road". Most areas use plot numbers that date to old Danish surveys and, since many have been subdivided, the result can be quite confusing. It's best to get complete directions before you set out. Keep a map in the glove compartment of your car, and if you get lost, don't be shy about asking directions. It's a great way to meet new folks.

In St. Croix all major roads are named and numbered and both are used. Some of the subdivisions will have street names with signs, some names but no numbers and some may have neither. While the houses all have plot numbers, you may find 5 next to 5-1 or even 7. In Christiansted and Frederiksted, the numbers start upward on one side of the street, cross over at the end, and begin downward on the other side. Don't be surprised to see 4 across from 42. Christiansted's numbering begins at the waterfront, runs inland to the old city limits and then returns on the other side of the street. Frederiksted's numbers begin at the north town limits or at the waterfront on the west. The main streets, and those that parallel them have long blocks. The cross streets have short ones. Corner plots usually take their number from the main streets, though the building's entrance may be around the corner.

St. Thomas is just as quirky. Though major roads all have names and numbers, most residents don't know the numbers. Some roads have been renamed and are referred to by both old and new names. Skyline Drive is a good case in point. Some years ago, the town fathers decided to name it after one of their own, Valdemar Hill Sr., but few people ever call the scenic road anything but Skyline Drive. In Charlotte Amalie, buildings have numbers, but they have no relationship to the number on the building next door. Remember to ask for a good map.

Some street names and town names may repeat themselves intra-island as well as inter-island. So you will have King St. and Mt. Pleasant in Christiansted as well as in Frederiksted, St. Croix; Bonne Esperance in both St. Croix and St. Thomas and Centerline Rd. in both St. Croix and St. John. It is therefore essential that you provide district names and zip codes as much as possible especially when applying for insurance or similar services.

## TRANSPORTATION TO AND AROUND THE ISLANDS

With tourism being such a critical source of revenue, transportation plays a major role. The influx of almost two million tourists and a professional or personal need to travel by islanders, has developed a network of the Major airlines and local commuters that blanket the Caribbean and all Points north, east, south and west.

The islands can be reached from anywhere in the continental U.S., the Caribbean, Europe or South America but it may take a few hours, and in some cases, two days. St. John has no airport, but both St. Thomas (Cyril E. King Airport) and St. Croix (Henry E. Rohlsen Airport) have airports capable of commercial handling jets. The Henry E. Rohlsen Airport expanded in 2002 to 10,000 square feet and 10 gates to attract new airlines and accommodate more passengers. Long-range flights were limited to St. Croix before the runway expansion due to fuel restrictions of smaller aircraft. Cyril E. King Airport has 9980 square feet over 2 floors and 11 gates.

The control towers are operated under the auspices of the FAA which contracts for private air traffic controllers.

The scheduling of flights to both islands are subject to seasonal and economic changes.

St. John, the smallest of the three islands, does not have an airport, but has a busy little seaport at its dock at Cruz Bay. Tourists can take one of the many inter-island ferries from Charlotte Amalie or Red Hook on St. Thomas.

*Cyril E. King Airport, St. Thomas, US Virgin Islands*

## Major Airlines - St. Croix

**American Airlines** – MIA/STX Boeing (148 seats) 5 weekly
1-800-474-4884 www.AA.com (adjusted seasonally; be sure to call)
**American Airlines** – Charlotte/STX Airbus A319 www.AA.com twice weekly (seasonal) 1-800-622-1015 (adjusted seasonally; be sure to call)

**Delta Airlines** – ATL/STX – MD88/CR9/E70 (143 seats) (4 weekly flights- Saturday, Sunday, Monday, Thursday) 1-800-221-1212 (adjusted seasonally; be sure to call)
**Spirit Airlines** – FTL/STX - 800-772-7117 www.spirit.com
**United Airlines** - 800-241-6522 www.united.com

## Regional / Commuter Airlines - St. Croix

**Air Sunshine-** 1 800-327-8900

**Cape Air** – SJU/STX – Cessna 402, twin-engine, single pilot aircraft (9 seater) up to 8 daily flights in season, also serving St. Thomas and Tortola. Departures are timed to meet jet departures to mainland U.S. 1-866-227-3247 www.flycapeair.com

**CoastalAir Transport** – Scheduled and chartered flights to Anguilla, Nevis, Dominica, St. Barths, and St. Eustatius. Call (340) 773-6862.

**Island Airline** 340-344-3900

**Seaflight** 340-714-3000

**Seaborne Airlines** – uses DHC-6-300 and Saab 340B. Seaborne offers daily nonstops to and between St. Croix, St. Thomas, San Juan, Vieques and the BVI. This airline also partners directly with Road Town Fast Ferry to offer connecting service from St. Croix to downtown Road Town, Tortola via St. Thomas. For full information about traveling with Seaborne, and to book online, visit www.seaborneairlines.com. You can also call them at (787) 946-7800 or toll free at 888-FLY-USVI. Charters available.

## Major Airlines - St. Thomas

**American Airlines**: 1-800-474-4884 (adjusted seasonally, be sure to call) MIA/STT – B757-200 (seasonal November to May two daily flights, then back to one) Boston/ STT – B757-200 scheduled service Jan – Apr on Tues & Sat JKF / STT B757-200 – one daily flight.

**Delta Airlines:** ATL/STT 1-800-221-1212 (adjusted seasonally, be sure to call) Two daily round trips (check with the airline) Additionally, there will be 4 weekly overnight flights – check with the airlines) 4 weekly round-trip same-day flights Copenhagen to ATL to STT: T/F/S/S JFK / STT: seasonal weekly on Saturdays (check with airline). Additional service during season Fridays and Sundays.

**Jet Blue -** 1 800 - JETBLUE (538-2583) www.jetblue.com

**Spirit Airlines:** Ft. Lauderdale / STT – MD-80 – daily non-stop 1-801-401-2222 www.spiritairlines.com..

**United Airlines**: Newark, NJ/STT – B737-700LR 1-800-231-0856 Four weekly flights (Saturday/Sunday/Wednesday/Friday)

**United Airlines:** 1-800-241-6522  www.unitedairlines.com Chicago /STT – 3 times per week, Sunday, Wed, Saturday Washington, DC/STT – one weekly service on Saturdays (adjusted seasonally, be sure to call)

## Regional Commuter Airlines - St. Thomas

**Air Sunshine:** Direct flights to San Juan, Vieques, Virgin Gorda, Nevis, St. Maarten and Tortola. Call (888) 879-8900.

**Cape Air** - about 8 daily flights, in season (call 1-800-352-0714)

**LIAT:** Anguilla, Antigua, St. Kitts and St. Maarten. Call (340) 778-9930
1-888-549-LIAT (5428).

**Seaborne Airshuttle** Daily nonstops to St. Croix, San Juan and Vieques and the BVI. Call toll-free at (866) -359-8784

# 19th Settler's Handbook  Infrastructure 5

## Downtown to Downtown
## Seaborne Seaplane –

The seaplane departs and arrives from the downtown Charlotte Amalie seaport and the downtown Christiansted seaport. Their aircraft fly under the same strict regulations as major US Carriers, with all-day availability on convenient morning, midday and evening flights. If you plan to travel between the islands frequently, or with your family, Seaborne SmartPaks are also available. For full information about traveling with Seaborne, and to book online, visit their website or call toll-free.

### Air Charters

| | | |
|---|---|---|
| Air Sunshine | St. Croix | (888) 879-8900 |
| Bohlke International Airways | St. Croix | 778-9177 |
| Caribbean Buzz | St. Thomas | 775-7335 |
| Coastal Air Transport | St. Croix | 773-6862 |
| Island Airlines | St. Croix | 344-3900 |
| Seaborne/Silver Airlines | Both | (866) 359-8784 |
| Sea Flight | Both | 714-3000 |

### By Sea

At press time, there is one ferry service between St. Thomas and St. Croix, the QE IV. St. Thomas and St. John are linked with a comprehensive

ferry transportation system. Ferries leave on the hour starting at 5:30 a.m. To midnite on weekdays between Red Hook, St. Thomas and Cruz Bay, St. John for the 20-minute each way trip and costs about $6 though small children are charged only $1 and seniors, $1.50 on either ferry, larger bags cost about $4 each. On all ferries you will share the trip with luggage, boxes of groceries, pieces of furniture and dozens of St. John residents returning from school, work or shopping in St. Thomas.

## Ferries Around The US Virgin Islands

| Name | Destination | Days | Times | Duration | Fare |
|---|---|---|---|---|---|
| Ferry QEIV | St. Croix | All except Wed | 8:00 am | 2:30 hrs | $60/30 |
| | St. Thomas | All except Wed | 3:00 pm | | |
| | Tel: (340)-473-1322 info@qe4ferry.com | | | | |
| Ferries | Red Hook/STT | All | 5:30 am - midnite | 20 min | $6 |
| | Cruz Bay/STJ | | | | |
| | Charlotte Amalie/ | All | 10:00 am - | 35 min | $12 |
| | Cruz Bay/STJ | All | 5:30 pm | | |

*All trips from downtown Charlotte Amalie to Cruz Bay have been suspended until further notice.*

If you miss the last ferry or want to travel to almost anywhere between St. Thomas, St. John or the British Virgin Islands, call for a high-speed boat for a quick trip to any where they can dock.
Ocean Dreams – (340) 998-6720 or Good News Charter - (340) 473-6795

### To The British Virgin Islands

Besides the two passenger companies ferrying between St. John and St.Thomas runs, TS-Transportation Services (776-6282) and Varlack Ventures (776-6412) and the inter-island boat service to the British Virgin Islands, there are other companies which provide barge service to/from St.Thomas: Boyson and Love City. Car/truck barges run every half-hour or so until about 7 p.m. Car rental companies in St. Thomas do not allow you to take the rental on the ferry to St. John. A car barge is about $30 one way, or $50 roundtrip. A port fee of $3 for cars and $4 for larger vehicles is payable in cash in St. Thomas. Some ferries charge $2.50 per baggage plus a $1.10 fuel surcharge. **(All rates subject to change**.)

Native Son and Smith's Ferry share the route between the Charlotte Amalie waterfront and either West End or Roadtown, Tortola in the British Virgin Islands. Service starts at 7:45 a.m. with departures scheduled for morning, mid-day and evening rush-hour. Times vary depending on the day of the week. The one-hour trip costs about $55 round-trip. Connections to other British Virgin Islands are possible. For information on the ferry trips to the British Virgin Islands, call Native Son at 774-8685 or Smith's Ferry at 775-7292. For vehicle transportation St. Thomas/St. John call Love City Car Ferries 779-4000.

From St. John, ferries leave the Cruz Bay dock for West End, Tortola, Jost Van Dyke and Virgin Gorda. Times vary by day. While you can go to West End, Tortola every day for about $35 for the 45-minute trip, the boat to Virgin Gorda leaves only on Thursdays and Sundays. The boat to Jost Van Dyke goes only on Saturdays and Sundays. Call to see if any of this has changed and also ask if you need a passport to get from the U.S. to the British Virgin Islands. You may NOT need one getting into the BVI but you may need one getting back! ALL rates subject to change.

**Public Bus Transportation**

The government-owned Vitran bus lines operates on all three islands. Look for these familiar blue and white buses. Stops located frequently across the islands have signs that carry the Vitran logo. Service usually runs from 5:30 a.m. till 8:30 p.m. Senior citizens and students get a discount if they present their identification. In St. Croix, Vitran operates bus routes between Christiansted and Frederiksted with a transfer station at La Reine and Golden Rock. All trips are about $1. In St. Thomas, Vitran buses run between Red Hook in the East and Bordeaux in the west. All buses go through Charlotte Amalie. Trips within the city limits cost about 75 cents The more distant locations run about $1 with no transfers.

Call **Vitran** at (340) 773-1664     (340) 774-5678 St. Thomas/St.John

**By Private Bus or Van**

In St. Croix, private taxi vans pick up passengers with unscheduled and unregulated service between Christiansted and Frederiksted. They stop only along the main road between those towns. Rates vary. Wait for them at shopping centers and bus pull-offs. If you are unsure whether they are a private taxi van or a regular regulated taxi, ask first.

In St. John you can make use of bus transportation service, but residents sometimes stand by the Boulon Center corner exiting Cruz Bay to wait for a kindhearted soul, or someone they know, to deliver them to points east. This personal service works well and gets many St. Johnians to and from school and work.

While you will soon get used to the sight of the familiar open-air safari buses packed with tourists on tour, they also serve as the main means of transportation between Red Hook and Charlotte Amalie. Drivers meet the ferry from Cruz Bay, St. John for the half-hour trip to Charlotte Amalie. Those Safari buses leave at about 20 minutes after the hour from 8:20 a.m.

# 19th Settler's Handbook    Infrastructure 5

till 3:20 p.m. Trips are about $3. The safari buses leave by the stop light at Market Square in Charlotte Amalie for Red Hook and points in between 15 minutes past the hour from 8:15 a.m. To 3:15 p.m.

## By Taxi

Taxis are unmetered, and fares are determined by destination. Fares are fixed by law, but it is best to agree on a fare before you go. If you want to travel solo or leave immediately, you will pay more— particularly at the airports and ferry docks since drivers wait till they have all the passengers they can fit. Because gypsy cabs do try to pick up passengers, especially at supermarkets, look for "P" as the second letter of the license plate to ensure you are taking a regulated taxi.

All major hotels are serviced by taxi associations. At smaller hotels, the reception desk will call one for you. If you are in town, look for a taxi at the marked taxi zones. In St. Croix and St. Thomas, call one of the taxi associations listed in the phone book for service. If the taxi association does not operate in your area, they will advise you who to call. You can call for a private taxi now in St. John. Tours that cover any or all of the island start at about $12 each for three or more passengers. A solo tour could be about $30. Fares include one suitcase or box and a small piece of hand luggage. Additional pieces cost $4.00 each. Pets must be caged. If you need to make several stops, negotiate with the driver in advance. After 10 minutes of wait time there will be an additional charge.

Should you have a problem, write down the driver number located above the windshield inside the vehicle or the license plate and call the government's Taxi Commission for help. When leaving the airports the taxi dispatcher will know the rates to where you are going. There are posted rates in some of the tourist publications too.

| **Call for a Taxi** | | |
|---|---|---|
| **St. Croix** | **St. Thomas** | **St. John** |
| St. Croix Taxi Assoc. | VI Taxi Assoc | St. John Taxi Service |
| 778-1088 | 774-7457 | 774-7457 |
| | **Taxi Commission  776-5354** | |

## Vehicle Rentals

It's a good idea to reserve vehicles well in advance. Expect car rentals to be in high demand during holidays and the busy winter months. The national chain rental companies have offices at airports, hotels and other locations on the three islands. Most locally owned independent car rental agencies will deliver to those same locations. Check the local tourist publications for any special discounts. Many car rental agencies will offer discounts on long-term rentals. When checking prices, remember that there are additional taxes & fees. Make sure the price quote you receive includes them. Read the rental conditions carefully to make sure you understand all charges, insurance coverage and liability limits. If you rent a motorscooter, the law mandates that you wear the helmet provided by the company. VI Motorcycle Safety Education Act 2009 mandates the establishment of standards for rider training courses, improvement of licensure requirements and promotion of motorcycle safety through education and public awareness.

## Dial a Ride

Persons with disabilities, elderly residents, and tourists with disabilities, may use Dial-a-Ride services. The service has wheelchair accessible vans. Please call 24 hours prior to schedule pick up. They also have a reference of hotels, restaurants, and attractions that have services for persons with disabilities. On St. Croix you can call Wheel Coach at 719- 9335 for a 24-hour in advance prearranged pick-up for handicapped. On St. Croix and St. Thomas VITRAN-PLUS, a public service, is available for persons with disabilities. To qualify, go to Public Works to submit an application. This application goes through an approval process for acceptability. On St. Croix call 773-1290 ext. 2238, and on St.Thomas, call 774-5678.

*VITRAN Bus*

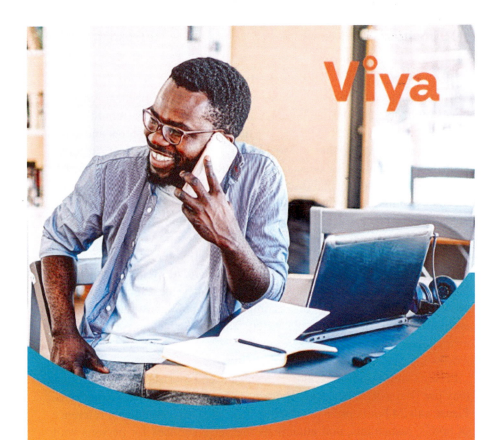

## UTILITIES

### VI Water and Power Authority

The Virgin Islands Water and Power Authority (WAPA) is an autonomous government body that produces and distributes electricity and potable water to approximately 55,000 electric customers and 13,000 potable water customers in the territory. WAPA also installs and maintains street lights. Considered a not-for profit public corporation, WAPA contributes directly to the territory's budget by an annual payment in lieu of taxes (PILOT) to the Virgin Islands Treasury.

The Virgin Islands Legislature created the Authority in 1964, and it is governed by a nine member board of public and private sector members. The governor of the Virgin Islands selects the three public sector members from his cabinet and nominates six private sector board members, who the legislature confirms for three-year terms. Private sector members come from each district.

### Electricity

Electrical service conforms to U.S. standards: 110/220 volts single phase or three phase, 60 cycle AC, making converters commonly required in Europe unnecessary. The Authority's power plants are located at Estate Richmond, St. Croix and at Krum Bay, St. Thomas. Customers on St. Croix and St. Thomas are served by both overhead and underground lines. Customers on St. John are provided power through underwater cables from St. Thomas.

Historically, WAPA relies exclusively on low grade fuel oil to power its electric generating units. Because of its reliance on fuel oil with its volatile prices worldwide, and its dual operations of producing water and power, plus the loathed Levelized Energy Adjustment Clause (LEAC), WAPA's customer rates are generally the highest rates charged by electric utilities in the United States. As always, monthly bills will vary according to customer usage and the prevailing fuel factor which is based on the cost of fuel oil purchased on the world market. The fuel surcharge (LEAC) which appears on the bill is a customer charge that allows WAPA to address increases or decreases in fuel prices. Customer rates, and adjustments to the fuel factor, are subject to approval by the Virgin Islands Public Services Commission.

To reduce rates, the Authority is moving aggressively to diversify its generation portfolio and will integrate 18MW of solar energy into its grid in 2015 and reduce dependency on fossil fuel by 60%. Wind studies are underway and the utility is pursuing a move to liquefied natural gas (LNG) as an alternative to fuel oil. To help its customers cope with fluctuating energy costs, WAPA has embarked on an aggressive customer education and conservation campaign to curb wasteful consumption and encourage investment in high efficiency appliances including solar water heaters. The utility often distributes Energy Star rated light bulbs at community events, as efficient lighting is one of the easiest ways to save energy.

Throughout 2015 rates dropped to more bearable levels to 33.3 cents/kWh on St. Croix and 36.3% 33.3 cents/kWh on St. Thomas. At press time WAPA had actually started converting to Liquid Propane Gas (LPG) first on St. Croix with St. Thomas and St. John waiting in the pipeline. With this conversion it is expected that there will be some 30% reduction in rates plus will allow the Authority to reduce its carbon monoxide emissions, nitrous oxide emissions, and particulate matter emissions incredibly, very welcome news for residents and environmentalists on these tiny land masses.

The Authority also supports netmetering, which allows consumers who install renewable energy systems, such as solar and wind, to reduce their bills by using less electricity from the grid. It also provides the customer with the potential to receive credit for electricity exported to the grid. Smart metering has been installed during the past two years to assist customers in digital monitoring and regulating their usage as a tool to ensure energy efficiency in their homes and businesses.

Additionally, a 2012 grant award from the U.S. Department of the Interior has established an energy services business unit which will provide energy audits, technology validation for best in class equipment and supplies, and a financing opportunity for utility customers to acquire energy efficient appliances and equipment.

Recognized as an Energy Star Partner of the Year in 2008, the Authority is an active member of the prestigious program created by the U.S. Environmental Protection Agency and the U.S. Department of Energy and partners with the Virgin Islands Energy Office (VIEO) to provide information and customer-focused services. In 2009, WAPA was designated an EDIN (Energy Development in Island Nations) partner. EDIN-USVI is a collaborative effort among many public and private sector representatives from the U.S. Departments of Energy and the Interior, the National Renewable Energy Laboratory, the V.I. Energy Office, the University of the Virgin Islands and local businesses. This partnership supports the territory's efforts to reduce fossil fuel usage in the electricity and transportation sectors 60% by 2025.

In recent years, WAPA has invested millions of dollars in upgrading its generating and distribution systems to improve reliability. But because WAPA is not connected to a national grid, as is the case with electric utilities in the mainland United States, periodic power outages may occur. Additionally, the threat of tropical storms and hurricanes from June through November leads many Virgin Islands residents to purchase back-up generators for their homes and businesses.

> More information about WAPA's projects and plans is available at www.viwapa.vi and www. edinenergy.org/usvi.
> Tel: (340) 773-2250 (340) -774-3552 or (340) 776-6446
>
> Customers are also invited to visit WAPA's customer service offices for information on no-cost, low-cost energy saving tips. These include:
> • Use ceiling fans to cool or be sure to use Energy Star-rated air conditioning units.
> • Wash clothes in cold water and only use full loads.
> • Hang wet towels, swimsuits and other items outside to dry in the sun rather than using an electric dryer.
> • Let dishes air dry in the dishwasher rather than use the automatic dryer mode.
> • Consider investing in a solar water heater.
> • Change out incandescent light bulbs with high efficiency, long-Life compact florescent bulbs (CFL) or LED (Light Emitting Diode) bulbs for the maximum savings.
> • Turn off all lights, appliances and electronics when not in use.

## Water

Recognizing that potable water is one of the most precious resources in the U.S. Virgin Islands, WAPA has taken a lead role in educating customers about water and energy conservation. The U.S. Virgin Islands have no freshwater bodies, so WAPA desalinates seawater for distribution to the most densely populated commercial and residential centers on St. Thomas, St. Croix and St. John, almost 13,000 users via waterlines and standpipes. The majority of water is currently produced by reverse osmosis plants at Richmond and Krum Bay. Residents also collect rain water in cisterns attached to their homes or businesses. With an average of only 45 inches of rainfall a year, water conservation has, by necessity, been developed into a fine art. If one has a cistern to collect rainwater, one might rush to launder slipcovers, draperies, rugs or the dogs if a storm should cause an overflow. Virgin Islanders talk about water or its shortage the way mainlanders talk about the weather, crab grass or heating bills. Potable and non potable water can also be bought and delivered from private companies.

Helpful water usage hints can be found at www.viwapa.vi, but consider the following:

• Cisterns must be kept clean and free of leaks and obstructions. All openings must be screened to keep out dirt, bugs, leaves and light. In the rare event more rain falls than a cistern can hold, an overflow will keep the water from backing up into your house.

• During power outages, the electric water pump will not work, but residents can often bucket water out of their cisterns or swimming pools for immediate needs. Knowledge of the workings of your water pump, water level and its flow and the quality of cistern water is a necessity. To access the cistern, which is more than likely located under your house, open the cover found in the floor of the home. If your cistern is free-standing, the opening should be fairly obvious.

• The flow at your faucet is produced by an air tank pressurized by an electrical pump. If the pump requires lubrication, stick to a schedule. Learn the sounds your pump makes. If it varies, investigate at once to avoid burning out the pump. If it seems to cycle too often, it may need bleeding or you may have a leak in the system. Call a plumber or ask a handy neighbor for help.

• Don't let the water run while you brush your teeth, shampoo, shave, shower or wash dishes. Wet everything down first, then TURN OFF THE WATER while you scrub. Rinse quickly. Since every flush uses five gallons of water, flush only when necessary and install water reduction devices such as dual flush toilets. Take a shower rather than a bath and install low flow showerheads. Remember to alert your guests that "in this land of sun and fun, we don't flush for every use for "number one".

• Fix every dripping faucet immediately and equip garden hoses with automatic shut-offs. Don't run clothes or dishwashers until you have a full load. In-sink garbage disposals use extra water and increase the build-up of solids in your septic tank which will hasten the day when it must be pumped out. Build a gray water cistern to catch runoff from patios, bathtubs and kitchen waters for garden or lawn use.

- Should your thirst outrun your capacity, private truckers will deliver water. Prices vary widely depending on where you live and how much water the truck carries. Water delivery companies can be located in the Virgin Islands telephone book or in online services directories.

## WASTE MANAGEMENT

The Virgin Islands Waste Management Authority (VIWMA) is responsible for the collection, treatment and disposal of wastewater and solid waste in the territory. This includes the operations and maintenance of the sewer collection system, wastewater treatment facilities and pump stations, landfills, and transfer stations.

On St. Croix, the Authority provides residents several types of solid waste services. Some locals receive house-to-house collection twice per week at their homes. For such folks, the pick-up days can be obtained from the Authority's Division of Solid Waste .

Those who do not receive this service are provided with waste disposal bin sites located throughout the island. There are three such sites on St. Croix: Cotton Valley, Mon Bijou and Concordia. A newly opened manned convenience center is located in Peter's Rest. This facility accepts household waste, household hazardous waste materials, and some recyclables.

St. Thomas residents receive limited house-to-house collection and there are 26 public disposal sites located island-wide. St. John does not receive any house-to-house service, as the terrain makes such service challenging, and there are 28 bins located island-wide for residential use.

Virgin Islands law requires commercial and industrial businesses to employ licensed haulers, who are permitted public disposal site acess, to dispose waste. Many small business owners and residents also use private haulers for their solid waste disposal. These haulers are permitted by the VI Waste Management Authority to dispose of waste at the landfill and transfer station, and must display a VIWMA sticker in their windshield to be allowed access to solid waste facilities, which include the Anguilla Transfer Station and Landfill on St. Croix, the Bovoni Landfill on St. Thomas and the Susannaberg Transfer Station on St. John, or wastewater treatment plants (WWTP), such as the Anguilla WWTP on St. Croix, Mangrove Lagoon or Red Point WWTPs on St. Thomas or the Cruz Bay WWTP on St. John. The Anguilla Landfill accepts solid waste, construction and demolition debris and scrap metal. A list of permitted haulers can be obtained from the Authority's Division of Compliance Management and Environmental Enforcement.

Each type of disposal practice requires adherence to various guidelines. House-to-house collection requires that residents place their waste in a closed bag within a large receptacle with a secure cover at the curbside on the day(s) of their neighborhood collection. Disposal at the bin sites also requires that the waste is placed inside of the bin and not on the ground adjacent to the bin. There are certain items that cannot be disposed of by either house-to-house collection or at the bin sites. The following items must be taken directly to the landfill for disposal: yard waste; scrap metal; appliances; junked cars; bulk waste, like furniture, bedding, and other bulky household goods; gas cylinders; and, construction & demolition (C&D) waste.

Littering is a criminal offense and individuals or businesses can be cited for violations at a minimum charge of $1,000 per violation and/or up to 180 days in jail. The VIWMA's Environmental Enforcement Officers monitor the waste disposal practices of residents and businesses and will issues littering citations.

## Keeping the V.I. Clean

The Virgin Islands continues to make strides in beautification efforts, and has supported various recycling projects to do so.

- There no local companies at this time that purchase aluminum cans and scrap metal for cash. The VIWMA also holds annual aluminum can collection contest in the local public and private elementary schools to educate and encourage students on the benefit of recycling.
- In March 2016 an Act was passed prohibiting certain business from providing plastic check out bags and non recyclable paper bags to customers. Plastic drinking straws are also no longer being provided at restaurants.
- Cell phones are accepted for recycling at local libraries as a fundraising opportunity.
- Scrap metal is currently being crushed and removed at the Territory's landfills.
- Lead-Acid Batteries are not accepted at the local landfills but are recyclable. To ensure they are recycled, return them to the place of purchase.
- Used tires are also not accepted at bin sites or local landfills. Tire dealers accept scrap or used tires, although many charge a small disposal fee.
- Aluminum cans are also recyclable.

- Used oil, if disposed of improperly, can contaminate soil, ground water, and surface water. Residents who change their own motor oil can dispose of no more than five gallons per month or two gallons or less of cooking oil at the VIWMA's Do-It-Yourself (DIY) Used Oil Collection Sites which are located on each island at sites listed in insert next page.

VIWMA has developed a campaign, "Preserving Paradise," that educates students, communities and businesses on ways they can help keep the islands clean. As part of the Preserving Paradise Kids' Campaign, VIWMA teaches students about the importance of preservation and encourages them to take what they learn and share it with their parents. Preserving Paradise Communities invites residents to enter into a partnership with the VIWMA to beautify their neighborhoods and common areas.

## At A Glance Landfill & Disposal Information
### St. Croix – (340) 712-4962

**Anguilla Landfill**
  Mondays-Fridays      6:00 am - 4:00 pm    Last load 3:30 pm
  Saturdays & Sundays  6:00 pm- 1:00 pm     Last load 12:30 pm
  Scrap Metal - Mon-Fri 8:00am – 4:00pm  Holidays 8:00am-1:00pm
  Used Oil   - Dept of Public Works - Anna's Hope
  Waste Water – Anguilla Waste Water Treatment Plant

  Bin disposal sites at Concordia, Cotton Valley, Mon Bijou, Peters Rest

### St. Thomas – (340) 715-9100

**Bovoni Landfill**
  Mondays-Saturdays 6:00 am – 4:00 pm  Sundays: 6:00 am - 2:00 pm
  Scrap Metal - Mon-Fri  7:00 am-4:00 pm
  Used Oil   -Dept of Public Works, Motor Pool in SubBase and Bovoni Landfill
  Waste Water – Mangrove and Red Point Water Treatment Plants
  Bin disposal sites – 26 throughout island

### St. John – (340) 774-2141

**Susannaberg Transfer Station**
  Mon-Fri 7:00 am- 5:00 pm        Sat & Sun 7:00 am-12 pm
  Used Oil is also collected here
  Bin disposal sites – 28 throughout island
      Contact (844) WMA-USVI (962-8784) to report a problem
        *For more details go to www.viwma.org*

New business owners on the island can become Preserving Paradise Business Partners. PPBP members work together to sponsor programs, projects and events that educate and inform the public about VIWMA's initiatives. Business Partners can make in-kind, monetary or other contributions to VIWMA's programs that introduce environmental educational information to students, community or civic organizations. There are numerous private carriers that provide bins for personal and commercial use.

## Cultural Tidbit
### Potato Stuffing - St. John, U.S.V.I.

*You will find this side dish, thanks to Angela Spencely of St. Thomas, delicious. It's a hit at virtually any West Indian gathering. An inexpensive investment in a potato ricer will make fluffy, not gluey, stuffing that is the perfect accompaniment for roast pork.*

**Ingredients**
• 6 large white potatoes, peeled and diced • 1 tbs. olive oil or bacon fat • 1 tsp. Salt • 1 large yellow onion, minced • ¼ cup butter or olive oil • 1 large sweet red bell pepper, minced • ¼ cup evaporated milk • ½ small habañero pepper, mince • ¼ cup whole milk • 1 tsp. dried thyme • 2 tbs. brown sugar • ½ tsp. dried marjoram •2 tbs. ketchup •½ cup raisins •1 tbs. tomato juice.

**Directions**
1. Place potatoes in a large, deep kettle or saucepan. Add salt and cover with water. Bring to a boil, reduce heat and simmer until potatoes are soft, about 20 minutes. Drain.
2. Run potatoes through a potato ricer or mash gently. Add ¼ cup olive oil, butter, milks, brown sugar, ketchup and tomato paste. Set aside.
3. Heat olive oil in a large skillet. Sauté onion, bell pepper and habañero pepper until soft, about 3 minutes over medium heat. Stir in thyme, marjoram and raisins. Simmer 2 min.
4. Preheat oven to 350°F. Combine onion with mashed potato mixture and spoon into a greased baking dish. Bake for 20 – 25 minutes until golden.

Yields 8-10 servings.

# Settler's Handbook Chapter 6

## YOUR BASIC NEEDS...

### Education

Public and private education is available for all Virgin Islanders from pre-school through college. The government operates Head Start centers on all three islands and there are numerous private pre-schools. It is best to ask around to find one that fits your needs. Students attend either private non sectarian, religious or public elementary and high schools.

Private and religious schools charge tuition. Government-run schools are free.

The government provides bus service for private and public school students in grades kindergarten through six who live over a mile away. It also has classes for handicapped students. St. Croix and St. Thomas also have vocational schools. Programs may include carpentry, computers, culinary arts, plumbing, hospitality, boat building, office skills, or practical nursing.

While most private school students wear street clothes, those attending religious or public schools wear uniforms.

### Home Schooling

Home schooling is an option for parents who so desire it. There are only about 60 or so utilizing this method at this book's writing. Some temporary residents home school their children while here. The Dept. of Education is about to embark upon updating its guidelines including stricter definitions, parameters and requirements for home schooling participants.

### St. Croix Private Schools

| | |
|---|---|
| **AZ Academy** Pre-K to grade 12, | 718-7909 |
| **Good Hope Country Day School** nursery - grade 12 | 778-1974 |
| **Rattan Montessori** | 773-8600 |
| **St. Croix Montessori** | 718-2859 |
| **Star Apple Montessori** | 773-8071 |

### St. Croix Religious Schools
**Church of God Holiness** 719-1220
**Free Will Baptist School**, Baptist, pre-school through 12,
elementary, high school 773-3179 778-8030
**Happy Children**- aka George's Christian Academy
K thru 6th 772-0635
**Iqra Academy** - Muslim, Nursery to Grade 12 772-4808
**St. Croix Christian Academy** 718-4947 or 718-6798
**St. Joseph's High School**, Roman Catholic,
grades 9 through 12 692-2455
**St. Patrick's School**, Roman Catholic, Grades
1 through 12 772-5052
**St. Mary's Catholic School**, Grades Pre-K through 8, 773-0117
**Seventh Day Adventists,** Holgers Hope, K to 12 773-6350

### St. Croix Public Schools 773-1095 www.vide.vi
**Elementary Schools**
Alexander Henderson 772-1330
Alfredo Andrews 778-1925
Charles H. Emanuel 778-0511
Claude O. Markoe 772-4510
Eulalie R. Rivera 692-2121
Juanita Gardine 718-0051
Lew Muckle 778-5286
Pearl B. Larsen 692-9336
Ricardo Richards 778-0612
**Junior High Schools**
Elena L. Christian Jr. High (*temporarily closed*) 718-4445
Arthur Richards Junior High Stoney Ground 772-1500
John H. Woodson Junior High Fredensborg 778-2710
**High Schools**
Central High School Grades 9 through 12 718-0123
St. Croix Educational Complex 778-2036
St. Croix Education Vocational 778-2216

### St. John Public and Private Schools
**Gifft Hill School** pre-school through 6th grade 776-1730
**St. John Christian Academy** ages 4 to 5th grade 693-7722

## St. John Public and Private Schools (cont'd)

**Julius E. Sprauve Public School**, to grade 9 - 776-6337
Many elementary and high school students take the ferry to St. Thomas to private or religious-affiliated schools and the public high schools such as, Ivanna Eudora Kean.

### St. Thomas Private Schools
**Antilles School**, pre-school through grade 12, 776-1600
**Beacon Schools ot the VI**   Drake's Passage 777-9300

**VI Montessori School**, accredited, ages 3 through 12, 775-6360

### St. Thomas Religious Schools
**All Saints Cathedral School**, Episcopal -pre k through 12 774-0231
**Bethel Baptist Day School**, kindergarten through 3 774-1378
**Church of God Academy** 775-1252
**Memorial Moravian School**, kindergarten through, 774-7579/774-2670
**Saints Peter & Paul School**, Catholic, pre-k-12, elementary 774-5662
High school 774-2199
**Seventh Day Adventist School**, kindergarten through 12, 775-3525
**Wesleyan Academy**, pre-school through 12, 774-5438

### St. Thomas Public Schools- 774-0100   www.vide.vi
**Elementary Schools**
Leonard Dober 774-5874
E. Benjamin Oliver 775-2000
Edith Williams 775-0820
Gladys Abraham 774-7385
Jane E. Tuitt 774-0520
Joseph Gomez 775-2354
Joseph Sibilly 774-7001
Lockhart 774-2133
Ulla Miller 774-0059
Yvonne Millner Bowsky 775-3220

**Junior High Schools**
Bertha C. Boshulte 7-8 775-4222
Addelita Cancryn Junior High School grades 7-8 775-4540

| St. Thomas Public Schools (cont'd) - 774-0100 www.vide.vi |
|---|
| **Public High Schools** |
| Charlotte Amalie High School grades 9-12      774-0780 |
| Ivanna Eudora Kean High Schoolgrades 9-12      775-6208 |
| Rafael O. Wheatley Skills Center - Vocational      774-6277 |

## UNIVERSITY OF THE VIRGIN ISLANDS

The University of the Virgin Islands (UVI) is a liberal arts, land-grant institution established by public statute to meet the higher education needs of people from the territory and throughout the Caribbean. The university is accredited by the Commission on Higher Education of the Middle States Association of Colleges and Schools, which is an institutional accrediting agency recognized by the U.S. Secretary of Education and the Commission on Recognition of Post Secondary Accreditation.

UVI has campuses on St. Thomas and St. Croix — with an Academic Center and Environmental Resources Station on St. John. The St. Croix campus is located at Golden Grove, midway between the towns of Christiansted and Frederiksted. Via the Queen Mary Highway, the entrance to St. Croix's Albert A. Sheen Campus is lined with royal palm trees leading to the residence halls, Student Center and the Melvin H. Evans Center for Learning. Other main buildings include the Research and Technology Park, School of Medicine Simulation Center, Great House, the Northwest Wing, the Nursing Complex, Agricultural Experiment Station and the Research and Extension Center, which contains administrative offices and the USVI Cooperative Extension Service.

The 388-acre St. Thomas campus is located three miles west of Charlotte Amalie overlooking Brewer's Bay. In addition to academic facilities, administrative and student service buildings, residence halls, the UVI Sports and Fitness Center and the 1,196-seat Reichhold Center for the Arts, the St. Thomas campus includes the Herman E. Moore Golf Course, Brewer's Bay beach and tennis courts.

Students who come to UVI choose from a broad array of associate and

bachelor's degree programs in more than 40 curriculum areas. The university maintains five colleges and schools: the College of Liberal Arts and Social Sciences, College of Science and Mathematics, School of Business, School of Education and School of Nursing, and offers master's degree programs in public administration, business administration, mathematics for secondary education, marine and environmental science, psychology social work and education. A new doctoral degree in Creative Leadereship is also being offered . UVI is one of few HBCUs to offer to offer undergraduate and graduate degrees in marine science.
The faculty is comprised of 228 highly qualified, full-time and part-time members. Seventy-one percent of the full-time faculty hold doctoral degrees Faculty members represent diverse ethnic and cultural backgrounds from the mainland U.S., the Virgin Islands and abroad.
Cooperative agreements between the University of the Virgin Islands and many other leading universities exist to allow UVI students to receive degrees not offered on the UVI campuses.

The Boston University School of Medicine cooperative agreement allows UVI students, who meet certain qualifications, provisional acceptance into the medical school at the end of their sophomore year. The College of Science and Mathematics has developed an articulation program in engineering with Columbia University, University of Florida and University of South Carolina. These articulation agreements allow students to begin their studies at UVI and then complete requirements for graduation at one of these schools.

UVI's 2,500 full-time, part-time and graduate students come from: the U.S.V.I., 34 U.S.states and about 14 other countries, primarily in the Eastern Caribbean. Undergraduate tuition for Virgin Islands residents is $4,630 per year. Non-resident tuition is $13,892 per year. Per-credit undergraduate tuition is $147 for residents and $441 for non-residents. Total room and board charges per semester average $4,275 double and $4,693 for a single room, depending on meal plan choice.

In addition to academics, UVI is home to the Virgin Islands' **Research & Technology Park (RTPark)**, an economic development initiative that leverages visions of the business community, UVI and the public sector. The RTPark also houses the College of Science and Mathematics on the Albert A. Sheen Campus. Chartered through legislation and affiliated with UVI, RTPark is a world-class, near-shore provider of technology solutions for knowledge-based, information technology and e-commerce companies. Its mission is to attract technology and knowledge -based businesses to the

USVI, foster a vibrant and sustainable technology sector, broaden the territory's tax base, stimulate creation of new jobs and career opportunities for residents, and strengthen UVI's academic and financial capabilities. RTPark can directly extend compelling benefits and incentives to qualifying knowledge-based businesses, including significant reductions – up to 90% – in income taxes for USVI-sourced income. Alternatively, in certain cases, knowledge-based businesses can obtain similar benefits from the USVI Economic Development Authority (EDA) if those businesses are first referred by RTPark. Other key strategic and competitive benefits include access to world-class broadband connectivity that leverages the USVI's unique concentration of switching facilities for undersea fiber networks, and legal protections for intellectual property, investments and contracts under federal law.

Current and incoming students are advised to contact UVI's Financial Aid Office to determine opportunities that exist with federal grant programs, other scholarship opportunities and loans.

| **UVI Directory (Area Code 340) (Voice / Fax)** | |
|---|---|
| **St. Croix Campus** | |
| Academic Affairs | 692-4022/4025 |
| Admissions | 692-4158/4115 |
| Agricultural Experiment Station | 692-4020/4035 |
| Alumni Affairs & Development | 692-4023/4027 |
| Bookstore | 692-4162/4004 |
| Campus Operations | 692-4170/4165 |
| Cooperative Extension Service | 692-4080/4085 |
| Financial Aid | 692-4193/4145 |
| Housing/Residence Life | 692-4194/4217 |
| Library | 692-4130/4135 |
| **St. Thomas Campus** | |
| Academic Affairs | 693-1200/1205 |
| Admissions | 693-1160/1167 |
| Alumni Affairs | 693-1040/1049 |
| Bookstore | 693-1561/1565 |
| Campus Operations | 693-1140/1175 |
| Financial Aid | 693-1090/1167 |
| Housing/Residence Life | 693-1110/1105 |
| Human Resources | 693-1410/1415 |

| St. Thomas Campus (cont'd) | |
|---|---|
| Library | 693-1367/1365 |
| Research & Public Service | 693-1367/1365 |

For information on UVI degree programs, tuition, fees and schedules, refer to refer to the website: http://www.uvi.edu/ or call 1-877-GO-TO-UVI.

For more on the RTPark, including application requirements, browse to *http://www.//rtpark.uvi.edu* or call (340)773-5000.

### Libraries

There are public libraries on St. Croix, St. Thomas and St. John. Library cards are free to residents and valid at each facility, which offer services for children, young adults and adults. There are also services to patrons remotely located via the bookmobile; in a major shopping center (the Sunny Isle Public Library); and from the Regional Library for the Blind and Physically Handicapped. In St. John visit the Sprauve Library.

The libraries are fully automated on the VIALS (the Virgin Islands Automated Library System) to include the Public Library Learning Center and access to the book/materials collections of all the public libraries and three of the four public high school libraries and two curriculum centers in the Territory. Internet access is free to the public.

Special collections on V.I. and Caribbean history, culture and related topics are housed in the Florence Williams Public Library Caribbean Collection and the Charles Wesley Turnbull Regional Library and Archives Von Scholten Collection. Researchers are asked to make appointments

## HEALTH FACILITIES

The hospitals on both St. Croix and St. Thomas are semi-autonomous agencies with the operations of each hospital overseen by a Board of Trustees. Medical assistance is available on St. Croix, St. Thomas and St. John for low-income patients at a variety of health facilities.

**ST. CROIX - Governor Juan F. Luis Hospital and Medical Center**

(JFL), centrally located in Estate Diamond Ruby, is the sole safety-net hospital on the island of St. Croix, US Virgin Islands and is licensed for 188 patient care beds. It offers our community a full array of medical and speciAlty healthcare services that meet all local and federal standards and cover all needed treatments including but not limited to acute, emergency, rehabilitative, and ambulatory care; most medical specialties including internal medicine, surgery, pediatrics, obstetrics, gynecology, psychiatry, physical medicine, acute and chronic hemodialysis and others. JFL is certified by the Center of Medicare and Medicaid (CMS); a member of good standing with the National Association of Public Hospitals and American Hospital Association. The Hospital Pharmacy and Blood Bank are licensed by the Drug Enforcement Agency; and the Pathology & Clinical laboratory is certified by "The Joint Commission. Additionally, the End Stage Renal Disease (Hemodialysis) Unit is certified by CMS and a 5 Diamond Patient Safety awarded program. All health professionals are licensed under Federal Regulatory Agencies and meet OSHA standards.

Following the damage caused to the facility by Hurricanes Irma and Maria in 2017, JFL began construction of a modular hospital as it projects the building of the new permanent hospital facility. Through this transition, it continues to provide full health care services for residents and visitors. The Emergency Room is open 24/7 and can/will refer patients as needed.

**The Virgin Islands Cardiac Center (VICC),** an adjoining structure of the Governor Juan F. Luis Hospital and Medical Center, was constructed To become the premier cardiovascular prevention and treatment center in the Caribbean. Following the damage caused to the Governor Juan F. Luis Hospital & Medical Center main building by Hurricanes Irma and Maria, the VICC will reopen in December 2020. During this transition, the VICC will Be outfitted with state of the art equipment to provide a wide range of Acute Care, Ambulatory Care, After Care and Preventive Cardiovascular Care.

On St. Croix, the Health Department is out-patient clinic at **Charles Harwood Clinic,** 718-1311, in Christiansted, provides services which include: primary care, obstetrics and gynecology, dental, mental health care, cardiac, allergy, dermatology, ear, nose and throat, eye care, food, handlers' exams, orthopedics, home care, immunization, Lamaze Classes, neurology, opthalmology, oncology, pediatric, sexually transmitted diseases, including HIV and AIDS, and urology.

**Frederiksted Health Care, Inc.** (all insurances accepted) is a private non-profit organization, whose principal offices are located in Frederiksted, with a School Based Health Center satellite clinic located at the St. Croix Educational Complex. The services of FHC, Inc., offered on an appointment basis, include: Comprehensive Medical Services of Family Medicine, Internal Medicine, Optometry, Prenatal/High-Risk Prenatal and Gynecological Services, Pediatric and Newborn Pediatric Clinic, Podiatry, Adolescent Health Services, Dietician Services, Lab Services and Immunization by appointment. HIV, Diabetic and Eye Screening Clinics. Walk-in services are offered at the Urgent Care Center to patients of various ages and levels of illnesses from minor to urgent with evaluation, treatment discharge and/or transfer to the Governor Juan F. Luis Hospital and Medical Center via Emergency Medical Services. The also provide laboratory and dietician services. FHC INC also offers on-site in-kind services which include: Community Health (STD/HIV/TB), Mental Health and Substance Abuse, Women, Infant and Children's Program (WIC), and Family Planning Services.

*April 2019 - Governor Albert Bryan, Jr. participates in Charles Harwood Medical Complex ribbon-cutting for new modular units*

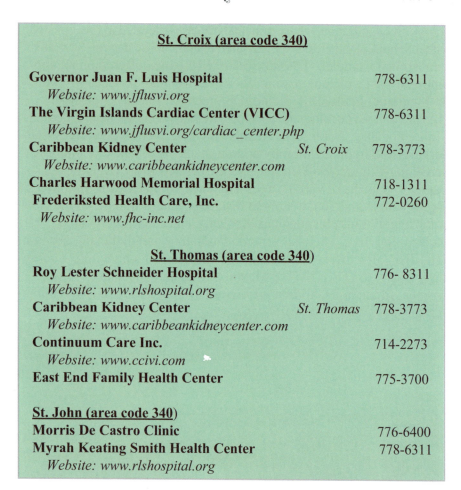

### St. Croix (area code 340)

| | |
|---|---|
| **Governor Juan F. Luis Hospital** | 778-6311 |
| *Website: www.jflusvi.org* | |
| **The Virgin Islands Cardiac Center (VICC)** | 778-6311 |
| *Website: www.jflusvi.org/cardiac_center.php* | |
| **Caribbean Kidney Center** *St. Croix* | 778-3773 |
| *Website: www.caribbeankidneycenter.com* | |
| **Charles Harwood Memorial Hospital** | 718-1311 |
| **Frederiksted Health Care, Inc.** | 772-0260 |
| *Website: www.fhc-inc.net* | |

### St. Thomas (area code 340)

| | |
|---|---|
| **Roy Lester Schneider Hospital** | 776-8311 |
| *Website: www.rlshospital.org* | |
| **Caribbean Kidney Center** *St. Thomas* | 778-3773 |
| *Website: www.caribbeankidneycenter.com* | |
| **Continuum Care Inc.** | 714-2273 |
| *Website: www.ccivi.com* | |
| **East End Family Health Center** | 775-3700 |

### St. John (area code 340)

| | |
|---|---|
| **Morris De Castro Clinic** | 776-6400 |
| **Myrah Keating Smith Health Center** | 778-6311 |
| *Website: www.rlshospital.org* | |

On **ST. THOMAS/ST. JOHN**, two medical facilities operate under the umbrella entity of the **Schneider Regional Medical Center: the Roy Lester Schneider Hospital (St. Thomas), and the Myrah Keating Smith Community Health Center (St. John).**

St. Thomas residents are served by the **Roy L. Schneider Hospital**, a 169-bed acute-care facility located across the street from the Lockhart Gardens Shopping Center. Provision of quality outpatient services is provided, including laboratory, radiology, rehabilitation and physiological testing. These services are in accordance with regulatory standards. The Schneider Hospital is a member of the National Association of Public

Hospitals, and has full accreditation by the Joint Commission on Accreditation of Healthcare Organizations.

**The Schneider Regional Medical Center** employs 600 employees and approximately 80 physicians, with specialties ranging from emergency room, intensive care, hemodialysis, radiology, laboratory, physical therapy, pharmacy, cardiology, catheterization, nephrology, general and laparoscopic surgery, gastroenterology, neonatology, neurology, obstetrics and gynecology, nursery, pediatrics, orthopedics, and nuclear medicine.

They also offer oncology, cancer chemotherapy, bone marrow aspiration, needle biopsy, evaluation and treatment of blood diseases, mammograms, skin tumors, lymph node, dissection, melanoma, and other cancer surgeries. The hospital is one of the few in the Eastern Caribbean that has a hyperbaric chamber to treat decompression sickness and wound treatment. There is a Community Wide Scheduling Center for outpatient services. By calling a central phone number, patients may make appointments and pre-register for a list of outpatient services. The system is designed to reduce the number of trips to the medical center, speed up the pre-admission process and to increase the level of customer satisfaction.

Also on St. Thomas, **The East End Family Health Center** provides many of the same services for residents of the eastern portion of the island. Call 775-3700. Family Planning and Maternal, Child Health and Crippled Children services are available in Nisky. Call 774-5256 for Family Planning, and 777-8804 for Maternal, Child Health and Crippled Children services. Mental Health Services are provided at Barbel Plaza South, 774-9000. Call 774-4912, the department's long-term mental health care facility, The Eldra Shulterbrandt Residential Facility.

**ST. JOHN - The Myrah Keating Smith Community Health Center:** in St. John, 24-hour emergency services, family practice, pediatrics, internal medicine, radiology and general laboratory services, high-risk OB/GYN services and women's health services can be found at the Myrah Keating Smith Community Health Center in Susannaberg (693-8900). Appointments are made Monday-Friday from 8 a.m. to 8 p.m. Patients needing hospital care go on the ambulance boat to the Red Hook ferry dock in St. Thomas, where the ambulance picks them up to go to the Schneider Hospital. The MKS helipad in St. John now provides direct acute emergency medical transportation between MKS and the Schneider Hospital in St. Thomas.

**The Morris F. deCastro** Clinic, St. John, provides general health services including dental and mental health. Open Monday thru Friday from 8 a.m. to 5 p.m., but after hours emergency can be accessed by dialing 911.

### Air Ambulance

If an unexpected injury or illness occurs that cannot be treated in the USVI, an air ambulance could be needed. These medically equipped jets can cost upwards of $9000 for services to Puerto Rico and about $20,000 to Miami. The planes are chartered from either here locally or Puerto Rico or Miami. While local primary health insurance coverage, or whatever you might bring from the states for primary insurance, say they include air ambulance, you may have to pay upfront and get reimbursed later. You may also have to meet a deductible. Also primary insurance companies may not be open 7/24/365 to handle those wee hours of the morning or weekend calls. These air ambulances want their money upfront first. Primary insurance companies may not pay your return trip home commercially.

### Staying Healthy

The best advice in the tropics? Drink plenty of fluids. Other hints until you have had a chance to acclimate: Why squint? Invest in a good pair of sunglasses, prescription, or not, to protect your eyes from sun damage. While many residents depend on photograys, optometrists say they do not provide sufficient protection for those who spend hours in the sun. Aside from wrinkles, the sun causes cancer and numerous other growths. Wear a hat and use heavy duty sunblock when out. The sun is strongest from 10 a.m. to 2 p.m., so avoid the beach during those hours. Since the rain water collected in your cistern lacks minerals found in ground water, a vitamin and mineral supplement every day is a good idea. Also, never ignore scratches and scrapes. Infection sets in quickly in the tropics. Wash with soap and water before covering loosely with a sterile bandage. If it's slow to heal, or the surrounding area becomes red, see your doctor immediately.

### Life and Health Insurance

Like everywhere, health insurance rates have skyrocketed. Private policies and group plans are available through local agents. Contact local insurance companies for more information. Several companies such as: Cigna Health Care, Elan Insurance Company, United Health Care write policies in the territory for small to large groups. Currently no individual insurance is available except for indemnity plans such as those offered by AFLAC or Ace American. Individual and group, Life, Disability and Annuities are available from several companies. If you qualify, expatriate insurance might be available from international websites but may not adhere to the terms of the Affordable Care Act. Ask local agents what is available here and where these policies are accepted. Be sure to check Department of Human Services (MAP) to see if you qualify for that income based option.

### Finding a Doctor/Dentist

Start your search by asking your new neighbors, or a business contact, or, look in the local telephone directory (www.viphonebook.com). Call first to be sure which island they are on. Each island has specialists, including: neurologists, cardiologists, chiropractors, dermatologists, ear-nose-throat specialists, radiologists, rehab centers, urologists, dentists, and many more. Some of them are associated with the local hospitals or clinics and/or may have their own practice. You might want to drive around to check for location of business signs and offices while you are familiarizing yourself with your new home.

### Taking Care of Your Pets

Animals are subject to all the creepy crawlies your garden or yard can muster and, like little kids, their curiosity will push their noses a little deeper into the bush or shrub. They will depend upon you for guidance and protection because the tropical climate will spawn a collection of interesting and unhealthy critters. Your pets are subject to the same diseases as those in similar warm climates where ticks, intestinal parasites and heart worm infestations are prevalent. It is important to control ticks with dipping preparations because ticks transmit blood diseases, can seriously threaten the health of your pet, and may set up residency in your home.

Intestinal parasites like hookworm are a constant threat because the warm weather conditions allow the larvae to persist in the soil. Heartworm is transmitted by certain mosquito species and may be treated successfully in most cases. Small monthly doses of medicine, prescribed by your vet, will prevent both heartworm and hookworm. Jack Spaniard stings can cause swelling and centipede bites can really hurt dogs. In both cases, get the animal to the vet. Medical attention is immediately needed if your dog gets entangled with an eight-to-ten inch toad called a "crappo." This toad exudes a substance from glands in the skin which may cause profuse salivation, nervousness with high fever, uncontrollable motions, and even death. In most cases, this toad is entirely nocturnal and can only be found in the daytime under some type of dark, damp cover. Cats are especially vulnerable to wild dogs and feral cats. If your pet has not been spayed, do so before you leave home to prevent encounters with these wild animals. In the islands there is an abundance of animals needing homes, so if your pet has babies, finding homes for them will be extremely difficult.

Two final thoughts on the care of your pets concerning the everyday life on the islands. For their sake, remember the tropics are too hot to leave animals shut in a car or in the back of a truck. And, if your pet becomes an ocean swimmer, wash off the saltwater from the pet's body afterward.
You rinse off after swimming in salt water, so do the same for them. Worthy of mention is the unwritten leash law. Dogs, where necessary, should be kept on leashes, and especially off beaches where turtles are nesting. Parrots, parakeets and fighting cocks must come from an area that is not under quarantine for psittacosis or Newcastle's Disease. For information on importing these birds contact any of the local animal shelters. The law mandates pets be registered every year, and new pets or pets brought into the territory must be registered with an identification tag within 30 days

In **St. Croix**, pets are licensed through the St. Croix Animal Welfare Center currently located in Clifton Hill. The AWC runs an on-line pet tag registry, for which fees are $5 plus $1 for shipping for a basic black tag. Personalized ones are available at an extra cost. Visit.www.stcroixawc.org /pet-licenses Licenses are also $5.00 and can also be purchased at any local veterinarian office.

The AWC shelter is open from 8:30 a.m. to 5 p.m. Monday-Saturday, but closed on Sundays and federal holidays. Owner phone numbers and names are kept at the AWC to help match lost pets. In addition to providing animal control services and operating a humane education program, the shelter works to reduce the huge number of stray and unwanted animals on St. Croix by requiring mandatory spay/neuter of all adopted pets, while offering a Low-Cost Spay/Neuter program to local residents. The adoption fee is $40 for adult dogs and cats over 6 months and $50 for kittens and $60 for puppies. All fees include heart worm or feline leukemia testing, vaccinations, spaying/neutering fees, and a microchip to aid in lost pets. The shelter is a non-profit organization that depends upon private fundraising, volunteers, and proceeds from their thrift store to keep doors open. This thrift store, called The Flea Market, is located in Richmond and open from 9 a.m. to 2 p.m. Wed. through Friday and on Saturday 9-4 p.m. Turn after Olympic Car and the Richmond Post Office to their alley.

In **St. John**, The Animal Care Center of St. John issues identification tags. Licenses on St. John are $85 for spayed animals and $124 for non-spayed to include spay/neuter. Dog licenses are not issued on St. Thomas. However, the Humane Society of St. Thomas issues an identification tag at $5 per tag. Their mailing address is 7041 Estate Nadir No. 26, St. Thomas, 00802 . They are open 7 days a week, 8 a.m. to 4 p.m.

**The Humane Society of St. Thomas** serves as the island's main animal shelter and adoption service. Potential adopters are welcome to come to the Humane Society's new Animal Campus, located on Weymouth Rhymer Highway across from Cost-U-Less. The adoption process is pretty straightforward. After filling out a questionnaire, staff will help you decide if the animal you want suits your lifestyle and will direct you to pets that may be appropriate. The shelter encourages prospective pet owners to allow everyone who will live with the animal (pets or housemates) to meet it before adoption. The Humane Society will require proof that you are allowed to have pets if you live in rental housing or in a condominium with animal restrictions in the bylaws. It is expected that adopters come prepared with landlord letters or lease copies that will verify that the animal does not violate rental or condo requirements. Adoption fees for cats are $75 which includes first vaccinations, de-worming, spay/neuter and flea treatment. Adoption fees for dogs/puppies is $105, which includes first vaccinations, de-worming, spay/neuter, flea treatment, license, a microchip and lifetime registration.

Below is information for veterinarian services on all three islands:

| | |
|---|---|
| **St. Croix** | |
| Stony Ground Critter Corner (Pet Supplies) | 772-4781 |
| Progressive Veterinary Hospital | 718-1256 |
| Sugar Mill Veterinary Center | 718-0002 |
| St. Croix Animal Welfare Center | 778-1650 |
| **St. John** | |
| Cruz Bay Canines, Cats & Critters | 693-7780 |
| All St. Thomas veterinarians make regular visits to St. John. | |
| Animal Care Center of St. John | 774-1625 |
| **St. Thomas** | |
| Moore Veterinarian Clinic | 775-6623 |
| Tutu Veterinarian Services | 777-7788 |
| Animal Hospital | 775-3240 |
| Humane Society of St. Thomas | 775-0599 |

# 19th Settler's Handbook  Basic Needs 6

There is a cool program that allows visitors traveling to the states to transport an animal to one of our partner shelters. On St. Croix it is called Pets from Paradise. Visit www.stcroixawc.org for details. The St. Thomas counterpart, Lucky Paws and Pets with Wings, can be found at www.hsst.com. and on St. John.

For more information on bringing your pet from the mainland double check "Bringing in your Pet", Chapter 3 in this *Handbook*.

**General and Special Interest Groups (all Area Code 340)**

| | | |
|---|---|---|
| A.A.R.P. | V.I. | 866-389-5633 |
| | St. Croix | 719-2277 |
| | St. Thomas | 776-8236 |
| Alcoholics Anonymous | V.I. | 776-5283 |
| | V.I. | 690-5283 |
| American Cancer Society | St. Croix | 1-800-277-2345 |
| | St. Thomas | 1-800-277-2345 |
| American Hibiscus Society | St. Croix | 513-2543 |
| American Red Cross | St. Thomas | 774-0375 |
| | St. Croix | 778-5104 |

# 19th Settler's Handbook  Basic Needs 6

| | | |
|---|---|---|
| Animal Care | St. John | 774-1625 |
| Animal Welfare Center of | St. Croix | 778-1650 |
| Bethlehem House for Homeless | St Croix | 777-4463 |
| | St Thomas | 777-5001 |
| Catholic Charities Services | St. Croix | 773-0132 |
| | St. Thomas | 777-8518 |
| Civil Air Patrol | St. Croix | 778-1280 |
| C.M. Cancer Institute | St. Thomas | 775-5433 |
| Continuum Care | St. Croix | 718-5683 |
| | St. Thomas | 714-2273 |
| Crime Stoppers | VI | 1-800-222-TIPS |
| Diabetes Association of the | VI | 693-1399 |
| Disability Rights Center | St. Croix | 772-1200 |
| Environmental Assoc. (SEA) | St. Croix | 773-1989 |
| Family Resource Center | St. Thomas | 776-3966 |
| Friends of Denmark | St. Croix | 690-7379 |
| | St. Thomas | 718-7017 |
| Friends of the Library | St. Croix | 773-5715 |
| | St. John | 776-6359 |
| | St. Thomas | 774-0630 |
| Found for Community Dev. | St. Croix | 773-9898 |
| Humane Society | St. Thomas | 775-0599 |
| Landmarks Society | St. Coix | 772-0598 |
| Legal Services of the V.I. | St. Croix | 718-2626 |
| | St. Thomas | 774-6720 |
| Lutheran Social Services | St. Croix | 772-4099 |
| Men's Coalition | St. Croix | 778-2161 |
| National Park Service, | St. Croix | 773-1460 |
| | St. John | 776-6201 |
| Orchid Society | stcroixorchidsociety@yahoo.com | |
| Queen Louise Home (children) | St. Croix | 772-0090 |
| Regional Library for the Blind and Physically Handicapped (Talking book Library) | St. Croix | 718-2250 |
| Rotary Club | St. Croix | 277-1126 |
| Rotary Club West | St. Croix | 772-5287 |
| Rotary Club Mid-Isle | St. Croix | 690-8246 |
| Rotary Club Harborside | St. Croix | 277-4788 |
| Rotary Clubs – | St. Thomas | 774-7304 |
| | St. Thomas | 513-0131 |

| | | |
|---|---|---|
| Salvation Army | St. Thomas | 776-0070 |
| St. Croix Bonsai Society | St. Croix | 778-9087 |
| St. Croix Seashell Society | St. Croix | 718-1910 |
| St. Croix Shrine Club | | 772-0030 |
| St. George Botanical Garden | St. Croix | 692-2874 |
| St. John Community Foundation | | 693-9410 |
| St. John Historical Society | | 344-4303 |
| United Way of | StT/StJ | 774-3185 |
| Women's Coalition | St. Croix | 773-9272 |
| VI Care (HIV/Aids) | St. Croix | 692-9111 |

### Art Groups

| | | |
|---|---|---|
| Arts Alive | St. Thomas | 776-8566 |
| Caribbean Community Theatre | St. Croix | 778-1983 |
| Caribbean Dance Company | St. Croix | 778-8824 |
| Caribbean Museum Center | St. Croix | 772-2622 |
| Island Center | St. Croix | 778-5271 |
| Music In Motion Dance | St. Croix | 772-5440 |
| Pistarkle Community Theater | St. Thomas | 775-7877 |
| Pointe Dance Company | St. Croix | 778-0317 |
| Reichhold Center for the Arts | St. Thomas | 693-1550 |
| St. John School of the Arts | | 779-4322 |
| V.I. Council on the Arts | St. Croix | 773-3075 |
| | St. Thomas | 774-5984 |

### Youth Programs

| | | |
|---|---|---|
| Boys and Girls Clubs | St. Croix | 778-8990 |
| Boy Scouts of America | St. Thomas | 774-2752 |
| F'sted Boating & Sailing Schl. | St. Croix | 772-2482 |
| Civil Air Patrol | St. Croix | 778-3371 |
| | St. Croix | 778-1280 |
| 4-H Club | St. Croix | 692-4087 |
| | St. Thomas | 774-0210 |
| Kids and the Sea (KATS) | St. John | 779-4994 |
| Swimming Assoc. | St. Croix | 719-7946 |
| Swimming Assoc. | St Thomas | 779-7872 |

### Labor

| | | |
|---|---|---|
| Am. Federation of Teachers | St. Croix | 778-4414 |
| Economic Dev. Community | St. Croix | 773-6499 |
| Economic Dev. Authority | St. Croix | 773-2161 |
| Job Corps. | St. Thomas | 777-9888 |

## Labor Cont'd

| | | |
|---|---|---|
| Lieutenant Governor's Office | St. Croix | 773-6449 |
| United Steel Workers of Amer. | St. Croix | 778-5634 |

### Business & Professional Associations

| | | |
|---|---|---|
| Advertising Club of the VI | St. Thomas | 774-8478 |
| Board of Realtors | St. Croix | 344-5618 |
| | St. Thomas | 866-598-1440 X234 |
| Casino Control Commission | St. Croix | 718-3616 |
| C'sted Retail & Rest. Assoc. | St. Croix | 778-9433 |
| Our Town Frederiksted | St. Croix | 772-3550 |
| Chamber of Commerce | St. Croix | 718-1435 |
| Chamber of Commerce | St. Thomas | 776-0100 |
| | St. John | 776-0100 |
| Hotel Association | VI | 774-6835 |
| Licensing & Consumer Affairs | St. Croix | 718-2226 |
| Taxi Association | St. Croix | 778-1088 |
| Taxi Association | St. Thomas | 774-0394 |
| Toastmasters | St Croix | 220-2318 |
| | St. Thomas | 473-2125 |
| V.I. Bar Association | St. Thomas | 778-7497 |
| | St. Croix | 778-7497 |

### Sports & Recreation

| | | |
|---|---|---|
| Cycling Federation/Triathlon | VI | 773-4470 |
| Marksmanship Assoc. | St. Croix | 773-8555 |
| Olympic Committee | VI | 778-2229 |
| | VI | 719-8462 |
| U.S. Coast Guard Auxiliary | St. Croix | 690-3280 |
| | St. Thomas | 998-9227 |
| Yacht Club | St. Thomas | 775-6320 |
| Yacht Club | St. Croix | 773-9531 |

## SPIRITUALITY

V.I. multiculturalism has led to diversity of spiritual culture here. Western religious tradition in these islands can be traced to the Moravians, who arrived in the 1700s with the blessing of the Danish governor. The Moravian missionaries were English speakers and taught their language to local slaves. Spanish services were also common, particularly on St. Croix.

Today there are more than 150 congregations and world religions in the territory, including hundreds of Christian denominations, Bahai, Islam, Hindu, Judaism and many more.

For a complete list visit www.viphonebook.com.

*Lord God of Sabath Lutheran Church, Christiansted*

*Meditating on the beach....*

# Settler's Handbook Chapter 7

## *COMMUNITY LIFE: ISLAND STYLE...*

### Folklore and Culture

Seven flags have flown over St. Croix and three over St. Thomas, a remarkable number for Caribbean islands since all were fought over for their agricultural advantages and strategic outposts on the trade routes to the New World. During the unending series of European wars and shifting alliances that lasted from the mid-1500s until the Napoleonic Wars in the early 1800s, settlers and Christian missionaries from about a dozen nations were merged to create the island culture. However, the dominant contributor was Africa, origin of the enslaved peoples who tilled the plantations in the Caribbean.

The definitive Virgin Islands form of music is quelbe, which is performed by scratch bands and makes use of gourds and washboards. Close to Christmas on St.Croix don't be surprised if one morning before dawn you find yourself jigging down the streets behind a truck of musicians. No, you are not in Hamlin – it's just St. Croix's Pied Pipers, Stanley and the Ten Sleepless Knights playing their infectious scratch music during their Annual 'fore Dawn Serenade, the local equivalent of mainland caroling. 'Jamesie and the Allstars were known as The Kings of Scratch music throughout the Caribbean' until his death at 79.

Another cultural music tradition is Cariso, a slave-pioneered, lilting music with words that tell a story. Not allowed communication as they toiled in the fields, the slaves sang as a way to pass on the news of family, friends and events to the other slaves. Cariso developed like the well-known calypso that now satirizes political figures and local issues and describes the folk medicine of the healers or "weed women" of long ago. One of the ingredients described for a particular problem was the aloe plant which now is included in many skin creams. Various teas and tisanes, or herbal concoctions, which will cure, sedate or stimulate are put to song. Story tellers today create their own theatre as they tell the folk tales from their African-West Indian culture. The island youngsters know all about Mickey Mouse but they also know of the "Bru Nancy" spider tales as well, which are the Caribbean equivalent to the Br'er Rabbit stories of Uncle Remus.

Virgin Islands traditional folk arts are still practiced by many devotees and you can catch the blowing of the conch shell heralding the start of some local observances and bamboula dancing. While fishermen continue to construct practical fish pots, it's only a few of the older generation, and even less of the territory's youths who continue to weave beautiful baskets, create original needle work or build mahogany furniture and fine caned chairs, though a tri-island woodworking group is growing. The social melting pot of the islands and the hardships endured during and after slavery have made Virgin Islanders a gracious and somewhat conservative people. They cherish privacy and are rather undemonstrative, at least by stateside standards, until you smile and say "good morning" and also that they know you are here for the long haul (except tourists) and will be part of and respect their homeland and culture. To a native islander, good fortune is nice but fragile, which is why the automatic quest-tion "how are you" often receives the reply "not as good as you".

**Mocko Jumbies**

These masked stilt walkers walk and dance the streets during parades or festive occasions and entertain with colorful, meaningful cost-umes..But the mocko jumb-ies have their serious side. Depending on whom you talk to, jumbies are supernatural beings for either good or evil. Never to be seen by nonbelievers, they reflect the islands' African heritage and are thought to be either one's ancestors or one's connection with the spiritual or superstitious world. That superstitious

---

*Cultural Tidbit*

Richard Allsopp in his text Dictionary of Caribbean English Usage, says the term mucko jumbie hails from African terms nsambi, 'God', and nsumbi, 'Devil', "the linking of good and evil with the same cos - mic powers."

My definition of a Jumbie is a chance en - counter of the living with a deceased relative, family or friend, in a guise recognizable to the seer.

Their intent for the most part is not to scare but to assist the living, or protect them from harm, bring them good news or luck, alert them of impending death of a family member, or to warn them of dangers. In this sense they are generally not haunts, al - though there are some "bad" Jumbies that are haunted and thereby are intent on doing harm. However, this is by far a rare occur - rence.

Then there are those who use Jumbies as a way to scare children into behaving. "Ima - ginary bogey man called on the frighten children." —from Wah a Jumbie Beh, by Dr. George Franklin force, called the Obeah, which creates those good and bad occurrences, is African rooted and similar in some ways to the more familiar Voodoo. While belief in Obeah has never been prominent in the U.S. Virgin Islands, it has been part of the territory's ambiance for years. You won't find many people who actually claim to believe in Obeah themselves, although the natives will tell you stories of something that supposedly happened to someone else. Some of the characters you see during Carnival or parades are mere interpretations of the spirits and superstitions of long ago.

## Carnival

Author Herman Wouk wrote the truth when he said "rain don't stop de Carnival. Indeed, all other activities cease when the Carnival comes through town. The event occurs on St. Croix, St. John and St. Thomas at different times, and each is unique. These celebrations begin slowly, as locals spend months building floats, sewing costumes, training horses, and selecting queens, princes and princesses. But on carnival days the action intensifies as groups gather for the hours-long parade through the streets with participants dressed in glitter and glitz. Look for floats, bands and twirlers, floupes, troupes and mocko jumbies. In the interim look for calypso contests, horse races, dances and night after night of fun, music and food at Carnival Village. Then there's J'Ouvert, a West Indian invention, which usually starts around 4 a.m. when thousands of people tramp through the streets behind their favorite bands. Boat races, baby contests and other events change from year to year depending on who's in charge and what the residents want. The entire event usually wraps up with a fireworks display. The newspapers and the local grapevine will let you know when and where the action starts. If you are not up to the crowds, be sure to catch the parades on television. The St. Croix version of Carnival, called the

> *Cultural Tidbit*
> Dr. George Franklin, cultural humorist, has volunteered the following instruction for newcomers to our islands.
> **Plural Nouns**
> What is the plural for mon-goose. No not mongeese, or mongooses, but mongoose dem.
> In fact, the plural for any-thing is the proper word fol-lowed by the suffix 'dem'.
> **Virgin Islands GPS**
> If you are a visitor and you are trying to find your way around our island using a map and the road signs you better forget it because none of us native have a clue about route this and route that. If you want to get from point A to point B you have to ask for landmarks (mango tree, a big white house with a lady sit-ting on the gallery, there's a red car in the yard, down by Cousin so and so house).

**Crucian Christmas Festival**, begins before Christmas and runs through Three Kings' Day or Epiphany on the religious calendar. Three Kings' Day is a major holiday for the numerous residents of Puerto Rican descent who live on St. Croix. Crucians first celebrated the festival during the final years of the Danish government. Although the holiday was abandoned over the years, residents revived it again in the 1950s. In some years, Carnival villages are erected near Frederiksted or near Christiansted. The parades (children's and/or adults) used to alternate yearly between the towns of Christiansted and Frederiksted, but are now all in Frederiksted.

Not to be outdone, St. John residents celebrate their **July 4th Festival** in a special style. Although smaller than Carnival celebrations on the other islands, residents enjoy it just as much. In fact it is growing yearly. Boatloads of sister-island folk crowd St. John. Just before the July 3rd parade, the ferries from St. Thomas run all day. Look for the Food Fair in Cruz Bay Park on the celebration's first Sunday.

St. Thomas has a lollapalooza of a Carnival. Usually held a few weeks after Easter, **St. Thomas Carnival** is second only to Trinidad's in scope and size. The tradition began in 1912 but subsequently lapsed. Revived in 1952 by Ron de Lugo, who later served as the territory's representative in Washington, D.C., the extravaganza consumes the minds and hearts of the islanders for weeks. Don't miss the parade through the streets of Charlotte Amalie. The costumes are known to rival those seen at the Mardi Gras in New Orleans.

## Entertainment and the Arts

Though not Broadway, there is plenty of entertainment in St. Croix and St. Thomas during the winter season. The pickings are slimmer on St. John, but late-running ferries allow residents to sample the St. Thomas night life. From major hotels to the corner bar, you will find a wide variety of musical entertainment during dinner and afterwards.

Since 1967, **Island Center for the Performing Arts** on St. Croix has headed the entertainment bill. A premier spot for artistic performances, Island Center has hosted such noted groups as the Boston Pops Traveling ensemble, Ebony Fashion Fair, Alvin Ailey, The St. Petersburg Ballet and the London Ballet. Such notable

Artistes as Eartha Kitt, Cab Calloway, pianist Awadagin Pratt, the Naumberg award winner Tomohiro Okumura, the Preservation Hall Jazz Band, Jose Feliciano, Third World and Victor Borge have headlined during the winter season. Island Center also hosts dance programs, theatre presentations, and youth activities, while serving as a community resource for special events, including performing arts workshops and public interest meetings. More than half of its 1100 amphitheatre seats are under cover. *Call 340-244-2036 for program information.*

Also on St. Croix, the **Caribbean Community Theatre** holds performances at #18 Orange Grove, behind Golden Rock Shopping Center. This non-profit performs Broadway-style musicals, comedies and local plays from October to July. Contact: 778-1983, www.cct.vi.

On St. Thomas, **Reichhold Center for the Arts** is celebrating 41 Years of in the arts. The center was the dreamchild of Philanthropist and businessman Henry H. Reichhold, CEO of Reichhold Chemicals, Inc. Reichhold endowed and oversaw development of a state-of-the-art amphitheater just west of the University of the Virgin Islands' St. Thomas campus. It has since grown a top regional performing arts center. Reichhold Center has hosted some of the world's top performers, including: Itzhak Perlman, Ray Charles, Sarah Vaughn, Puerto Rico Symphony Orchestra, Alvin Ailey Dance Company, Beres Hammond, George Benson, Chris Botti, and McCoy Tyner, just to name a few.

*Beres Hammond*
*Courtesy Reichhold Center*

Artists and audience members alike are enthralled by the theater's natural setting, nestled within the lap of a natural valley whose mouth opens to the crystal blue waters of John Brewer's Bay. Performances take place under the stars and moon, adding a unique ambience to each performance in this nearly 1,200-seat theater. The Center's season runs from October to June each year. However, at press time the center is being rebuilt as it was seriously damaged in the 2017 storms, IRMARIA, and is scheduled to be completed by October 2020. For performance schedule and ticket information, call 693-1559 or visit www.reichholdcenter.com. In addition to the Reichold Center, St. Thomas has a community theatre called **"The Pistarkle Theatre Group,"** which performs at **Tillett Gardens.**

The government-supported **Virgin Islands Council on the Arts** provide matching yearly grants, funded through the National Endowment for the

Endowment for the Arts, to artists and organizations. The Council on the Arts participates in and sends exhibits and musical groups throughout the the world. Anytime you are in the islands look and listen for Calypso, steel bands, quadrille dancing, marching bands and baton twirlers as well as ballet and modern dance performances. Check local newspapers for the latest entertainment updates.

## Holidays

If it seems like there is a holiday every time you turn around, you are probably right. Many of the local holidays are celebrated on Monday to give workers a three-day weekend. Local government offices are closed for those listed below. Banks and Federal offices close only for those marked with an asterisk (*). The Governor usually gives workers a day or half-day for Carnival activities.

**Usual Annual Holidays**
This is 2020. Dates in subsequent years will be similar. *Banks may be closed most of these days.

| Date | Holiday |
|---|---|
| Jan. 1 | New Year's Day |
| Jan. 1 | Crucian Festival Children's |
| Jan. 2 | Crucian Festival Adult's Parade |
| Jan. 6 | Three King's Day observed* |
| Jan. 20 | Martin Luther King's Day* |
| Feb. 17 | President's Day* |
| Mar. 31 | Transfer Day, V.I. |
| April 9 | Holy Thursday |
| April 10 | Good Friday |
| April 13 | Easter Monday |
| April 30 | St.T Carnival/ J'Ouvert |
| May 1 | St.T Carnival Children's Parade |
| May 2 | St.T Carnival Adult's Parade |
| May 25 | Memorial Day* |
| July 3 | Emancipation Day V.I. * |
| July 4 | Independence Day* |
| July 4 | St John Festival parade |
| Sept. 7 | Labor Day* |
| Oct. 12 | Columbus Day / USVI-Puerto Rico Friendship Day* |
| Nov. 1 | D. Hamilton Jackson Day |
| Nov. 11 | Veteran's Day* |
| Nov. 26 | Thanksgiving Day* |
| Dec. 25 | Christmas Day* |
| Dec. 26 | Boxing Day |

## Newspapers & Magazines

To quickly get an understanding of the islands and know what's going on, read the two local newspapers, the St. Croix Avis, and the V.I. Daily News. Both newspapers carry wire services reports on breaking stateside and world news. For more in- depth world coverage, read the New York Times, the Miami Herald, Washington Post, the Wall Street Journal or the San Juan Star. They are available of course online, and at outlets in the islands at prices quite a bit higher than stateside. The Sunday New York Times will arrive a day later because the plane comes in the next day. A good selection of national magazines is available at many convenience stores, supermarkets, Kmart and at news outlets. The prices run about a dollar more per issue.

## Newspapers

The *St. Croix Avis*, a St. Croix daily, except Mondays and major holidays, Box 750, Christiansted, VI 00821 718-2300, (fax) 718-5511. (call for subscription). (In St. Thomas it is sent there as The Avis.)
*Virgin Islands Daily News*, St. Thomas and St. Croix daily, except Sundays and Christmas Day, 9155 Estate Thomas, St. Thomas, VI 00802. 774- 8772 St. Croix Bureau, 714-9123.

### News On-Line
https://stcroixsource.com •www.virginislandsdailynews.com
https://viconsortium.com

### Tourist and Island Information Websites
•www.gotostthomas.com •www.gotostcroix.com
•www.gotostjohn.com •www.stcroixhotelandtourism.com
•www.virgin-islands-hotels •www.visitstcroix.com
•www.visitthevi.com •www.vinow.com

### Local Periodicals
*Island Trader*, free weekly, call for classified rates, (contact Daily News).
*St. John Tradewinds*, bi-weekly news of St. John, P.O. Box 1550, Cruz Bay, St. John VI 00831, 776-6496.

### Tourist Publications
*Marine Guide* (Media Marketing Inc.), 774-0920, all three islands, British Virgin Islands and Puerto Rico. www.vimarineguide.com
*Places to Explore* (Media Marketing, Inc.) 774-0920, all three islands.
*Places to Eat Map*, *St. Thomas and St. John* (Media Marketing, Inc.) 774-0920. www.viplacestoexplore.com; stthomasdining.com
*St. Croix Explorer*, an annual tourist guidebook with information on shopping, dining, accommodations, activities, and watersports, with map, P.O. Box 2797, Kingshill, St. Croix VI 00851 718-5128. www.stcroixexplorer.com
*St. Croix This Week*, 774-2500 published monthly: events, shopping, maps, tourist information, Box 224477, Christiansted, St. Croix, VI 00822-4477, http://www.stcroixthisweek.com.
*St. Thomas/St. John This Week*, 774-2500, Saturday, weekly. P.O. Box 11199, St. Thomas, VI 00801, http://www.stthomasthisweek.com.

### Books
Many wonderful books have been written about the Caribbean and in particular about the U.S. Virgin Islands. Some of the older ones could be out of print although you may find them at a local library. Below is listed but a mere selection of good books written about the U.S. Virgin Islands.

You can also go on-line and conduct searches. Additionally, when you arrive at your chosen island, visit some of their local book stores, gift shops, university libraries, visitor centers, airports and market places.

### Architecture / Living Here
Architectural Heritage of the Caribbean – Andrew Gravette
Caribbean Elegance (exotic furniture from the sugar islands)
Caribbean Houses, both – Michael Connors
Gardening in the Caribbean – Bannochie and Light
Historic Buildings of St. Thomas and St. John – F.C. Gjessing, F.C. & W.P. MacLean
Life in the Left Lane – Emy Thomas

### Children's
A Caribbean Journey from A-Y – Mario Picayo
Caribbean Capers – J&M Santomenna
Caribbean Colors of Rainbow – Skylon & Woodruff
Daniel and the Christmas Festival– Denise Bennerson
It's Not About You, Mr. Santa Clause - Soraya Diase Coffelt
It's Not About You, Mrs. Turkey - Soraya Diase Coffelt
It's Not About You, Mr. Pumpkin - Soraya Diase Coffelt
Lenny the Lobster – Katherine Orr
Look A Moko Jumbie – Opal Palmer Adisa
My Island and I - The Nature of the Caribbean – A. Silva Lee
Pabi, Beega & The Mongoose Monster – Patricia Gill
My Grandma - Winnifred Loving
The Illustrated Animal Folk Tales (Anansi Stories) – P. Sh
The Lame Shepherd Boy and Other Stories - Anne Marie Danet
The Adventures of Jean-Pierre Mongoose - Anne Marie Danet

### Cookbooks
A Taste of the Virgin Islands– Angela and Richard Spencely
Crucian Confusion Cooking – St. Croix Landmarks Society
Just Add Rum – Angela Spenceley (other similar ones by her)
My Little Virgin Islands Cookbook– Kathleen Querrard
Native Recipes – UVI Cooperative Extension Service
Virgin Islands Cooking – Carol Bareuther

## Culture / History
A Brief History of the Caribbean – Rogozinski
A History of the V.I. of the U.S. – Isaac Dookhan
Alexander Hamilton: American – Richard Brookhiser
Annals of the Big Island, both – Robert Hoffman
Collection of Writings: French Heritage - The People, History and the Culture - Anne Marie Danet
Fireburn – Angela Golden Bryan
From Columbus to Castro – Eric Williams
Fruits and Vegetables of the Caribbean – Seddon
Hidden Secrets of St. Croix – Clarice Clarke
I am Not a Slave – Eugene LaCorbiniere
I am The Virgin Islands - Tiphanie Yanique
Kallalo – Richard A. Schrader, Sr. *(plus others by Schrader)*
Me and My Beloved Virgin – Guy H. Benjamin
Negotiating Enslavement – Arnold Highfield, George F. Tyson
Peter Von Scholten– Hermann Lawaetz
Pirates of the Virgin Islands – Fritz Seyfarth
Romantic History of St. Croix – Florence Lewisohn
St. Croix Historic Photos – Elizabeth Rezende, Anne Walborn
Saint Croix 1770-1776 – Robert Johnson
Say It In Crucian – Robin Sterns
The Night of Silent Drums – John L. Anderson
This Little Island Mine – Richard A. Schrader, Sr.
Time Longa Dan Twine – Arnold Highfield

## Fiction
A Bunch of Real Jumbie Stories, Meh Son – George Franklin
A West Indian Fish Tale – A. Anduze
Andy Browne's Departure – S. B. Jones-Hendrickson
Buddhoe and Cape of the Arrows – Patricia Gill
Caribbean – James Michener
Don't Stop the Carnival – Herman Wouk
How to Escape a Leper Colony - Tiphanie Yanique
Land of Love and Drowning - Tiphanie Yanique
Lagoonieville Series – Bert Emrick
The Caribbean Writer - Volume 1-22 – Erika J. Waters
The Glass Bottom Boat – Everett Freeman
The Mangoes Series – R. D. Dowling
Transfer Day– Sophie Schiler

### Fiction (cont'd)
The Mangoes Series – R. D. Dowling
Transfer Day– Sophie Schiler

### Nature/Wildlife
200 Tropical Plants of the Caribbean – John Kingsbury
A Guide to the Birds of P.R. and the V.I. – Herbert Raffaele
Caribbean Wild Plants & Their Uses – P. Honychurch
Diving Pioneers and Innovators – Bret Gilliam
Guide to Corals & Fishes – Idaz Greenberg
Island Peak to Coral Reef – Toni Thomas & Barry Devine
Traditional Medicinal Plants – Toni Thomas
Tropical Trees of Florida and the V.I. – T. Kent Kirk
U.S. Virgin Islands – National Park Handbook

### Poems
Sugar Is All – Annette Walwyn Michael
Under the Taino Moon – Arnold R. Highfield /Richard Schrader

---

### Annual Events Sampler
### www.virginislandsthisweek.com

**January:**
**St. Croix** - Crucian Christmas Festival (includes Three Kings DayParade on or close to Epiphany); Candlelight Concerts at WHIM (run Nov-April); Martin Luther King Annual Run; Krewe de Barkus canine parade; Sunset Jazz, Frederiksted 3rd Friday; Dolphins Annual Swim, Artists Guild Art Exhibit

**February:** Miss UVI Pageant;
**St. Croix** – Agricultural Fair; House Tours by St. Croix Landmarks Society thru March; Agricultural Fair; Jump-Up Christiansted Block Party (streets closed and stores stay open late 4 per year); Mardi Croix; Orchid Society Show;
**St. John** - St. John Race, Eight Tuff Miles (last Saturday);
**St. Thomas** - Valentine's Ball (Fur Ball) to benefit Humane Society

**March:**
**St. Croix** - St.Patrick's Day Parade; University of the Virgin Islands Golf Tournament;
**St John** – St. John Blues Festival

## Annual Events Sampler (cont'd)
## www.virginislandsthisweek.com

### March (cont'd):
**St. Thomas -**
Arts Alive Festival Tillett Gardens; Hibiscus Society Show; VI History Month

### April:
**St. Croix** - LPGA Pro-Am Tournament, Carambola Golf Club; Golden Hook Fishing Tournament; Taste of St. Croix (fantastic wine/Food sampling!)
**St. Thomas** - St. Thomas Carnival; Intl. Rolex Cup Regatta ; Easter Bonnet Contest, Blackbeard's Castle Hotel

### May:
**St. Croix** - Memorial Day Race, St. Croix Yacht Club; Amer. Cancer Society Walkathon:
**St. John** - Beach to Beach Swim by Friends of the Park;
**St. Thomas**: Spring Charter Yacht Show - (alternates each year between USVI and BVI –call 774-3944 for info)

### June:
**St. Croix** -Annual Women's Race for Women's Coalition

### July:
**St. Croix** - Mango Melee, SGVBotanical Garden; Summer World Music Series July/Aug/Sept at WHIM plantation, St. Croix Landmarks Society;
**St. John** - July Festival Celebration;
**St. Thomas** - Open Sport Fishing Tournament; French Heritage Week; Bastille Day King-fish Tournament; St. Thomas Billfish Tournament, American Yacht Harbor

### August:
**St. Thomas** - Arts Alive Festival, Tillett Gardens; Texas Chili Cookoff; Atlantic Blue Marlin Tournament

## Annual Events Sampler (cont'd)
### www.virginislandsthisweek.com

**September:** St. John Love City Triathlon, Aquathon; St.Thomas - Women's Laser Regatta, Bee Buzzaar

**October:**
**St. Croix** – Fall Heritage Day; Virgin Islands/Puerto Rico Friendship;
**St. Thomas** – October Sunday Music Fest; Columbus Day Regatta;

**November:**
**St. Croix** – International Sailing Regatta, Yacht Club; Starving Artists Fair, Whim Museum; Dine VI
**St. John** – Annual Thanksgiving Regatta; Veteran's Day in the Park;
**St. Thomas** -Arts Alive Festival, Tillett Gardens; Evening in the Courtyard Party; Agricultural Fair; Paradise Jam Basketball Tournament ; Fall Charter Yacht Show, Taste of Two Islands Food Festival

**December:**
**St. Croix** – Ironman 70.3 Triathlon; Crucian Christmas Festival kicks off; Boat Parade of Lights, VI Pace Runners Marathon & Half Marathon, Botanical Gardens Christmas Dinner and Auction;
**St. John** –Annual All Island Holiday Party;
**St. Thomas** - Hibiscus Show; Carlos Aguilar Match Race; Las Vegas Night Fundraiser VI Montessori; Miracle on Main St.

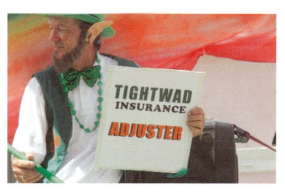

"Post Ir-Maria St. Patrick Leprechaun"

*Courtesy Mike Hanne*

# Settler's Handbook Chapter 8

## *THE GREAT OUTDOORS....*

With an endless array of sunny days, a climate unsurpassed, and the blue Caribbean at your feet, playing in the outdoors is a natural way of life. It's just how do you decide what to do! You can bask on the beach, float in the gentle surf, hike, ride horseback through a rain forest or on the beach, play a championship golf course, dabble in tennis, sail, snorkel, SCUBA dive, cast a line in the turquoise waters, or play softball or basketball with a local league. The more sedate or curious person might want to do some bird watching in bushes, or watch the sugar birds right from a porch. A lazy afternoon could be spent collecting shells along the beach. The choices are endless.

## WATER SPORTS
### Boating

Whether you are an old salt or a novice, under power or sail, boating in the U.S. Virgin Islands offers spectacular sparkling waters, cozy anchorages, tradewinds and plenty of little islands to visit. Sheltered bays dotted with palm trees, and white sandy beaches invite you to drop anchor. This part of the Caribbean is a favorite cruising ground. St. Croix, the biggest island, offers good anchorages in both Christiansted and Frederiksted harbors. Buck Island Reef National Monument, just a few miles north of St. Croix, has an underwater national park with fabulous snorkeling, swimming and anchor sites. Getting into Christiansted harbor, especially at night can be very tricky. While there are channel markers and buoys, there are many shallow reefs surrounding this area. From St. Thomas, head up the Pillsbury Sound, going east, into the sheltered Windward Passage between St. John and Jost Van Dyke to the stellar anchorages in the British Virgin Islands.

If you are a novice boater, take a boating safety course from the U.S. Power Squadron or U.S. Coast Guard Auxiliary. While these waters and islands are all too inviting, let the sailor beware that dangerous squalls can come up fast.

On the average, swells run from one to five feet; waves are one to three feet and the wind up to 20 knots. In the winter, the winds blow from east to northeast with northerly swells. While in the summer, the wind shifts south to east to southeast with swells from the south.

As with any large investment, try before you buy. Sail with friends, charter, or visit boat yards to see what's available. Check the classifieds, and also *Triton, All at Sea* and *Island Trader*. If you find a "favorite boat" back home, arrangements can be made with them, or locals, to set up a delivery crew.

Call the U.S. Coast Guard Auxiliary in St. Thomas for a free safety check of your boat. They will advise you as to what needs to be fixed up. Other useful numbers are the Resident Inspection Office on St. Croix 772-5557, and St. Thomas, 776-3497.

Since there were not any pump-out stations anywhere in the territory, The Department of Planning and Natural Resources worked with marinas to ensure their installation. At the present time, there are pump-out stations at several marinas on both islands, or boats can go beyond the three-mile limit to empty their holding tanks.

If you sail into the U.S. Virgin Islands on a vessel registered on the mainland or in a foreign country, you can cruise for 60 days without registering here. You can anchor for 14 days in any one bay. If you want to stay longer, you must apply for an anchoring permit at the DPNR. Anchoring permits run $2 a foot per month. If you want a mooring, you must apply to the DPNR. Mooring fees are $5.00 per foot per year. They will pro-rate your registration fee since all boats must register in June. Noncommercial boats pay $25 under 16 feet, $50 for boats 16 to 25 feet, $100 for boats 26 to 39 feet, $150 for boats 40 to 65 feet, and $200 for boats over 65 feet. Commercial vessels pay $37.50 under 16 feet, $75 for boats 16 to 25 feet, $150 for boats 26 to 39 feet, $225 for boats 40 to 65 feet, and $300 for boats over 65 feet. Call DPNR at 773-5774 in St. Croix, or 774-3320 in St. Thomas for more information.

### Chartering

To experience boating first hand, charter a boat, with captain and crew, or bareboat, by yourself and friends. That of course means you do the navigating, swab the decks and cook. For a little more dollars, you can let someone else do all the work while you relax on deck or jump in for a snorkel .You can sign up for a day or for a week. There are many charter companies and different size boats available for small or large groups. Check with tourist publications, or your travel agent, or for a spur of the

moment trip, walk along the dock and see who is in port.
The Spring Charter Yacht show is May in St. Thomas with a much larger show in November to kick off the season.

### Charts

Charts from the U.S. Coast and Geodetic Survey will help you find your way around these islands. All marine stores sell selected charts, but Brad Glidden Charts and Books at Caribbean Inflatable Service has the most complete selection in St. Thomas, and in St. Croix see St. Croix Marine. Frequently used local area chart numbers:

Anegada - No. 25609
Christiansted Harbor - No. 25645
Culebra - No. 25653
Frederiksted Roadsted - No. 25644
Pillsbury Sound (St. Thomas/St. John) - No. 25647
Puerto Rico - U.S. Virgin Islands - No. 25640
Roadtown Harbor, British Virgin Islands - No. 25611
St. Thomas Harbor - No. 25649
Virgin Islands - No. 25649
Virgin Gorda, British Virgin Islands - No. 25610
Virgin Passage, Culebra, Vieques - No. 25650
200 moorings in National Park waters around St. John to protect coral reefs

### Marinas

On St. Croix, boats can be docked at St.Croix Marine, Green Cay Marina or the Salt River Marina. Permanent moorings are allowed in Christiansted and Frederiksted harbors, Chenay Bay, Cotton Garden Bay, Salt River and Teague Bay. St. Croix Marina, a full service marina has a marine railway and a 60-ton travel lift, and is the only place to haul your boat. You will find launching ramps at Altona Lagoon in Christiansted, and at the foot of Fisher Street in Frederiksted; also at Cane Bay and the Great Salt pond, and several coves along the southshore.

There is no boat docking in St. John. Permanent moorings are permitted only in Cruz Bay, Great Cruz Bay, Chocolate Hole, Coral Bay or Johnson Bay. The Friends of the National Park organization have set up more than

and sea habitats from anchor damage. There is a small marine store near the Coral Bay dinghy dock. St. John Hardware near the Enighed Pond should have a small selection of marine parts. All Coral Bay is a launching ramp. Currently the Virgin Islands National Park allows boaters to use the Park's launching ramp in Cruz Bay.

On St.Thomas, Crown Bay Marina in Subbase, Saga Haven, Independent Boat Yard, Compass Point Marina, American Yacht Harbor, Yacht Haven Grande Marina, Pirates Cove Marina, Frenchtown Marina CYOA and Sapphire Marina have dock space. Permanent mooring is permitted at Elephant Bay, Honeymoon Bay, Flamingo Bay, Frenchtown/Villa Olga, Careening Cove, Long Bay, Hull Bay, Bolongo Bay, Jersey Bay, Benner Compass Point, Secret Harbour, Vessup Bay and Red Hook in St. Thomas.

To haul your boat call Independent Boat Yard at the Benner Bay Lagoon. Gas and water are available at Crown Bay, Saga Haven and American Yacht Harbor. The new Yacht Haven Grande Marina is another place to get fuel and water. Trailer boaters can launch their craft from shore at Red Hook, Magens Bay, Hull Bay or Crown Bay. The Virgin Islands Port Authority will allow small boats to tie up for a few hours without charge, space permitting, at its harbor facilities on all three islands, but check with them first. You should leave a dinghy ashore since there is no launch service.

Visit www.vimarineguide.com for information on marine industry and services.

## Yacht Clubs

**St. Croix Yacht Club** at Teague Bay offers club privileges and guest memberships to visiting boaters. Racers gather at the Yacht Club for the prestigious St. Croix International Regatta over Veteran's Day Weekend, and the winner takes home their weight in Cruzan Rum! The course is laid out between the Yacht Club, Buck Island and, at times, through Christiansted Harbor, permitting a great view of the race for spectators situated in town and along the north shore of the island.

They encourage members to participate in inter-island racing and also teach Junior sailing. These young sailors often participate in Opti, Laser and Sunfish Regattas on other islands, the mainland, or even internationally. While there are no yacht club facilities in St. John, the **St. John Yacht Club** and the **Coral Bay Yacht Club** do have meetings. Call Skinny Legs Bar and Restaurant at 779-4982, for Coral Bay Club info or Connections at 779-4994 for St. John Club info. The clubs sponsor the annual Thanksgiving Weekend Regatta which draws casual and serious Racers.

The **St. Thomas Yacht Club** at Vessup Bay provides reciprocity to visiting yacht club members. On Easter weekends, or close to that time frame, the club hosts the acclaimed Rolex Cup Regatta, which draws competitors from the States and all over the Caribbean. St. Thomas has top-notch sailor Peter Holmberg who has participated in many world-wide races such as the America's Cup.

## Diving

Crystal clear waters with visibility up to 100-feet invites the new diver to learn about exploring its depth, and the experienced to add to their diving log. With thousands of coral reefs, rocky pinnacles, drop offs and ledges, the Caribbean Sea especially around these three islands, are home to an abundance of marine life and shipwrecks. For a lot of vacationers it is the number one reason to visit. *Diving Magazines* rate the clear, azure waters of the Virgin Islands as the *"most beautiful in the world for diving"*. Take lessons from some of the finest instructors in the Caribbean. If you can swim, you can dive. If you like the water, you can learn how to dive. Each of the three Virgin Islands offers its own unique spots for diving and they all have great dive shops who know their areas well. For a fascinating experience in this undersea world, take an introductory SCUBA diving course from any of the local dive shops. They teach to national and world standards and will walk you through the basics step by step from the pool to the beach, to a boat dive. You will soon discover the sea gardens that boast a myriad of flora and fauna, sea fans, feather dusters, colorful fish, reefs, slopes, walls, crevices, canyons and shipwrecks. After a resort course, advanced certification courses can be obtained. All instructors here promote safety for yourself and the environment. They enforce "take pictures and leave nothing but bubbles". For safety's sake there is much to learn before you go off on your own. (Of course, never dive alone, but always with a Buddy.)

You should especially learn about which sea life can sting. If you are certified, the local shops will rent you gear. Please use them as Dive guides because they know the areas. They fly the red with white Diagonal diver down flag, or the blue/white alpha flag to warn boaters that divers are in the area. You should fly one if you are diving from a float. Each of these Virgin Islands has its own great diving spots. St. Croix has wall, wreck and reef diving. St. Thomas is more flat, with great reefs and shipwrecks. St. John has great reef diving, and the St. Thomas/St. John dive shops will take you on certain days to great diving in the British Virgin Islands, especially to the wreck of the Rhone.

**Wall Diving**

St. Croix is famous for The Wall, a section of the Puerto Rico Trench that Runs about 7 miles wide and 3,200 ft deep, along the North side waters of the island. It makes for exciting, but potentially dangerous wall diving. To give you an idea of the depth of t he slope, several hundred feet off the western shore near Frederiksted, the U.S. Navy used to conduct submarine and airplane night detection training. The most popular wall diving sites are off the north shore at Annaly Bay, Cane Bay, Davis Bay, North Star and Salt River East and West Walls.

The Frederiksted Pier is known for its abundance of sea life, for you are apt to find: seahorses, Christmas tree worms, sponges, puffer fish, trumpet fish and needle nose fish. You can't dive when cruise ships are in. This pier is also very popular for night diving. To the south of the Pier, Kings Reef reveals a gentle slope full of corals, fans and sponges. There are several dive shops on island of course to assist with rentals, and boat diving or a snorkel guide tour. Most of them have boats to take you to wrecks at Ham'Bluff. West End shore diving usually has calmer water then the rest of the island's shores.

The dive shops in St. Croix, in conjunction with a group called the Island Conservation Effort, established mooring areas around and near the dive sites. For an example, visit www.stcroixscuba.com.

Those mooring sites, Cormorant Reef, Eagle Ray, Luv Shack, Scotch Banks, and win Anchors (to name a few), were set up to prevent damage to the reefs by not anchoring just anywhere. There are over 60 moorings to dive, both on the west end and north shore.

The **Buck Island National Monument** offers extra crystal clear water and is marked by signs on an underwater trail to identify local flora, fauna and fish.

**St. John**
The rocky ledges at Carvel Rock are decorated with gorgonians, seawhips and sponges.
**Stevens Cay and Watermelon Cay** offers excellent shallow water diving.
**Trunk Bay** has an underwater trail that offer an abundance of coral formations and marine life.
**Salt Pond** has a small reef in the middle of it with an array of marine life, sure to be a snorkelers delight.
**St. Thomas**
**General Rogers** and **Grain Wreck,** boast the best wreck diving on the north side, popular dive sites include:
**Coki Beach, Hans Lollick, Thatch Cay, Outer Brass.**

Off the south side you will find good diving at **Cow and Calf Caverns Capella Island French Cap Cay and Fortuna Beach, Sail Rock…** the **Ledges at Little St. James,** and the **Stragglers at Great St. James.**

SAFETY TIP:
If you have an open cut, stay out of the water. Do not drag around your "catch of the day". Curious barracuda are attracted by smell, as well as shiny objects like jewelry. Also, when the water is warmer, jellyfish may drift through the waters. If you have an allergic reaction from any of these type of stings, see a doctor immediately.

### Fishing
The fishing waters in the U.S. Virgin Islands are considered some of the finest in the world for tuna, marlin, sailfish, kingfish and wahoo. You will

find lots of challenges whether you fish from the family yacht, a chartered fishing boat or a rented runabout. Major fishing tournaments, in the Johnny Harms' Tournament Series, are held annually on St. Thomas July through October. The tournaments in the Johnny Harms' Series include three Billfish events in St. Thomas, one in the British Virgin Islands, one in Puerto Rico and, The Golden Hook Challenge in St. Croix.

The Golden Hook Challenge, held in late February, is one of four annual St. Croix tourneys. The three other Crucian tournaments include the Dolph-

In Tournament, mid-April; the Guy/Gal Reel Challenge, early October; and the Wahoo tournament, ocurring in late Nov-Ember. Call 778-0487 for information on Crucian sport fishing.

In St. Croix, championship marlin, yellow fin tuna or wahoo can usually be found several hundred feet off the north shore, along the northeast corner to the southeast corner of Lang Bank (extending nearly 15 miles). The drop off near Sandy Point just south of Frederiksted is also a popular spot. Local fishing professionals will tell you to go out about a half mile and drop your line.

About ten miles north of St. Thomas and St. John, head for the famous North Drop to look for blue and white marlin, wahoo, sailfish, dolphin and yellow fin tuna. About 20 miles north of St. John and St. Thomas is the Puerto Rico trench, at 25,000 feet the second deepest trench in the Atlantic ocean. Ten miles south of St. John and St. Thomas, is the south drop, another popular spot. Reefs closer to shore are where you can find smaller fish like bonito, rainbow runner, jack, grouper, snapper and mackerel.

Check tourist publications or the hotel bulletin boards to see who is going out.
You won't need a license from DPNR to fish with hook and line or your bare hands. You do need one to use a net or trap. Spearfishing is prohibited in any of the Virgin Islands National park waters. Commercial fishermen will need a license.
You can fish for conch in local Virgin Islands National Park waters from November 1 to May 30. The take is six per day and they must be mature adults. Fines can be high. The whelk season runs October 1 through March 31. They must be more than 2-7/16 inches in diameter. There is a 12 inch

minimum on Yellow Tail.

It is against the law to take or bother sea turtles or their eggs. Turtle meat will not be found on the market because it is illegal to sell or import. The U.S. Fish &Wildlife Service has ruled that even if it is grown in captivity, it still is on the endangered species list. Lobsters must measure 3-1/2 inches long along the carapace and you can take an unlimited number from local waters. Within the boundaries of the Virgin Islands National Park waters, you can take two but they must be captured in ways that will not injure them, whether by hand, trap or noose. Females with eggs cannot be taken at any time. Virgin Islands Fish & Wildlife issues commercial fishing licenses for the skipper and each crew member at $5 a year. Each commercial fisherman chooses a color code patch for his boat, traps and other gear to assist in identification and enforcement. There is no fee for recreational fishing licenses. To make certain your catches for the above are withing legal guidelines you can pick up a measuring gauge from the Fish & Wildlife office.

### Spearfishing

Spearfishing is popular everywhere but prohibited within the waters of the Virgin Islands National Park. Virgin Islanders hold about 30 world records including: speedy prey such as mackerel, kingfish, snapper, pompano, and sharks over 200 pounds!

### Swimming

Virgin Islands' law states that the beach area is measured 50 feet from the low water mark, which means that all beaches in the Virgin Islands are open to sunbathing or swimming for locals or visitors. This law ensures that the beaches will never be closed. The hotels on the islands do not own the beach on their property, but it pays to use discretion and common sense when using any of those beaches. Several beaches as well as marinas have received the Blue Flag certification, which is awarded throughout the world when beaches must meet 32 strict requirements including water quality, environmental management and safety services. If you have to cross private property to get to that beach, permission is necessary. Everyone has a right to use the beaches, but please help keep it clean for others too.

New residents to the islands will likely frequent the beaches as much as possible, but believe it or not, this novelty will wear off, as you either enjoy different recreation, or your back-yard pool. The longer you live here, the more you will find that even you will think the water temperature is colder in the winter months. The water is in fact about 10 degrees cooler in the winter months. For local divers that means using a shorty wetsuit!

Snorkelers feel comfortable in a lycra suit or, even a t-shirt to prevent some sunburn and to keep a little warmer. The sun is still sun is still at its strongest between 10 a.m. and 2 p.m. That's because we are closer to the Equator here. Just like vacations, don't overdo it, always wear good sunblock, and a hat and take a break and sit in the shade.

Sun reflection from ocean and sand can give you a faster burn that you may not realize until later. Ouch! You'd probably rather not want to look for the Aloe! Everyone always asks locals where their favorite beaches are. You will get mixed reviews, because every island has its share of great beaches.

### St. Croix beaches
Bucaneer Beach, Cane Bay Beach, Carambola Beach Resort, Chenay Bay Beach Resort, Cramer Park, Club St. Croix, Divi Resort (east end southshore), Ha'penny, Hibiscus Beach Hotel, Hotel on The Cay, Shoys, Tamarind Reef Hotel, The Palms (north side), and all the sandy beaches along the shore at the west end such as Dorsch, Sandcasteles, Rainbow. Sandy Point, when it is open is spectacular!

### St. John beaches
National Geographic says Trunk Bay is one of the most beautiful beaches in the world. Other notable beaches-Cinnamon Bay Hawksnest, Honeymoon

### St. Thomas beaches
St. Thomas' Magens Bay is the most favored by locals and tourists while the east enders prefer Secret Harbor, Coki Point or Sapphire.

Local swimming associations offer lessons for infants through adults. Check the handy Association listing later in this chapter for swim clubs.

**SAFETY TIP:** Every week, Dept. of Planning and Natural Resources publishes a safe beach advisory to protect your health, so check the news before you go swimming.

## Shell Collecting

While shell collecting has been a favorite pastime of many over the years, one may soon come to realize that it can dwindle the resources, and those pretty shells you might want to take home in a suitcase, or to your residence here, will soon smell if not cleaned properly. While some like to collect souvenirs and some scientists like to collect "live specimens", legal clarification on what can or can't be taken should be queried with the Department of Planning and Natural Resources. Beachcombers should be conservative. An old saying holds true, "take nothing but pictures, leave nothing but footprints."

## Snorkeling

The United States Virgin Islands of St. Croix, St. John and St. Thomas were listed in the SCUBA Diving Magazine's Readers Choice Awards as "one of the finest spots in the world for snorkeling" (and SCUBA diving too!) There is great beauty and fascination under the waves here. If you didn't bring your own snorkel gear, check out the many local dive shops to buy your own personal gear, or rent it. They would be the best place to start either for quick lessons or for advice on the best places just to snorkel. There are techniques for beach diving, like either putting your fins on near the water's edge and walking backwards, or walking in waist deep and slipping your fins on there. As for the mask, one must either use a defog rinse, or spit into the mask and rinse it around. You want a clear mask to see everything. You can float along the surface and just breathe out of your snorkel, but if your snorkel goes below the surface you should leave enough air in your lungs to blow out the water in your snorkel when you surface.

Dive shops will tell you what not to touch underwater. They also stress not removing any souvenirs. Leave something for the next person to see and try not to disturb the eco-system. The best thing is to float, not stand, on any of the coral heads since they are pretty delicate and can be crushed. It is always recommended to swim with a buddy. If you can't, stay close to the shore and avoid any place with a current. Try not to touch anything because it can leave a substance on your fingers which may result in itchiness or even being poisonous. Don't step on those spiny sea urchins, and be careful of yellow hard coral with white trim. That's fire coral and it can burn the skin.

If you should cut yourself on coral, wash with soap and water as soon as possible. Infections develop more easily in a warmer climate so apply antiseptic cream as soon as possible. For stings, neutralize the cut with ammonia, baking soda or a piece of papaya.

## LAND ACTIVITIES

### Baseball/Softball

From Little League for boys and girls, to softball for men, girls and women, to baseball for young men and the over 40s crowd, baseball/softball is one of the most organized and popular sports in the U.S. Virgin Islands. Major league players on vacation often conduct clinics to introduce the game to the kids on the islands. Virgin Islander Horace Clarke of New York Yankees fame and former Pittsburgh Pirates player Elmo Plaskett (since deceased) worked in St. Croix to give youths a shot at the big time.

### Basketball

Basketball has been a strong sport for a long time, producing such top notch players as Tim Duncan (San Antonio Spurs) and Raja Bell, helping to put the Virgin Islands on the national sports map.

Since 2000, the University of the Virgin Islands has been hosting the USVI Annual Paradise Jam, a pre-season College Basketball Tournament for women and men. Participating colleges over the years have included Duke, Rutgers, Notre Dame and Georgetown. The event is usually held in late November.

### Golf

On St. Croix, residents and visitors can play at the Buccaneer Hotel Golf Course, the Carambola Golf and Tennis Club or the Reef Condominium Golf Course. The uphill third hole overlooking the ocean at the Buccaneer Course offers a real challenge. This 18-hole course and provides rental equipment and carts. Stop by the 19th Hole bar for post-game refreshments. Call their Pro Shop at 773-2100/778-5638 for reservations. Nestled among the lush hills of the rain forest, Carambola Golf and Tennis Club is home to an 18-hole Robert Trent Jones world-class championship course You might find a well known golfer teeing off, since it is a popular tournament spot and hosts an annual LPGA Tournament in the Spring. Its facilities include a pro shop with equipment rentals and fashions, a restaurant, and an after-golf bar overlooking a spectacular view. For tee times call 778-5638.

On St. Croix's East End, the nine-holed Reef Golf Course is a nice warm-up for spot for pros or a fine course for the less ambitious golfer, as its 568-yard, par-five, 5th hole can be a challenge. In 2015 The Reef installed equipment for 'disc golf' at its course. At press time it was the only such facility in the Caribbean. Call 773-8844 to reserve.

Also on the East End, check out The Links Miniature Golf Course by Divi Resorts.

In St. Thomas, set amid a beautiful valley and coastal cliffs, the Mahogany Run Golf Course is tough, particularly at Devile's Triangle, three Hellish seaside holes where golfballs frequently sail over the edge. The golf course has a pro shop with equipment rentals and lessons.

The University of the Virgin Islands in St.Thomas has a nine-hole golf course situated alongside the road that runs through the campus. It is mainly a practice course, with no amenities and golfers can play any time.

### Hiking

There is good hiking on all three islands. In St. Croix, you can hike through the rain forest, Salt River National Park, or along many beautiful beaches. You can also walk along specifically marked trails on Buck Island. In St. John, the Virgin Islands National Park has many maintained trails winding through the vegetation and ruins of old plantations. In St. Thomas you can hike along the north side and to the beach for spectacular views. Views looking north and east are the best. Read "A Walking Guide to the Caribbean" by Leonard M. Adkins for some tips.

### Running

The Virgin Islands Pace Runners organizes over 20 road races and related running events annually. The events are for the fitness-minded, recreational and competitive runners. There are road races, track races, cross-country races and beach runs for particpants of all ages and levels of fitness. Some of these events also serve as fundraisers and charity events. Distances for the events range from the mile to the marathon. V.I. Pace Runners produces an annual Virgin Islands Running Calendar. Log on to: http://virginislandspace.org

## Tennis

In planning a tennis match remember it is hotter at midday. Most people like to play early morning, or later in the afternoon after work. Most major hotels in the territory have tennis courts. There are fees for playing and for lessons. Hotels charge around $18 per court per hour, daytime, and $22 per court per hour at night for guests, and $9 per person per hour daytime, and $11 per person per hour at night for non-guests. Lessons are about $70 an hour and $36 for a half hour. Check with local hotels, or their pro shop to sign up. Annual memberships are about $295 single, $525 family and $12 per person per hour if not a member, but a guest..

The local government's Parks and Recreation Department operates public courts in St. Croix at the D.C. Canegata Ball Park, call 773-3850; and at the Isaac Boynes Park, Sion Farm Park, and Stoney Ground Park near the old fort in Frederiksted. The public courts are on a first-come, first-serve basis. In St. John, the Parks and Recreation Department operates public courts across from the Fire Station in Cruz Bay, on a first-come, first serve basis.

In St. Thomas, the Parks and Recreation Department operates public courts at Subbase and Bordeaux on a first-come, first-service basis. Here are some numbers to help you get oriented with tennis in the Virgin Islands. The association has trained junior and Davis Cup teams, and is affiliated with the United States Tennis Association, as well as the International Tennis Federation.

## Track and Field

The Virgin Islands Track and Field Federation is the governing body for the sport of track and field. The disciplines include: Track running, field events. road running, cross-country running, race walking and mountain running in the Virgin Islands. The Federation is the Virgin Island's affiliate to the International Association of Athletic Federations (IAAF), the world governing body and the Virgin Island's Olympic Committee.

The Federation implements the development of the sport including athletes of all ages for competition on V.I. national teams in local, regional and world championships to include: the Central American and Caribbean Games, the Pan American Games and the Olympic Games. The Federation facilitates the certification of coaches, technical officials and insures the continuity of the sport in the Virgin Islands.

Log on to: http://virginislandspace.org

## Olympics

The U.S. Virgin Islands Olympic Committee puts together a V.I. National Team for the Central American Caribbean Games, the Pan American Games and the Summer/Winter Olympics. The committee represents 24 sports federations from across the territory. While most participants compete in warm-weather sports, Occasionally the Committee sends a bobsled team to the Winter Olympics. The V.I. Olympic Committee has boasted numerous medal winning athletes in Olympic games since its inception in 1966.

In 1988 Virgin Islander Peter Holmberg won a silver medal in the Men's Finn Class in the Summer Olympics.

In 2002 the Olympic Committee sent the first black women Olympians to compete in luge events. The Virgin Islands has been sending a Winter Olympic team to events since 1988 with the first black woman skier.

In 2008 the USVI had athletes competing in the Beijing Summer Olympics in boxing, sailing, swimming, track and field, and one shooter. They competed in the Central American Games in 2010 at Mayaguez, Puerto Rico, in about 12 sports. In 2010, Ian Barrows won gold in sailing at the Youth Olympics. The territory has sent seven Olympians to London in the summer of 2012 to compete in laser sailing; 100, 200, and 400-meter track;100-meter freestlyle swimming; and the triple jump. In the 2014 Sochi Winter Games we were represented in the Giant Slalom and Slalom alpine skiing events and had an active Skeleton atheletc.

In 2015, some 3 dozen athletes from the VI participated in the Special Olympic World Games. For more information log on to: *http://www.virginislandsolympics.org*

## Government Sports Facilities

The local government runs a summer youth program which includes:

Baseball, basketball, track, softball, soccer, swimming, cooking and dancing. The staff also runs the sport activities at the various recreation facilities. Below is listed the recreation facilities on all three islands.

### St. Croix

All parks listed can be contacted and events scheduled through the main number of Parks and Recreation 773-0271 or 773-0160 and Canegata Ball Park 773-5588 or 773-3850. All parks are open daily at 8:00 a.m., but the recreation leaders are there from 1:00 p.m. to 9:00 p.m.

**Campo Rico:** Basketball and tot play area.
**Cramer's Park**: beach, picnic area, camping, restrooms, volleyball. - 773-9696
**D.C. Canegata Complex**: baseball, volleyball, basketball, tennis, softball, to play area, bandstand, board games, billiards, table tennis and restrooms. softball, tennis, basketball, restrooms, lights, bleachers, tot play area. A building for games, exercise classes. (East of Christiansted);
**Estate Glynn**: tot play area, picnic and basketball;
**Fort Frederik:**:basketball, tennis, volleyball, tot play area, lights, beach, picnic area.
**Horace Clarke Complex:** baseball, basketball, handball, tennis;
**Issac Boynes Complex:** (Grove Place) baseball,
**Pedro Cruz Complex**: (at Estate Profit), softball, bleachers, restrooms, lights, basketball and playground area 778-4369.
**Renholdt Jackson Complex:** softball, volleyball, tot play area, football, basketball, field and restrooms.
**(Estate Whim);** Paul E. Joseph Stadium in Fredriksted is undergoing major renovation as of press time. Rudy Kriegger Complex: softball, basketball, soccer, tennis courts, handball courts, tot play area, shaded benches, picnic tables and rest-rooms 719-9223.
**(Sion Farm);** LaValle Complex: Center in 2008.
**Terence Martin Field:** softball Mon Bijou/Frangipanni rec park: softball, basketball and picnic area.
**Winston Mason Pool Resort (Frederiksted - west end, beach area):** junior olympic salt water pool, open 9-5 play-ground, picnic tables, table Games. (Temporarily out of commssion due to hurricanes)

## Cultural Tidbit

St. Croix is home to the annual Ironman 70.3, one of The world's premiere destination triathlon's—and a virtual local holiday. Triathletes begin the course at Hotel on the Cay, where they dive into the warm,clear Caribbean for a 1.24-mile swim. Rising from the sea at Christiansed Harbor, they then begin a 56-mile bicycle course that wind through the island's north and south shores and natures a grueling steeply sloped hill known as "the beast." The cherry atop this exhausting race is a 13.1 mile run that finishes in the town of Christiansted. Top finishers can qualify for Ironman Hawaii or the Ironman 70.3 World Championship.

### St. Thomas

Number for all Sports, Parks and Recreation:     774-0255
**Joseph Aubain Ball Park** (Frenchtown): softball, Little League, Ladies League,     774-9477
**Bordeaux:** tennis, basketball, tot play area;
**Emile Griffith Park** (Charlotte Amalie:) basketball, softball, tot play area and games,     775-6435
**Frydenhoj:** basketball, softball;
**Kirwan Terrace Complex** (Lindbergh Bay): basketball, volleyball, baseball     775-7363
**Alvin McBean Complex** (Tutu): softball, Little League baseball, tennis, softball, basketball, handball and paddle ball,     775-7183
**Mandahl:** basketball
**Nadir (Bovoni)**: softball and basketball and horse racetrack;
**Winston Raymo Complex** (Charlotte Amalie) basketball, indoor recreation baseball, paddleball, handball and tot area,     774-2640
**Lionel Roberts Stadium** (Charlotte Amalie): baseball, softball, cricket, boxing shows, high school football, soccer and concerts.
**Savan**: basketball
**Lionel "Smut" Richards** (Smith Bay): softball, basketball (Little League)
**Subbase** (Charlotte Amalie): tennis, handball and paddleball.

### St. John

General # for Sports, Parks & Recreation, 776-6531 Coral Bay: baseball, basketball, tot play area; Cruz Bay: tennis, basketball, softball; Little League Park (Cruz Bay): baseball and tot area; Pine Peace: basketball and volleyball Winston Wells Park (Cruz Bay): baseball and softball.

### Firearms and Hunting

To own a gun, you must have a Public Safety Department permit. In order to get this, the department will conduct a background search. To carry a gun or keep it at your business, you need an additional permit, for which must submit your business license when applying.

If you try to bring a gun into the territory with other personal effects, it will be confiscated. Weapons must be declared to the U.S.Customs inspector, who will request that you leave the gun in police custody until your permit comes through. If you plan to purchase a gun here, don't go shopping until you have your permit. Perhaps leave your gun behind with a licensed firearm dealer till you have one. He can then ship the weapon to you. Call 774-2211, ext. 5563 for information.

Hunting is allowed for mountain doves, and white-tailed deer with bag limits in season, dictated by DPNR. The season for dove and duck hunting is set by the U.S. Fish and Wildlife and is September and December. No hunting is permitted within the boundaries of the National Parks or in the Virgin Islands Wildlife Refuges.

### Horse Racing

The Randall "Doc" James Race Track, near the airport is home to a favorite pastime of Crucians. As of press time, only a few live horse races have been held in 2015, but the track has a simulcast room where thoroughbreds, greyhounds, and harness races are broadcast 365 days a year, rain or shine. Two native Crucians, Victor Lebron nad Kevin Krigger, made history by qualifying to race in the Kentucky Derby in 2013 after winning the Arkansas Derby and the Santa Anita Derby respectively. www.stcroixracetrack.com. On St.Thomas check out the Clinton E. Phipps Race Track where live races are still being run.

| Sports Federations/Associations (All area code 340) | |
|---|---|
| Baseball: V.I. Federation, Dennis Brow | 332-3827 |
| Basketball: V.I. Basketball, Usie Richards | 772-9524 |
| Bowling: V.I. Bowling Federation, Ronald Moorehead | |
| Boxing: St. Thomas Amateur Boxing Fed. Jose Rosario | 227-3158 |
| Cycling: V.I. Cycling Federation, Scott Fricks | 513-8281 |
| Equestrian: V.I. Equestrian, Virginia Angus | 773-0289 |
| Hiking: St. Croix Hiking Association | 772-2073 |
| Running: VI Pace Runners, W Williams | 778-8255/643-2557/777-0258 |
| Soccer: V.I. Soccer Federation, Derrick Martin | 719-0037 |
| Softball: V.I. Softball Federation, Warren Brooks | 718-7026 |
| Swimming: V.I. Swimming Federation, Brent Mays | 773-7374 |
| Track & Field: VI Track & Field Federation – W. Williams | 643-2557 |
| Tennis: VI Tennis Association - William McComb | 774-8457 |
| Triathlons: Ironman 70.3, other local, Angel Morales | 719-8462 |

## WILD LIFE

While there are not many species of wildlife on isolated tropical islands, you will see a small furry, speedy critter known as the mongoose. Heavily populated on St. Croix (the mongoose capital of the world), 'de mongoose dem' are about the size of a squirrel and were first imported by plantation owners years ago to keep down the rat population in the cane fields. But since the mongoose loves sunshine and rats are nocturnal, their paths seldom crossed. You might also see "shy" deer in the bush. They are popular to St. Croix and St. Thomas. You might even find a variety of insect, fruit or fish-eating bats.

 A variety of birds stateside keep bugs in check, but in these islands it is the lizards! There are two different groups of these. In the daytime the Anoles, like chameleons, change color from green to brown (to match their background), and prowl everywhere to nab bugs. But in the evening hours they leave this prowling to the Gecko, a chunkier lizard with fat toes effective for climbing. The Gecko's eyes are like cats eyes with a vertical pupil. These two breeds average 3 to 6 inches and are totally harmless to humans. If you are 'citified', do not find them particularly cute and don't relish the thought of waking up with one of them staring you in the eye, there are humane ways to keep them outside where you are adamant they belong. Home and Garden stores sell naturally derived repellent that you can spray around your entryways at regular intervals to keep them at bay, but if one happens to get inside your house, remember they are afraid of you. One of the best ways to catch one is to chase them into a container, put the lid on it, then drop them back outside!

While the lizards mentioned above live on all three islands, there seems to be more of the smaller ones on St. Croix, and more iguanas on St. Thomas. The big iguana (see photo above) still inhabits some parts of these islands. They are vegetarian and range from bright green, as a juvenile, to a grassy brown. In less populated areas, you will see them sunning themselves along road sides midday or in trees on long heavy branches. Some hotels have a few in their ponds as pets. Do keep an eye out for them because they may try to cross the road in front of a car.

Another type of little lizard, a striped one, the Ameiva, lives on St. Croix, Mostly at Hotel on the Cay. No cats or dogs are allowed there in order to protect this endangered specie. The azure striped St. Croix Ground Lizard which was native to St. Croix before Europeans got here but was eradicated over time, was reintroduced to Buck Island according to the National Park Service.

Any snakes are the small harmless types that combat bug problems and are rarely seen. If you happen to bring in pet such as a boa and are relocating back to the states, please do not release it into our wilds. If you do not plan to take it back with you, please call DPNR or the Animal Shelter for assistance.

**Birds**

The most common and visible bird here is the snowy egret. Often called the "cattle" egret, snowy egrets perch on the backs of cows or horses to feed on insects. Also very popular, and native to most islands, are the yellow and black bananaquits and green hummingbirds. To welcome bananaquits (sometimes called sugar birds) to your home, merely put out a saucer of sugar or sugar water. Related to honey-creepers, bananaquits are year-round residents. To attract hummingbirds, buy a feeder for them locally. The pearly- eyed thrashers, known as trushees by locals, are bigger pests. They resemble a dirty brown robin and might eat food off your plate if you aren't careful.

An avid birdwatcher would recognize the Mockingbird, Kestrel (called Chicken Hawks here) and Red-tailed hawks. The Lesser Antillean Bull Finch has migrated northward and now makes the U.S. Virgin Islands its home. The male is a small black bird with red under its chin and rust under the tail. The female is brown with a speck of rust under her tail. The smooth-billed big black ani resembles a parrot's profile. You will notice the slate and white kingbirds that chatter loudly from telephone wires as they grab bugs mid-air. Along roadsides you will find zenaida doves (resembling mourning doves) and smaller ground doves as they bob along the dirt in search of insects. Herons and egrets can be seen walking along the shore. The brown pelicans resting on boats or dock pilings are very entertaining as they dive bomb the waters in search of fish. Frigate birds somewhat resemble Japanese kites. They tend to hover from overhead, where they patiently wait to pounce on birds with prey in their beaks.

Life in the tropics is unique. The beautiful blue waters, the tropical vegetation, the great climate, trade winds, and multitude of experiences, provide a beautiful and wondrous playground for lovers of the outdoors.

## Cutural Tidbit

**The Cocks Have Clocks**. . . of their own: Be aware that roosters in these islands can sometimes crow "All day and all night Miss Maryann." Yes, it can be very rritating. However it seems like these rooster have a lot to crow about. Do like the locals do, show him a box with a picture of fried chicken. Hint, hint.
**Sounds of The Chain Gang**: At night you will hear the sounds of the crickets and the frogs "working on the chain gang." Don't worry be happy. You will soon become anesthetized to those sounds and after awhile it will grow on you . . . like everything else island.
**Mongoose Dem:** Do not attempt to pet the mongoose dem if you want to leave the islands with your fingers and toes connected to your body. These little critters can be very feisty. *by Dr. George Franklin*

# 19th Settler's Handbook — Great Outdoors 8

# Settler's Handbook Chapter 9

## *BUSINESS CLIMATE... A PROFILE OF TODAY*

The official government of the United States Virgin Islands continues its territorial relationship with the government of the United States of America. While some residents desire statehood and others want greater autonomy, in the general election in October 1993, a low voter turnout of 31.4% of voters in the islands regarding a referendum on status guaranteed the US Virgin Islands would remain an unicorporated US territory for the time being. The issue is expected to resurface in the future.

The general organization of the Virgin Islands government was created through the Revised Organic Act passed by the Congress in 1954 with some powers left in the hands of the Federal government. The affairs of the islands are controlled by the Governor and the Legislature.

In January 1993, the territory was given more responsibility when the courts in the islands took over jurisdiction from the Federal Government of major felonies.

The governor of the Virgin Islands has asked Congress for an increased return of excise taxes on products developed here. The move is seen as not only a way to develop more self-sufficiency for the islands but to also reduce the burden of Federal payments for services. The Federal government now returns over $72 million in excise taxes on St. Croix-made rum and this amount is on the rise due not only to the not only Cruzan Rum products but as stated earlier with Capt. Morgan Rum.

Like island nations in the Caribbean, the USVI is economically dependent on tourism. Assets, like special tax incentives, a duty-free status, foreign trade eligibility, good commercial rental rates, a marvelous climate and the security of the "Stars 'n Stripes", all add to a favorable business atmosphere.

While the economy is heavily dependent on tourism the territory seeks to diversify through further development of light to medium industry. With that in mind, the islands offer comprehensive tax benefits and a well-developed infrastructure that includes some of the finest ports, best roads and airports in the Caribbean. Furthermore, state-of-the-art telephone service enables almost instant communication with any point in the world.

And the Virgin Islands Water and Power Authority produces and distributes electricity and desalinated water from plants on all three islands.

The territory is well served by the U.S. Postal Service as well as UPS, Federal Express, and DHL Worldwide Express. Most businesses are open from 9 a.m. to 5 p.m. Monday through Friday. Retailers stay open Saturdays, and in some cases, Sundays. The local government operates from 8:00 a.m. to 5 p.m. Federal offices. U.S. Postal Service and banks close for all Federal holidays. Schools and government offices also close for all Federal and local holidays. For a comprehensive look at the business picture, contact the Economic Development Commission at 773-6499.

**Tourism**

As winter grasps North America, Virgin Islanders hope that tourists will flock here for island warmth and beauty. Seventy-eight percent of the hotel guests and 65 percent of cruise ship visitors come from the U.S. mainland. However, many come from all over the world.

A government bond issue was passed to address the specifics of revitalizing St. Croix as a tourist destination. The Bond issues identify several main areas for consideration: airport modernization, construction of a shopping area, King's Alley, and a Boardwalk, both on Christiansted Harbor are now complete, as is the airport. This also included renovation of Government House in Christiansted, and the renovation of Frederiksted as an authentic Danish West Indian town. The St. Croix Community Foundation in Christiansted receives block grants and Federal funding for renovation projects and has undertaken a lot of old building renovation in Christiansted. The Frederiksted Economic Development Authority, the PFA (Public Finance Authority) and Our Town Frederiksted have assisted with the revitalization of the Frederiksted and its waterfront and the Dorsch Theatre.

In a 1994 referendum, St. Croix voters, the only island interested, indicated they wanted casino gambling on their island to see if it would assist in the development of hotels and create jobs. While casino gambling will bring some tourists, most of them will likely view the pastime as an additional amenity like fine dining or fun shopping to go along with their day at the beach or the golf course. The first casino in the Virgin Islands, Divi Carina Bay Resort and Casino opened on St. Croix March of 2000, and a few more investors have applied for their licenses. Three years ago, The Caravelle Hotel renovated and opened a smaller casino in downtown Christiansted, The Caravelle Arcade Casino. On St. Thomas, one can try their luck on VLT's (Video Lottery Terminals) located at various locations on the islands.

In an effort to improve its marketing strategy as a tourist destination, the V.I. government has recently started marketing each of the three islands for their own uniqueness and personality. The official marketing song 'Virgin Islands Nice' can be frequently heard throughout the territory and on the USVI tourism commercials. Google 'Virgin Islands Nice' to listen and purchase. Other local artists have also made patriotic songs such as Bill Bass' Welcome to St. Croix'. The highly developed world class water sports industry namely boating and scuba diving and the number of quality hotels and restaurants combine to make the Virgin Islands an attractive destination. The government's promotional plan is to market and capitalize on each of these three islands' specific specialties.

St. Thomas, with its deep-water harbor, is the number one cruise ship destination in the world, with over a million passengers a year looking for great duty-free shopping. Tour companies are ready to whisk the passenger off for an island tour, beach tours, air tours, harbor tours, or Scuba diving. Its many beautiful hotels attract almost half a million visitors a year to enjoy the beaches and bargains in designer name shopping. You can find great prices in liquor, linens, electronics and jewelry. St. Thomas has upscale tourist attractions like Coral World with its Aquarium, and a tramway which runs above Charlotte Amalie. A must see is St. Peter's Great House, a renovated old estate house built on the side of a mountain, with a spectacular view and beautiful tropical gardens. It is available for tours and functions.

There are about 15 major hotels, 35 smaller hotels and guesthouses and some of the best world-class restaurants located on St.Thomas. A network of private homes and villas entices visitors to stay a week or several months during the winter. Check with the U.S. Virgin Islands Hotel & Tourism Association at 774-6835.

St. Croix's uniqueness exists in its old-world charm and the blending of the historical culture of seven different nations who governed her. Mix that charm and culture with the quaintness of Frederiksted's waterfront park, cosmopolitan Christiansted, the charming boutiques, the talented local craftsmen and artists, an array of outdoor activities (diving, sailing, kayaking, horseback riding, hiking, golfing), with a smothering of friendliness and relaxation, and you could discover an island like no other. St. Croix is known for its light industry, some agriculture, cozy bed & breakfasts, small hotels, nice beaches, top-notch restaurants, its culture heritage, its heritage trails and recently, a rekindling of the jazz spirit with the Blue Bay Jazz Festival in November held every few years. Call Landmarks Society at 772-0598 for its Heritage Trail Map.

St. John is three-quarter national park and boasts some of the most beautiful beaches in the world. Tourists visit St. John for its scenic beauty. It has currently one major hotel, the Westin Hotel & Resorts (Caneel Bay was the second but has been closed since the hurricane)., as well as a handful of small budget guesthouses and amany private luxury homes for rent.
Two campgrounds, both within the Virgin Islands National Park, have covered campsites and nature-trail hiking. Cruise ships may stop at its west end town of Cruz Bay (en route to St. Thomas). Passengers are tendered in from the big ships to shop, dine and tour. At its east end, Coral Bay was more badly damaged by the 2017 hurricanes than Cruz Bay, and so it is undergoing extensive reconstruction making it fertile ground for property purchase and investors.

### Duty Free Status

The territory's free port status, a provision of the treaty between Denmark and the United States which accompanied the 1917 sale of the islands, is still in effect. This means the territory lies outside the U.S. Customs' zone, allowing goods to enter tax free regardless of where they originated. Otherwise, most countries, including the United States, impose import tariffs, or quotas to protect local industries. The islands are almost a true free port in that goods manufactured in the U.S. or its possessions enter duty free, while those from elsewhere are charged a low uniform rate of six percent. It is not the brand name which determines an object's duty-free status, but its country of origin. Comparable to other parts of the world, the Virgin Islands is a shopper's paradise with the duty-free prices available. However, pricing benefits for the consumer under this free port status are not as meaningful as they once were. Today's merchants and suppliers have to pay various taxes to the government on imports, excise taxes and gross receipt taxes, as well as take into consideration the cost of goods imported for resale and shipping costs. While there is no sales tax, these charges and expenses are included in the retail price of the goods. Thanks to U.S. Customs laws, residents and visitors returning to the U.S. can bring, or mail, $1,600 worth of goods per person duty-free. A family of four can bring $4,800 duty-free. That's a rate twice as high as the $800 allowed duty-free from other Caribbean countries and four times higher than the $400 allowed from most other countries. If you exceed the $1,600, you pay a flat rate of five percent on the next $1,000. For those who travel back and forth between the mainland and the U.S. Virgin Islands, remember that the $1,600 duty-free allowance can only be used once in a 30-day period. You can send as many gifts as you want to friends and relatives as long as you don't spend more than $100 a day for any one address. These do not have to be declared. U.S. citizens over 21 can enter the States with four litres of liquor as part of their $1,600 duty-free allowance; one extra if they are brands such as Cruzan Rum and Captain Morgan, which are produced in the U.S. Virgin Islands. U.S. citizens can also take home five cartons of cigarettes and 100 non- Cuban cigars per person.

Be sure to keep your sales slips or invoices for items purchased. Even though you have declared items you are shipping, when you re-enter the States, you will need proof of value for each package when your articles arrive. It would be wise to check with your local U.S. Customs office if you are planning to mail goods. All articles must be strictly for your personal use and not for re-sale. Goods made in the U.S. Virgin Islands are not included in the $1,600 allowance, but if any item is worth more than $25, you must fill out a Certificate of Origin form 3229 which is available where you purchased the items. You can take back those gorgeous anthuriums you bought along the road, but check in advance with the U.S. Department of Agriculture to find out about the other flowers and vegetables you may have discovered during your visit that you can take out.

There are also specific rules and regulations for importing animals. Here are the addresses for finding out what's allowed from FAPHIS (Federal Animal and Plant Health Inspection Service) regarding plant protection and animal quarantine. Henry E. Rohlsen Airport, St. Croix, VI 00820, 778-1696. Cyril E. King Airport, St. Thomas, VI 00801, 774-5719, Federal Bldg., Charlotte Amalie, St. Thomas 00801, 776-2787. *For the "ins" and "outs" of shopping, ask the U.S. Customs office where you live, for a copy of "Know Before You Go" handbook.*

## The Light and Heavy Industrial Scene

The Economic Development Authority oversees activities at industrial parks on both St. Croix and St. Thomas. Located one mile from the Henry E. Rohlsen Airport, and Southshore Port facility, the St. Croix Industrial Park has 50,000 square feet of space.

With acres of flat land and specific tax incentives for businesses, St.

Croix is ripe for the development of light industry. The Authority is actively seeking and encouraging new light, non-polluting industries. HOVENSA, now an oil storage and refining facility owned and operated by Limetree Bay Terminals, LLC, and Limetree Bay Refining, LLC, had until early 2012 operated a refinery on the south shore of St. Croix, which included a new Catalytic Cracking Unit constructed to manufacture reformulated gasolinet to meet the requirements of the Federal Clean Air Act.

An alumina processing plant in the same area, was opened by Harvey Aluminum in 1965, was later purchased by Martin Marietta, then the VI Aluminum Company (VIALCO), and finally Alcoa Aluminum. Aluminum production ceased in December 2000, due to a downturn in that industry. As stated earlier, the property was purchased by The Renaissance Park to develop it for light industry and renewable resources.

In St. Croix, small manufacturers produce, soda, electronics, garments and boats. Companies benefiting from the EDC programs discussed further on include Call Centers, financial services, hospitality and technology. The territory is poised to capitalize further on the recently upgraded undersea fiber optic cabling system via viNGN (Virgin Islands Next Generation Network), which now has capability of providing upload and download internet speeds of over 1000 megabytes per second. St. John has few light industries other than one or two person entrepreneurial ventures. They include fiberglass cistern construction, herbs and spices and artistic ventures.

The St. Thomas Industrial Park at Subbase, with an area of 20,000 square feet, is close to shipping docks and the airport. There are few light manufacturing companies in St. Thomas with the exception of fragrance manufacturers and artistic ventures.

### The Economic Development Authority

The US Virgin Islands is unique and offers many benefits. Besides the beautiful setting, the territory offers the stability of U.S. currency and the protection of the U.S. Flag and U.S. court, never mind that the constitution preamble could now begin - "We de people dem...". Manufacturers have duty-free, quota-free access to the U.S. mainland with "made in the USA" labels on many items. The USVI offers a business-friendly environment; an educated work force; easy air access; world-class telecommunications; shipping advantages; and prime rental space.

Our Economic Development Commission helps qualified companies reduce taxes and increase profits.

# 19th Settler's Handbook  Business Climate 9

### Cultural Tidbit

Whether visiting or moving to the Virgin Islands, one way to invest in the local economy is to buy Leatherback Beer, Cruzan or Captain Morgan's rum or Mutiny Vodka.

Here's a simple, yet fantastic, tropical rum punch recipe that'll keep you cool in the island heat. Ingredients:
3 oz pineapple juice / 2 oz dark rum
3 oz orange juice
Splash of cranberry juice, Pineapple pieces, Splash of grenadine

**Preparation:** Pour rum, pineapple juice, orange juice in a shaker. Pour in glass with ice. Top off with a splash of cranberry juice and grenadine. Enjoy. Cheers!

For the sake of our economy, as long as you are the designated drinker - not the driver, please have another!

---

The Virgin Islands Economic Development Authority (EDA) is semi-autonomous and is responsible for promoting and enhancing the economic development in the USVI. Its four major components are:

> The Economic Development Bank,
> The Economic Development Commission,
> The Virgin Islands Economic Park Development Corporation,
> The Enterprise and Commercial Zone program.

To expand its economic base, and create jobs for residents, the federal and local government enacted a series of incentives to create tax benefits for eligible businesses. By locating your business, or part of your business, to the USVI, you may be eligible to apply for tax benefits and receive substantial reduction in, or exemption from, your business and personal taxes. Companies that qualify receive either a substantial reduction, or an exemption from many of the standard business taxes. The list of some types of companies that could qualify would be: raw materials processing, financial services sector, assembly operations (i.e. jewelry), hotels/guest houses, certain services/businesses that provide goods and services to customers both inside and outside the territory, transportation and telecommunications, high tech businesses.

Since the tax incentive program is industry or sector non-specific, various other companies or organizations may be eligible if they prove beneficial to the territory's economic well-being.

Incentives and benefits for new businesses include:

90% exemption on local income taxes;
90% exemption on local income taxes paid by resident stockholders on dividends and interest received from the company
A maximum reduction from 6% to 1% on custom duties;
100% exemption on property and gross receipts taxes;
100% exemption on Excise taxes.

The IRS has imposed source-income requirements, which make the benefits offered by the EDC tax-incentive programs to those businesses operating "wholly" in the V.I. and who ship their commodities (hard manufactured goods) to places outside the mainland. These requirements fall under the Federal Jobs Creation Act. The EDC is looking at international markets for those companies who are smaller high-tech manufacturers, software developers and investment bankers to encourage economic development in the U.S. Virgin Islands.

EDC tax exemptions are offered for 10 to 30 years, depending upon the location of the business and industry in the territory. Companies may start the benefits package at any point in the first five years of business operations. These benefits may be extended in five to ten-year increments. The basic qualification is an investment of $100,000, exclusive of inventory, in an approved industry that the EDC has determined will advance the economic well being of the VI and its people, and employment of at least ten employees on a full-time basis, of which 80% have resided in the USVI at least one year.

For **Small Business Financing** the EDA administers business development programs through its "Lending Unit" consisting the **Economic Development Bank**. It provides access to capital for small and medium-sized businesses to be used to start a business, expand a business, purchase an existing one, purchase inventory, machinery, equipment, supplies, furniture, fixtures employment, etc. Loans are issued at competitive interest rates with competitive terms. Residence requirements may apply. The applicant must own 50% of the business and be active in the management *(see site for in-depth details or call 714-1700 St. Thomas* *or 773-6499 St. Croix).* The **Industrial Park Development Corporation's**, basic function is to provide rental space for EDC beneficiaries as restricted by the agreement between the Federal Government and the IPDC. These include The Virgin Islands Industrial Park on St. Thomas and The William D. Roebuck Industrial Park, St. Croix.

The **Enterprise Zone** on September 14, 1999 Act No.6294, mandated that blighted areas that are historical in nature with many buildings over 150 years old, and having had some of the oldest families in the VI from these areas, be revitalized. Many of the oldest families in the VI are from these areas, but a lot of these buildings have fallen into disrepair. This applies to areas in Christiansted and Frederiksted in St. Croix, and Savan in St. Thomas. The law provides for tax incentives and calls for public, private and non-profit organizations to develop these areas.

**Capital Project Financing**:
The VI Government enacted Tax Increment Financing (TIF) in 2008 to stimulate economic growth and public infrastructure. It can be used for affordable housing and schools, demolition, utilities and planning costs. The funding comes from USVI with the use of real property tax increment revenues and gross receipts tax increment to pay for, or finance the cost, or portion of capital improvements to those underveloped areas and areas in need of redevelopment, etc., designated as TIF by the Authority and approved by the Legislature.

Requirements do change, so for more information see the EDA website www.usvieda.org or call : 340-773-6499 St. Croix ;340-774-1700 on St. Thomas or 1-877-432-USVI

**Offshore Companies**
Act 6490, Bill No. 24-0187 passed in December 2001, changed FSC's (Foreign Sales Corporations) to the VIFSC (Virgin Islands Foreign Sales Corporations). The franchise tax is either $400 or $900 depending on the volume of sales. The registration requirements are: Articles of Incorporation and a Consent of Agent Form. Once the Lieutenant Governor's office has received and approved this paperwork the foreign-owned company can register here as an exempt company for a $1,000 annual franchise fee. For a copy of the VI Code visit www.michie.com. For further information call the Lieutenant Governor's office at 776-8515.

## Marine Industry

With hundreds of boats throughout the Virgins, the marine industry accounts for 10 percent of the territory's economy. Several large charter companies rent boats to sailors. Crewed yachts provide luxury vacations for less intrepid vacationers and fuel a myriad of other businesses including grocery stores, marine parts and service companies, to mention a few. The local government in 1994 canceled a tax on boats and parts, so marine industries pay no tax on that portion of their business.

St. Thomas is the center of marine activity in the Virgin Islands. Boasting numerous marinas and boatyards, it is the hub of the charter yacht industry of the USVI. Basing their operations at Yacht Haven, is the Virgin Islands Charter Yacht League (VICL). The VICL, www.vicl.org, holds two boat shows annually for the vessels under their umbrella, one in the spring and a larger one in the fall. The fall show has about 100 vessels for charter brokers to meet the captain and crew and inspect the vessels before booking clients. Call them at 774-3944 for further info.

The two primary marinas on St. Thomas are Crown Bay Marina, located in Sub Base next to the cruise ship docks, and American Yacht Harbor on the east end of the island. American Yacht Harbor serves as the gateway to St. John and the BVI's. Famed for its annual Boy Scout Fishing Tournament in July or August, AYH is the fishing Mecca of the USVI due to its close proximity to the famed "North Drop." Anglers and vessels come from all over the world for the opportunity to catch a "trophy" Blue Marlin, although these days most vessels are strictly catch and release, a picture and measurements will get you an artificial replica of the monster you landed.

Crown Bay Marina, primarily caters to Mega Yachts during the busy winter season. Crown Bay Marina is capable of berthing vessels up to 200' long and has a 315' fuel dock with dispensers that fuel at a rate of 150 gallons per minute! Both marinas cater to the cruising sailboat enthusiast during the busy winter season. Other marinas include the Sapphire Beach Marina, Independent Boat Yard, Yacht Haven and Compass Point Marina, among others. Enjoy all that the Virgin Islands marine industry has to offer.

There is plenty of fishing, diving, daily boat rentals, day sails and overnight charters available. Just go to one of the marinas and ask! Also, be sure to visit the Yacht Haven Grande Marina in the Charlotte Amalie Harbor to the east side of the harbor and just past the Havensight Cruise ship docks, for provisioning, restaurants and shopping.

### Film Industry

Crystal clear water, white beaches, lush mountains and everyday sunshine set the stage for the territory's film industry. From the box-office hit, "Weekend at Bernie's II," to segments of the soap opera "The Young and Restless", with nearly, 1,000 commercial shots (including the Pepsi beach shots) in between, and reality shows such as "The Bachelor," hundreds of filmmakers have shot miles of footage here plus a few episodes on HGTV and Bizarre Foods America. The territory has some full-service production companies and a handful of supporting companies who offer complete facilities including casting, lighting, grip equipment, trucks, motor homes, generators, helicopters with special mounts, underwater camera housing and video editing suites. Companies can hire members of the Screen Actors Guild for many "extras" as they need them. Call the Department of Tourism at 774-8784, and their Film Promotion Office.

### Agriculture

Although land suitable for commercial agriculture on St. Thomas and St. John is limited, St. Croix's plains and rolling hills support beef, dairy cattle, sheep and goats. The government maintains agriculture stations on all three islands to help small farmers. On St. Croix, small farmers sell fruit, vegetables and root crops at roadside stands and in the Agriculture Department's farmers' market. Two companies producing beef, and a few farmers raising goat and sheep farmers for local consumption sell to local grocery chains and at Annaly Farms. The companies also breed and export Senepol cattle, which has global demand. The cattle, genetically engineered in St. Croix, were successfully and secifcally bred for use in warm tropical climates.

A St. Croix company farming the freshwater fish "Tilapia", in conjunction with hydroponic gardening, opened in the last few years. A Tilapia fish farm is part of the Fisheries studies at UVI. In St. Thomas, success has come through the growth of herbs and spices sold to island supermarkets, at roadside stands, and the government's market at Market Square in Charlotte Amalie and farmer's market on weekend at Yacht Haven Grande. Exports of bush tea products to the mainland, used locally for medicinal purposes, are increasing. Farmers also grow root and garden crops for sale at open markets.

### Finding a Job

Life in the tropics is more than palm trees and pina coladas, so you will need a few dollars for necessities. If you have decided to live out your dream, plan on enough money, depending upon your standard of living, to see you through until you are settled. Taking a temporary job is a good idea until you have been here long enough to know if you like island living. Unless you are recruited from the mainland, employers will want to make sure you will stay awhile before they invest in you.

   USVI law requires that all job openings be posted through the Department of Labor. The Labor Department matches the local labor supply with jobs, providing placement, referral, training, information and counseling services. Jobs for accountants, mechanics, bakers, bartenders, bookkeepers, carpenters, chefs, cooks, electricians, pastry chefs, plumbers, secretaries, and servers are always available.
(See www.vidol.gov/https://www.vidolviews.org  Check also the local newspapers, and in St. John, the bulletin boards placed around town.
Though it maybe difficult to find a job from off-island, you may try requesting a local phone book from VIYA Communications.
Call 779-9999 or go to www.viphonebook.com. The same book covers all three islands, and you can get a start in employment research.

Another easy way to seek employment is job postings on Indeed.com. The website offers hundreds of job listings from across the Virgin Islands and opportunities for employers to provide applicants with feedback. Like in the mainland ,Craigslist (http://virgin.craigslist.org) is also a main source for employment classifieds.
This being a US territory, you will of course have to present proof of US citizenship, Alien status or other valid work permit. If you are legal, look to smaller restaurants, tour companies or charter boats for instant jobs, particularly in the busy winter season.

Professionals and other tradespersons need licenses as follows:

**The Dept. of Licensing and Consumer Affairs**
774-3130, St. Thomas     773-2226 St. Croix.
Barbers, beauticians, construction contractors, draftsmen, electricians, plumbers, real estate brokers

**The Divison of Banking, Insurance and Financial Regulations**
774-7166 St. Thomas     773-6459 St. Croix
Banks, insurance and other financial professionals and institutions

**The Department of Health** 774-0117 St.Thomas or 713-9924 St.Croix . Doctors, dentists, nurses and pharmacists and other medical personnel. They will also issue health cards for workers who are employed in a food service position.

Attitude counts. If you are a self-starter, you may find yourself in your home-based business with an opportunity to grow.
You will probably have to pay your own way here if you manage to land a job in advance of your arrival. If you get a key position, you might be able to negotiate relocation costs with your company.

## The Work Force

At the beginning of fiscal year 2019, 38,368 persons were employed compared to 40,614 at the end of 2019, a 2.1pts drop in unemployment during that year non farm payroll increased 1664 territory wide with the largest gains in the service providing sector with 1064 jobs and goods-producing sector including construction with 600 jobs.

At end of 2019 St. Croix's unemployment rate was 5%. 19,431were eligible to work and 18,459 were employed.

On St. Thomas/St. John. Unemployment rate was 5.3%. 23,402 were Eligible to work, while 22,155 were employed.
By comparison, the national unemployment rate for the same month was 3.5%.

The local government, and the service industry are the largest employers In the territory, with others in construction, manufacturing, finance, insurance, real estate, transportation, communications, public utilities, and in the wholesale business. The Labor Department matches the local labor supply with jobs. It provides placement, referral, training, information and counseling services. Jobs for accountants, auto mechanics, bakers, bartenders, bookkeepers, maintenance, carpenters, chefs, electricians, cooks, sports instructors, Maintenance mechanics, pastry chefs, plumbers, secretaries, cocktail waiters and waitresses are always available.

## Training

The Virgin Islands has a fairly well-educated work force. A large number complete high school. Many continue their education at The University of the Virgin Islands or travel to mainland colleges. The Labor Department oversees federally-subsidized training for interested citizens through the Workforce Investment Act. The program repays employers up to 50 percent and financial stipends. The Department works closely with private industry for on-the-job training and will, in some cases, offer classroom programs to custom tailor training programs that meet their needs. Call them at 776-3700 ext. 2081.

### Federal Unemployment Tax

All employers pay a federal unemployment tax called FUTA and pay 0.8 percent of the first $7,000 paid to employees. They must fill out Form 940 and then file with the Federal Internal Revenue Bureau in Philadelphia. The current unemployment insurance tax rate for new employers is 6.0 percent of the taxable wage base, which is subject to change yearly. In 2009, the wage base was $21,800. Rates for existing businesses vary. It's based on how often they laid off workers in the previous twelve quarters. Employees can collect when they are laid off or unfairly fired. For details on the various surcharges, computations and filing requirements go to:
www.vidol.gov/unemployment-taxes-overview

### Wages

Overall, wages here are lower than on the mainland. The minimum wage for most jobs is $10.50 per hour. Tipped employees must earn at least $10.50 an hour, as long as tips bring it up to that. Tipped employees will be required to be paid at least 70% of the minimum wage rate. Check the Dept. of Labor website for current updates.

### Benefits

Although a comprehensive benefits package is not required in the private sector, most businesses provide a minimum of health insurance which because we are not part of the Affordable Health Care Act state Exchange programs, is in high demand by individuals and families. Larger businesses also offer pension plans and other perks. Naturally, employees will gravitate to firms where they will get the best benefits.

### Worker's Compensation

Workers compensation insurance is mandatory for all businesses with premium rates varying by job. Workers compensation insurance is available only through the Department of Labor, but Part B Employers Liability and Part C Other States may be available from private carriers. Ask your agent.

### Social Security

Businesses contribute to the employee's social security at the same rate as in the States. They pay 7.65 percent (1.45% Medicare and 6.20% is for old-age) and the employee pays 7.65 percent on wages up to $113,700 (2013). Self-employed residents pay 15.3 percent (consisting of a12.4% component for component for old-age, survivors, and disability insurance, and a 2.9% component for Medicare on wages up to $113,700 (2013). However, they must fill out form 1040 SS, rather than the usual 1040 SE, Form 1040 SS and the payment is filed with the Internal Revenue Service in Austin, Texas. All benefits are the same as on the mainland except there is no supplemental security income. In summary, Social Security taxes are still paid to the United States Treasury, while withholding is paid to the U.S. Virgin Islands Government.

The VI Bureau of Economic Research had conducted a study in 2014 of the state of the territory. For an in depth review of statistics related to various segments of the economy visit www.viber.org

### Financial Help

If your business needs financial help, check with your bank, the Federal Government's Small Business Administration at 340, or with the local government's Small Business Development Agency at 714-1700. The three organizations offer counseling and financial assistance. The Small Business Development Center at the University of the Virgin Islands offers counseling, research and technical assistance to eligible businesses. For more information please call St. Croix Office 340-692-4294 and St. Thomas 340-693-1694 and 340-774-8530.

### Business Insurance

For business insurance purposes, local agents can arrange for coverage of your needs with various packages and can often finance your premiums. Rates depend on business gross receipts or other type of exposure.

### Bonding

U.S. Customs, bid and performance, fidelity and surety, and court bonds are available to those who qualify, but the process is slow. Only a few agents offer this service. Whenever possible, have a certified financial statement prepared and confer with your agent long in advance of need.

### Getting a Business License

Once you have evaluated the local economy, the labor market and the territory as a whole, and you decided you want to do business here, you need a business license. The fee schedule varies with a range of $1.00 for commercial farming license, $50 for an itinerant vendor, $100 for retail shops, $200 for restaurants with more than 25 seats, $300 for business and management consultants, and $400 for hotels and guest-houses over 100 rooms. Businesses are responsible for renewals since the department does not send notices. Those who plan branches on more than one island must file separate applications. Also if you have two different businesses and two different names, you must file two applications. The USVI adheres to the Uniform Commercial Code (UCC), a copy of which is available from the Lieutenant Governor's Office.

## Basic Business License Requirements
1. A completed application form;
2. Certificate of Trade Name/Partnership & Corporation Registration; http:ltg.gov.vi/corporations-and-trademarks.html
3. Tax Clearance letter from The Bureau of Internal Revenue www.viirb.com;
4. Police Records Check www.vipd.gov.vi/departments/officeofthepolice/commissioner/recordsbureau.aspx
5. Zoning approval - www.dpnr.gov.vi/pages/about-dpnr-1
6. Fire Inspection;
7. Health inspection (certain businesses only)
8. Liability and/or Professional Insurance for some types of businesses Board certifications are required for some fields such as architects, Barbers, Construction contractors Real estate appraisers, social workers.

*Renewing your licenses is much easier and can also be done online. Call the Licensing department in St. Thomas at 774-3130, for St. Croix call 718-2226. www.dlca.gov.vi*

## Business Taxes Corporate Income Taxes

In addition to the usual income taxes, corporations registered in the U.S. Virgin Islands pay a 10 percent surcharge due to a 1985 act passed by the local Legislature. It is paid with your quarterly tax return.

## Corporate Franchise Tax

Every incorporated business, whether domestic or foreign must pay tax on the amount of capital used in the business. The tax is $1.50 for every $1,000 of capital stock. The minimum tax is $150. A penalty of 20%, or $50, whichever is greater, for failure to pay by June 30th, and 1% interest compounded annually for each month beyond June 30th is imposed.

### Entertainment Tax

A five percent tax is levied on the gross receipts for performances or entertainment, including, motion pictures, shows, boxing matches, circuses and concerts where admission is charged unless the performance is sponsored by a recognized non-profit organization.

### Excise Tax

Pretty much anyone doing business in the Virgin Islands, except those that are specifically exempt, must pay excise tax on all goods, merchandise, or commodities manufactured in or brought into the Virgin Islands for business purposes. The excise tax is based on the invoice value of such merchandise, plus a mark-up of five percent. Rates of tax depend upon the applicable category, and range from two percent to twenty-five percent.

The following rates apply to the following categories of goods: Drugs, medicine, and clothing, 2% percent; tires, 5%; self-propelled vehicles, firearms, ammunition and bicycles, 10%; U.S. beers, $1.55 per case; foreign beers, $2.08 per case; liquor, $6.00 per case; wine, $2.50 per gallon; tobacco (exclusive of cigars), 20%. More info on rates is available in the *Tax Structure of the U.S. Virgin Islands* booklet, available at viirb.com.

### Gross Receipts Tax

Businesses pay a five percent gross receipts tax on all money earned from all transactions including services and may not deduct expenses. If you earn under $120,000 a year you must file annually at the Internal Revenue Bureau. If you earn more than $120,000 you must also file monthly. Businesses that earn under $225,000 per year are entitled to a $9,000 per month exemption as are some categories of businesses such as fishermen.

### Hotel Room Tax

Those who stay in hotels, guest houses, apartments, condominiums, or residences for less than 90 days are charged a Hotel Room Tax. The rate is 10% of the gross room rate, which is the total sum charged to a guest for room use plus additional charges, such as an energy surcharge or a maintenance fee, but not charges for food, beverages, and gratuities.

### Business Organizations

The Chambers of Commerce in St. Croix and St. Thomas/St. John work hard to improve the business climate and overall community. Membership is open to business and non-business people. Both Chambers have small staff/or volunteers guided by a board of directors. Feel free to call them with questions.

Staff members will either know the answers or tell you where to find them. Both Chambers provide and publish information packets, newsletters, business notifications, membership guides, and directories. The Chamber groups also have monthly luncheons and "Business-After-Hours" meetings for members and the public. Visit the St. Croix Chamber of Commerce at www.stxchamber.org; e-mail: info@stxchamber.org. The St. Thomas-St. John Chamber of Commerce is located at 6-7 Dronningens Gade. Visit them at www.usvichamber.com, e-mail: chamber@islands.vi.

---

### Other Professional Organizations

| | |
|---|---|
| Advertising Club of the Virgin Islands: | 774-8478 |
| American Institute of Architects: | (St.C) 772-5904; (STT) 777-1600 |
| Christiansted Retailers/Restaurant Association: | 773-2148 |
| St. Croix Chamber of Commerce: | 718-1435 |
| St. Croix Hotel & Tourism Association: | 773-7117 |
| St. Thomas -St. John Chamber of Commerce: | 776-0100 |
| St. Thomas - St. John Hotel Association: | 774-6835 |
| St. Croix Board of Realtors: | 334-5618 |
| St. Thomas Board of Realtors: | 866-598-1440 ext 234 |
| V.I. Territorial Association of Realtors: | 773-1855 |
| V.I. Taxi Association: | 774-4550 |
| V.I. Bar Association, vibar@viaccess.net, | 778-7497 |

### Labor Associations

American Federation of Teachers: (STC) 778-4414; (STT) 776-1825
Our Virgin Labor Union     St. Croix   719-1464

---

For the record, if you hear the exclamation 'Cheese and Bread!' (sometimes followed by 'Mi son!'), it has nothing to do with victuals (though a St. Croix restaurant had that name). Rather, it could mean either 'Gee Whiz' , 'Golly' or 'What the @$#&!'

# Settler's Handbook Chapter 10

## YOU AND THE GOVERNMENT...

The U.S. Virgin Islands is governed by the Revised Organic Act passed by the United States Congress in 1954. In this document, U.S. Congress defined the three branches of the territorial government, set debt limits, and spelled out voting rights. It includes a bill of rights that substantially extends the same rights enjoyed by U.S. mainlanders to the islands. Under the U.S. Constitution, the Federal government reserves any powers not expressly granted to the States and the people. In this unincorporated territory, the government has only such powers as Congress may give or take away. While autonomy has increased over the years, residents first elected a governor in 1970, but voted in a 1993 referendum that they wanted no change in their status. The referendum options ranged from independence to statehood.

There have been five attempts to pass a Virgin Islands Constitution, the last one in 1980, but the Virgin Islands electorate each time has turned down the measure in the hopes that the next draft will be perfected to meet the majority's acceptance. In 2007 another Committee to redraft a new Constitution was formed and it has also fizzled.

The Federal government maintains a presence here through various agencies. A Federal Inspector General, appointed by the Interior Department keeps watch over local use of Federal government revenues and expenditures.

### Income Taxes

Islanders use familiar federal forms to pay income taxes. The rate is the same as in the states, but the funds remain in the U.S. Virgin Islands. When income is earned here, on the mainland, or anywhere else in the world, taxes are paid where the taxpayer declares his bona fide residence on December of that year. If you reside here, but earn money elsewhere you pay your entire tax on any world-wide income to the U.S. Virgin Islands, but you need to report it on a 1040-SS information form. If you are a U.S. resident with some island income, complete Form 1040 and Form 8689 to determine your tax liability to the U.S. Virgin Islands. This means you allocate taxes between both jurisdictions. File by April 15. Be aware that a local holiday may mean that the filing date is different than that on the mainland.

All tax forms are available at local Internal Revenue Bureau offices located at Estate Diamond, Lot 7B, Christiansted, St. Croix, VI 00820, 773-1040. Administrator's Office; The Battery, Cruz Bay, St. John, 00830, 776-6485, and Mandela Circle, 9601 Estate Thomas, St. Thomas 00802, 774-5865.

### Social Security

Social security taxes are deducted from all paychecks. Self-employed residents pay their social security tax at the same rate as mainlanders, but unlike residents of other U.S. territories, use form 1040-SS.

### Other Taxes

All U.S. citizens who move here from the U.S. mainland are subject to Federal estate tax laws no matter where the assets come from, whether it be England or Kansas. Since usual stateside exemptions apply here, most people who inherit small estates pay no taxes. If you are born here or naturalized in the U.S. Virgin Islands, Puerto Rico, or other U.S. territory, your assets on the U.S. mainland are taxed but not those here or elsewhere in the world. The taxes are payable to the U.S. Treasury Department. A 2% stamp tax is paid on real property transfer. That would be 2% on value up to $350,000; from $350,001 to $1 million it is 2.5%, and from $1 million to $5 million it is 3%. Anything over $5 million is 3.5%. Contact the Recorder of Deeds in St. Thomas/ St. John at 774-9906 and in St. Croix at 773-6449.

### Voting

U.S. Virgin Islanders cannot vote for the President and Vice-President of the U.S. However, the local Republican and Democratic parties are active with their respective national committees. While these islands cannot vote for the President and Vice President, we do however vote for our Delegate to Congress every two years here in the territory. This position does have an office in Washington and does serve on various house committees. There is an office in St. Croix and St. Thomas for this office. Residents elect the Governor and Lieutenant Governor to four-year terms and Senators to two-year terms. We vote for seven senators on St. Croix, seven on St. Thomas, and one "at-large' senator from St. John. Members of the Board of Education and Election Board are also elected. To register bring passport, birth certificate, or naturalization certificate PLUS your social security card.

Years ago, the individual islands had more autonomy through municipal councils, but now the reins of government rest with the territorial government. While there are no elected mayors or other municipal officials, periodically residents in St. John and St. Croix push for more home rule. Register to vote at Elections Board offices at: St. Croix: 93 Sunny Isle Annex, 773-1021. Mail to: 1499 Kingshill, VI 00851, St. John: The Battery, Cruz Bay, St. John, VI 00801 776-6535 (open Tuesday/Thursday), St. Thomas: 212 Crystal Gade, Charlotte Amalie, St. Thomas 00802, 774-3107, Mail to: P.O. Box 6038, St. Thomas, VI 00801-6038.

## EXECUTIVE BRANCH

The Governor and Lieutenant Governor, elected to four-year terms, may serve two terms. The Lieutenant Governor acts in the Governor's stead when he is off-island. When both are temporarily out of the territory, the Finance Commissioner is next in line. The Attorney General, Budget Director, Education Commissioner, Public Works Commissioner, Housing Commissioner, and Police Commissioner follow. Should the Governor and Lieutenant Governor permanently leave office, the Legislature's president and vice president are next in the line of succession. They are followed by the same line of government officials as when the Governor and Lieutenant Governor are temporarily absent.

The Government's cabinet consists of Commissioners from each of the executive branch's many departments. The Lieutenant Governor's office has the responsibility for tax assessors' offices, recorder of deeds offices, regulates the banking and insurance industries and is the repository for all official documents. Administrators on each island are the Governor's representatives.

### Government Officials

**Governor:** St. Thomas 21-22 Kongens Gade, Charlotte Amalie, VI 00802, 774-0001
**Legislative Bldg.,**
**St. Croix:** No. 2, Lagoon St. Complex, F'sted, 772- 1000
**Govt. House**, St. Croix: King St., Christiansted, 00820, 773-1404
**St. John:** The Battery - Cruz Bay, Box 488, 00830 776-6484
**Lieutenant Governor:**
**St. Croix** 1131 King Street, Christiansted,00820, 773-6449
**St. Thomas** -18 Kongens Gade, Charlotte Amalie, 00802, 774-2991
www.ltg.gov.vi
**Office of the Lieutenant Governor, Divisions:**
**Banking & Insurance:** 773-6459 *St. Croix* 774-7166 *St. Thomas*

19th Settler's Handbook     You and Government 10

**Corporations & Trademarks:** 773-6449 *St. Croix* 776-8515 *St. Thomas*
**Passport Office:**    773-6449 *St. Croix* 774-4024 *St. Thomas*
**Recorder of Deeds:** Office records property deeds –
**St. Croix**: King Street, Christiansted, 773-6449
**St. Thomas** - Kongens Gade, Charlotte Amalie, 774-9906

**Tax Assessor:** Office responsible for appraising property value:

**St. Croix** - King St., C'sted, 773-6449 ; No. l Lagoon St., F'sted, 772-3115
**St. John** - The Battery, Cruz Bay, VI 00830, 776-6737
**St. Thomas** - No. 18 Kongens Gade, Charlotte Amalie, VI 00802 776-8505,
**Cadastral** (office that houses property maps) St. Croix 773-6549
St. Thomas 776-8505

**V.I. Medicare/ State Health Insurance Program (SHIP),**
772-7368, St. Croix St. Thomas; 714-4354

**Administrators' Offices**: Government House, St. Croix: King St., Christiansted, 00820, 773-1404
St.Thomas: Government House, Charlotte Amalie, 00802, 774-0001

## LEGISLATIVE BRANCH

The territory has a unicameral, 15-member Legislature with all the members elected to two-year terms every two years. Elections are held in even-numbered years. Senators take office the second Monday in January of the following year. The territory is grouped into two districts: St. Thomas/St. John and St. Croix. Voters in those districts elect seven senators each. Voters on all three islands elect a senator-at-large, who by law must be a resident of St. John.

The Legislature meets throughout the year for committee meetings or sessions. The Governor or the Legislature's President can call specific sessions so Senators may address specific issues. While the main Legislature offices are in Charlotte Amalie, where all sessions are held, Senators may also have offices and hold committee meetings in St. Croix and St. John.

The Senate has nine standing committees that deal with issues and pending legislation related to the government's various departments. It also has final approval on all zoning and variance changes and trust land permits. Bills are passed by majority vote. They become law when the

Governor signs, or if he fails to sign, within 10 working days. While he can veto bills, the Legislature may override his veto with a two-thirds vote.

## U.S. Virgin Islands Legislature

**St. Croix:** Lagoon St. Complex, Frederiksted, 00840 Mail: Box 4800, Christiansted, 00822, 773-2424

**St. John:** #9 Enighed, Cruz Bay, St. John, 00831 Mail: Box 1690, Charlotte Amalie, St. Thomas 00801, 776-6285 The mailing address is: P.O. Box 7789, Charlotte Amalie, St. Thomas, 00801 774-0880

## JUDICIAL BRANCH

The U.S. Virgin Islands has two judicial levels, the local and Federal judiciaries. Most of the cases go to the Superior Court, which handles all criminal and civil matters from litter to murder.

There are five judges in St. Thomas and four in St. Croix. A judge visits St. John for traffic, litter, family, and small claims cases. The judges are appointed by the Governor and confirmed by the Legislature. U.S. District Court tries federal crimes and may elect to try serious local crimes including murder. Assaults on Virgin Islanders.

Islands National Park officers and crimes involving interstate transfer of funds are among those tried by a federal court. Federal judges are appointed by the President and confirmed by the U.S. Congress. There are two judges and two magistrates sitting here with mainland judges assigned when the case load is more than the sitting judges can handle. A federal grand jury hands down indictments. Appeals from the Superior Court are heard by a three-member appeals panel consisting of one territorial and two federal judges. Cases from the appeals panel are heard by the 3rd Circuit Court of Appeals, Philadelphia. The U.S. Supreme Court is the last step in the appeals process. Defendants who can't afford an attorney are represented by a public defender or a court-appointed attorney in both Superior and U.S. District Court cases. All the territory's attorneys are on a list. When their name is at the top, they get the next case.

**Legal Services of the Virgin Islands Inc.:** This non-profit agency handles many civil and immigration matters for those who need legal advice and cannot afford the cost. Call St. Croix at 718-2626, or in St. Thomas at 774-6720.

**Traffic tickets** can be paid by mail or in St.

Croix and St. Thomas at Superior Court. In St. John, they are payable at the Police Department's motor vehicle inspection lane.
**Superior Court locations:** Alexander Farrelly Justice Center, Veteran's Drive, or Box 70, Charlotte Amalie, St. Thomas 00804, 774-6680. Hall of Justice, Box 929, Christiansted, St. Croix 00821, 778-9750
**Superior Court Public Defenders**: Company St., Christiansted, St. Croix

### POPULAR FEDERAL and LOCAL GOVERNMENT OFFICES
There are many Federal agencies and local government departments and commissions with offices on both St. Croix, St. Thomas and infrequently, St. John. Most local department Commissioners are based in St. Thomas. Federal information www.usa.gov
**Alcohol, Tobacco, Firearms and Explosives Bureau** St. Croix 773-3920; St. Thomas 774-2398
**Agriculture, VI , Dept. Of:** This local department sells plants and assists farmers with their plants and livestock, provides veterinary services, heavy farming equipment and builds farm ponds. Estate Lower Love, Kingshill, St. Croix, 00850, 778-0997 Estate Carolina, Coral Bay, St. John 00830, 776-6274, 7944 Estate Dorothea, St. Thomas, 00802, 774-5182
**Agriculture: U.S. Dept Of:** Federal agency oversees various Federal programs and enforces Federal agricultural laws. Agricultural Research Service, Box 3008, Kingshill, St. Croix 00850, 778-1312.Animal and Plant Health Inspection Service, Box 8119, St. Thomas, 00801, 776-2787. Plant Protection & Quarantine, Henry E. Rohlsen Airport, St. Croix, VI 00820, 778-1696. Cyril E. King Airport, St.Thomas, 00802, 774-5719.Waterfront, St. Thomas 00802, 774-2561. Natural Resources Conservation Service, Federal Experiment Station, P.O. Box 4399, Kingshill, St. Croix 00851, 778-1312
**Arts, VI Council on the Arts:** Reports to the Governor and disburses Grants, promotes arts and holds exhibits. Strand St., Christiansted, St. Croix 00820, St. Thomas 774-5984 / St. Croix 773-3075
**Coast Guard, US:** Federal agency patrols the territory's waters, works in drug interdiction, U.S. maritime laws, marine safety. Inspection Office— Frederiksted, St. Croix, 772-5557. Cutter Point Ledge, Charlotte Amalie, St. Thomas 00802. Marine Safety Detachment — Waterfront, Charlotte Amalie, St. Thomas 00802, 776-3497 Search and Rescue Coordination Center, San Juan, P.R., 1-787-729-6770 Customs and Border Protection St. Croix 773-1490; St. John 776-6741; St. Thomas 774-2510

19th Settler's Handbook  You and Government 10

**Coastal Zone Management Program:** Anna's Hope, Christiansted, St. Croix, VI 00820, 773-3450, Cyril E. King Airport, St. Thomas,VI 00802, 774-3320

**Congress, Delegate to Congress: US:** Represents the U.S. Virgin Islands in the House of Representatives as a non-voting Delegate. 60 King St..,F'sted St. Croix, VI 00840, 778-5900. 9100 Havensight, Port of Sale, Charlotte Amalie, St. Thomas 00801, 774- 4408. 2404 Rayburn House Office Building, Washington DC 20515 - (202) 225-1790 Wasshington, D.C., 20515-5501, [1-202-225-1790]

**CRIME STOPPERS: to report anonymously a crime or lead, call : 1(800)222-TIPS (8477)**

**Defense, U.S. Dept. of Defense**: Federal agency recruits armed forces members and runs support centers. Army Recruiter, Nisky Center, St. Thomas 008022, 714-3027. Recruiter St. Croix, Sunny Isle Mall 719-9077

**Education, VI, Dept. of** : Oversees Federal and local money that funds the public school system. Each island's Board of Education and insular superintendent implements policy planning and operation for each public school system. 2133 Hospital St. Christiansted, St. Croix, 00820, 773-1095. No. 44-46 Kongsbergite, St. Thomas, 00802, 774-0100

**Energy Office, VI:** Promotes energy-saving programs, provides information to residents and publishes a newsletter for residents. Located at Mars Hill in Frederiksted, St. Croix 00840, 772-2626 or 713-8436; St. Thomas 714-8436. Visit their website at www.vinenergy.org for energy related matters and information. The site offers many ways to conserve gasoline and tips to lower water and power (WAPA) bills. Speakers are available to discuss subjects such as: energy efficiency, renewable energy applications to include: solar power, wind energy, and net metering; global warming, rebate incentives, and building an energy efficient home to catch

*St. Thomas Legislative Building*

the sun and wind for huge energy savings. The VIEO is a division of the Office of the Governor and they are serving you to save energy dollars!
**Fire Service: VI**: (340) 692-2410
**Farmers Home Administration (USDA):** Federal agency finances loans for first-time home owners and makes farm loans. Room 14B, Ville La Reine, Kingshill, St. Croix 00850, 778-5224
**Federal Aviation Administration:** This agency controls the airport tower and maintains navigational equipment on St. Thomas Cyril E. King Airport, Box 302120, St. Thomas 00803, 774-1836. The airport in St. Croix is privatized on a contract basis. Henry E. Rohlsen Airport, Rt 1, Airport, Kingshill, St. Croix 00820, 778-4826
**Federal Bureau of Investigation**: Investigates Federal and major local crimes. Federal Bldg., 3013 Estate Golden Rock, Christiansted, St. Croix 00820, 773-7922. Al Cohen Plaza, Charlotte Amalie, St. Thomas 00802, 777-3363. If no answer call San Juan, Puerto Rico: 1-787-754-6000
**Federal Highway Administration**: Federal department funds road
*St. John*: Cruz Bay 776-6333; Coral Bay 776-6365
**General Services Administration:** Federal agency manages all Federal buildings and leases space for Federal agencies. Federal Building 5500 Veterans' Drive, Rm.107, Charlotte Amalie, St. Thomas 00802 714-1367. Federal Building, Rt. 75 Northside Road, Golden Rock, St. Croix, 00820-4355, 773-4636
**Fish & Wildlife Division:** 45 Mars Hill, Frederiksted, St. Croix, 00840, 772-1955. Estate Nazareth, St. Thomas, VI 00802, 775-6762
**222-TIPS (8477)**
**Health, Department & Clinics:** Operates local clinics, extensive outpatient services, alcoholism and drug treatment centers, public health services, environmental health, mental health, family planning, maternal and child health and crippled children's services. The Myrah Keating Smith Community Health Center on St. John, 693-8900, is operated by the Hospital on St. Thomas. Community Health Clinic—774-7477. Department of Health, Commissioners offices, Sugar Estate, St. Thomas 00802, 774-0117. St. Croix: Charles Harwood Medical Complex 718-1311
**Homeland Security/Immigration, U.S,:** Federal agency is responsible for enforcement of immigration laws and naturalization. Sunny Isle Shopping Center, Box 1468, St. Croix, VI 00823, 778-6559. Nisky Center, St. Thomas, 774-1390, T. S. A. Transportation, Security, Administration 715-2271 St. Thomas
**Human Services Department, US:** Federal agency manages all Federal

health and social services programs. Social Security Administration, Federal Building, Charlotte Amalie, St. Thomas 00802, 774-0930, Sunny Isle Shopping Center, Professional Building, Christiansted, St. Croix 00820-4423, 773-2323 (Social Security office). Disability Programs, Federal Building, 5500 Veterans' Drive, Charlotte Amalie, St. Thomas, VI 00802, 774-7375

**Human Services, V.I. Department:** Administers federal and local welfare and food stamp programs. Oversees various youth, adult and senior citizen programs. 20A Strand & 5BB Smith St., Christiansted, St. Croix 00820, 773-2980 and 773-2323. St. John (mail goes to St. Thomas address), 776-6334. Knud Hansen Complex, Building A, Hospital Ground, St. Thomas 00820, 774-0930

**Interior U.S. Department of the Interior, Inspector General's Office:** St. Thomas, 774-8300   St. Croix 778-9012

**Justice, US Dept. Of:** This Federal office provides Federal court security, transports Federal prisoners, administers warrants and subpoenas. Federal Building, 3013 Estate Golden Rock, Lot 13, Christiansted, St. Croix, VI 00820, 778-2051 U.S. Marshal's office, 773-1072, Federal Building, 5500 Veterans' Drive, St. Thomas, VI 00801, 714-1761 U.S. Marshall's office, 774-5999

**Justice, V.I. Department of:** Headed by the territory's Attorney General, this local department prosecutes most of the territory's criminal and civil cases. It oversees appeals, administration law, ethics, conflicts of interest for the territory's jails and prisons, the Criminal Justice Complex, the Medical Examiner and the Civil Rights Commission. 6040 Estate Castle Coakley, Christiansted, St. Croix 00820 773-0295. 48B-50C Kronprindsens Gade, GERS Building, Charlotte Amalie, St. Thomas, VI 00802, 774-5666

**Labor, V.I. Department of :** This local department can help you find a job and pay you unemployment compensation if you are laid off or unfairly fired. It also deals with training, youth employment, labor relations, wage and hour management, occupational safety and health, workers' compensation, and fair employment practices.
St. Croix 773-1994, St. Thomas,776-3700

**Labor Statistics, The Bureau of:** provides an in-depth and graphic picture of the local labor picture. Church Street, Christiansted, St. Croix 00820, 773-1994. Box 2606, Charlotte Amalie, St. Thomas 00803 776-3700

**Licensing and Consumer Affairs V.I. Department of:** Reviews, issues and enforces all matters pertaining to licensing, weights and measures and consumer protection. It oversees the Public Services Commission, Taxi and

19th Settler's Handbook  You and Government 10

Real Estate Commission and Architects and Engineers, Electricians, Plumbing, Alcohol Control, Contractors, and Barbers and Beauticians boards. Golden Rock Shopping Center, Christiansted, St. Croix, VI 00820, 718-2226. No. 1 Sub Base, Rm. 205, St. Thomas, VI 00802, 774-3130

**Management & Budget V.I., Office of :** This local office is responsible for the territory's budget. It parcels out money from the local and federal revenues. St. Thomas, 774-0750. St. Croix, 778-8925.

**Motor Vehicles. VI Bureau of:** This office is responsible for managing most matters related to the acquisition or renewal of driver's licenses and vehicles: St. Croix , Golden Grove; 713-4268 ;  St. John, Cruz Bay  776-6262; St. Thomas, Subbase 774-5765

*Offices*: St. Croix, 45 Mars Hill, Frederiksted 778-2211
St.John Leander Jurgen Command, Cruz Bay  693-8880

**National Guard, V.I .:** The territory's National Guard is called out in case of disaster. Run by the adjutant general who also oversees the territory's civil defense operation, the Virgin Islands Territorial Emergency Management Agency unit has about 800 members on both St. Croix and St. Thomas. 774-5919 Adjutant General, 4031 La Grande Princesse,   Lot 1B, Christiansted, St. Croix 00820-4353, 712-7711. VITEMA, Leonard B. Francis Armory, St. Thomas, 774-2244 ; St. Croix 773-2244 Government on all three islands.

**National Parks Service, US:**
Thesre are parks run by the Federal Government on all three islands.
On St. Croix, the park  oversees Christiansted Historic site, Buck Island Reef National Monument, and Salt River Bay National Historic Park and Ecological Preserve. On St. John, Virgin Islands National Park has a campground, visitor's center, biosphere reserve, and about 12,000 acres of land and sea. On St. Thomas, the park has a visitor's center at Red Hook and oversees Hassel Island, a historic cay in Charlotte Amalie Harbor. The superintendent's office is at the Red Hook visitor's center.

**St. Croix:** Fort Christianvaern, 773-1460
**St. Thomas:** Old Barracks Yard, Charlotte Amalie, St. Thomas
**St. John:** Cruz Bay Visitor Center, 776-6201, Cinnamon Bay Campground information, 776-6330. For reservations, call 1-800-539-9998, Biosphere Reserve (U.S. Geological Survey), 693-8950

**Personnel, V.I. Division of:**  This local department administers, recruits, classifies, trains and keeps the records on all government employees. Orange Grove, Christiansted, St. Croix 00820, 773-0341 48B-50C Kronprindsens Gade, St. Thomas 00802, 774-8588

**Planning & Natural Resources, (known as DPNR); V.I. Department of:** is responsible for coastal zone planning, capital development, historic preservation and archaeology, issuance of construction permits, libraries, archives and museums, environmental protection, fish and wildlife, boating and mooring permits. 6003 Anna's Hope, Christiansted, St. Croix,VI 00820, 773-3320 **DPNR - Enforcement Division:** 6003 Anna's Hope, Christiansted, VI 00820, 773-5774. Cyril E. King Airport, St. Thomas 00802, 774-3320

**Police Department: VI** The territory's prime law enforcement body has offices on all three islands. St. Croix 45 Mars Hill, Frederiksted 778-2211, Wilbur Francis Command, Frederiksted 772-3566, Anselmo Marshall Command, Christiansted (Basin Triangle) 773-2530. St. John Leander Jurgen Command, Cruz Bay 693-8880. St. Thomas Richard Callwood Command, Norre Gade, Charlotte Amalie 774-2310 Bassanio David Command at Lindberg Bay 775-3445:

**Port Authority, VI:** This entity develops and operates public air and marine ports. It is a major engine of economic growth and helps maintain the Virgin Islands' position as a major tourism destination. Persons interested in learning more, leasing VIPA's facilities, or doing business with VIPA may contact (340) 774-1629 or info@viport, or www.viport.com.

| | |
|---|---|
| Box 1134, Christiansted, St. Croix 00821 | 778-1012 |
| Box 1707, St. Thomas 00803 | 774-1629 |
| Manager, Cyril E. King Airport, St. Thomas | 774-5100 |
| Marine Manager, St. Croix | 778-3131 |
| Marine Manager, St. Thomas | 774-2250 |

**Public Safety (Police Department), V.I. Dept. of:** Responsible for all anti-crime activities, including drug interdiction, Special Operations Bureau as well as the Motor Vehicle Department. Call 911 for all emergencies. If you are using a cell phone, for emergencies call 911.

**Property & Procurement, V.I. Department of:** Purchases, warehouses, controls inventory, distributes materials used in all government departments, and executes contracts and leases; runs the central motor pool, government mail service, printing plant and administers the Federal surplus property program. Suppliers can ask to be on the mailing list for bid notices. Bidding practices favor USVI enterprises that meet the qualifications. St. Croix 773-0370; St. Thomas 774-0828.

**Public Services Commission:** Regulates telephone, electric and cable television rates. Complain to them when you have a problem with the telephone, electric or cable television companies. Barbel Plaza, P.O. Box

40, Charlotte Amalie, VI 00804 776-1291. On St. Croix call 778-6010

**Public Works Department, V.I.:** Oversees activities concerning roads, solid waste, utilities, signals, and bus routes. 6002 Estate Hope, Christiansted, VI 00820, 773-1290 #6 Suzannaberg, St. John, VI 00830, 776-6346, 8244 Sub Base, St. Thomas, VI 00802-5805, 776-4844

**Sports, Parks & Recreation, VI:** This local department runs local parks and recreation programs. LBJ Gardens, Christiansted, St. Croix, VI 00820, 773-0160 / 773-0271, Box 122, Cruz Bay, St. John, VI 00831, 775-6531, Sub Base, Bldg. No. l, Rm. 206, St. Thomas, VI 00802, 774-0255 00801 Mail: Box 1690,Charlotte Amalie, St. T, 00801 774-0880

**VI Territorial Emergency Management Agency (VITEMA):** The agency with primary responsibility for ensuring the territory's resilience to disasters. VITEMA partners with federal, state and local government agencies, and with the private sector to assess, prepare, and ensure effective responses to disasters. St. Croix 773-2424; St. John 776-6444; St. Thomas 774-2244 Alexander A. Farrelly Criminal Justice Complex, Charlotte Amalie, St. Thomas 00802 774-2211 (commissioner's office)

**Small Business Administration:** This Federal agency makes loans to small businesses. Sunny Isle Professional Bldg., Suites 5&6, Christiansted, VI 00820, 778-5380, 3800 Crown Bay, St. Thomas, VI 00802, 774-8530 Sunshine Mall lower level, St. Croix, 692-5270

**Small Business Development Center:** Assists with the set up and development of businesses, and runs courses to assist new business owners. Sunshine Mall lower level, St. Croix, 692-5270, 8000 Nisky Center, Ste. 720, St. Thomas, VI 00802, 776-3206

*Lieutenant Walton J. Jack, Jr., Police Chief William Harvey and Deputy Police Chief Herman Lynch, Jr. - St. Croix VIPD*

**Tourism, V.I. Department of:** This local department oversees all activities concerning tourism, domestic and foreign offices. King Street Chrisitansted, St. Croix (Government House) 773-0495, Strand Street, Fredriksted, St. Croix, 772-0357, Cruz Bay, St. John, VI 00830, 776-6450 Waterfront, P.O. Box 6400, St. Thomas, VI 00801, 774-8784
**Offshore Offices, Washington DC**, 444 North Capitol Street NW, Suite 305 Washington, DC 20001
• (T) 202-624-3590 • (F) 202 624 3594 • (E) tlbertrand@usvitourism.vi
**Massachusets**, P.O. Box 812247 Wellesley, MA 02482• T 508-507-8097 • F 770-745-2757
• E usvi@judithakerman.com
**Miami,** 18495 South Dixie Highway, #160 Miami, FL 33157-6817
• T 305-322-2740 • F 770 7452757  E jhodge@usvitourism.vi
**Chicago** 4100 N. Marine Drive, Suite 14-F Chicago, IL 60613 • T 312 -670 8784 • F 312-670-8788 • E awartenberg@usvitourism.vi
Atlanta 3961 Floyd Road, Suite 300-391Austell, GA30106 • T 404-688 0906 • F 770-7452757• E kmilliner@usvitourism.vi
**U.S. Attorney:** This office prosecutes all Federal crimes. King Street, Box 3239, Christiansted, St. Croix 00822, 773-3920 Federal Building, 5500 Veterans' Drive, Charlotte Amalie, St. Thomas 00802-6424 774-5757
**U.S. Customs and Border Protection:** An arm of the Federal Treasury Department which enforces U.S. Customs regulations. Old Post Office Building, 1 Church St., Christiansted, VI 00820, 773-5650, The Creek,
**Water and Power Authority (WAPA)**: This semiautonomous agency, called WAPA by locals, provides electricity and desalinated water. P.O. Box 1009, Christiansted, VI 00820, 773-2250, Cruz Bay, St. John, VI 00830

19th SETTLER'S HANDBOOK

# Services Directory

This Services Directory is but a small sampling of the professional organizations and local businesses who offer goods and services commonly needed by newcomers, visitors, investors, or potential residents to the USVI.

This section is divided by islands: St. Croix, St. John, St. Thomas, and, there are some who service all three of these islands. Ask when you call.

Please support our advertisers. If you have any questions or need their services.

19th Settler's Handbook

ST. CROIX

*Your Style* IS STUNNING

shop in-store at
4200 United Shopping Plaza | Christiansted, VI. 00820 | +3407786440

shop online at
Ashley.com.vi

# Services Directory - St. Croix

## ACCOUNTANTS/CPA

Theo Broodie - (340) 643-3434 (see display ad below)
Lil's Bookkeeping Service - (340) 778-2857 (see display ad below)
Travel Tax - (866) 272-7871 (see display ad below)

---

### THEO T. BROODIE, CPA, PC.
*Forensic Certified Public Accountant*

Auditing • Bookkeeping
Cost Accounting/Cost Analysis
Economic Damages • Financial Probability Analysis
Financial Forensic (Fraud) Examinations
Insurance Casualy Claims Analysis
Litigation Support • Tax Preparation

#2B Mount Pleasant, across street from Plaza West (ample parking)
Telephone: (340) 643-3434 / Email: ttbcpa@aol.com

*Theo Broodie, CPA, CFE, FCPA, CGMA*

---

### LIL'S BOOKKEEPING SERVICE

*Lelia Stephen - Sole Proprietorship*

**Preparations of all Taxes and Training of Peachtree Software**

P.O. Box 5239 Kingshill, St. Croix USVI 00851
Phone: (340) 778-2857 or (340) 690-4072

---

### TAXES!
*Made you look! Didn't it?* ☺

www.traveltax.com
866.272.7871
info@traveltax.com
Skype available

Moving to or working in the USVI? The Virgin Islands are treated as a foreign tax entity by the US and special rules apply. We specialize in territorial and international tax planning and filing.
- Mainland based
- Work by email, fax, and phone
- Flexible appointment times

**TravelTax**

US, Canada, Puerto Rico, USVI, and International

# Air Ambulance ~ Architects     19th Settler's Handbook

## AIR AMBULANCE

**Evac USA** - 1-844-464-4277 (see display ad page 203)
**SkyMed** - • Direct to St. Croix  866-349-1494 • St. Thomas  866-349-1494
SkyMed Air Ambulance Membership Plans —A must when living in the USVI for unexpected injury, or illnesses that can't be treated here.
      Join today! www.skymedusvi.com  (see display ad below)

**ST. CROIX**

## ARCHITECTS

**Design Engineering. LLC** - (340) 690-8759 (see display ad below)
**Steve Crane** - (801) 560-5369 (see display ad below)

## ATTORNEYS

**McChain, Miller, Nissman** -(340) 719-0601;773-6955 (see display ad below)
**Kiture Law Firm** - (340) 773-4590 (see display ad below)

## BANKS

**Banco Popular -** All branches (340) 693-2777
**Bank of St. Croix** - (340) 773-8500 (see display ad page 189)
**First Bank** - 866-811-2700
**Oriental Bank -** (340) 778-5350

Banks ~ Churches  19th Settler's Handbook

### BOWLING
Tropical Ten Pins - (340) 778-3994 (see display ad below)

### CAR RENTALS
Budget Rental Car - (340) 778-9636 (see display ad below)

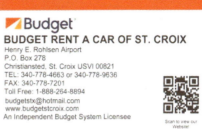

### CHURCHES
St. Croix Reformed Church - (340) 778-0520 (see display ad page 190)

Churches - Distilleries     19th Settler's Handbook

## St. Croix Reformed Church
### St. Croix, U.S. Virgin Islands

On the hill just North of the Kingshill Post Office
Sunday Worship at 9:30 a.m., Sunday School 9:45
Fellowship hour begins at 10:30
The St. Croix Reformed Church is part of the
family of Presbyterian and Reformed Churches.
Reverend Rodney J. Koopmans, Pastor
RR 01 - Box 6125, Kingshill, VI 00850
Telephone/Fax 340-778-0520
Church Website www.stcroixreformed.org

### COMMUNICATION SERVICES
**VIYA** - (340) 777-8492 www.viya.vi (see display ad page 90)

### CONDO RENTALS (SHORT TERM)
Inter-Ocean Views - www.airbnb.com/rooms/4502975
Turquoise Properties - www.airbnb.com/rooms/1762784

### CONSTRUCTION
**Castle Glassworks** - (340) 773-2464 (see display ad below)
**Zefo's Crane Rental** - (340) 277-8246 (see display ad below)

### DISTILLERIES
**Cruzan Rum** - (340) 692-2280 (see display ad page 191)
**Leatherback Brewing Company** - (340) 772-2337

Distilleries - Furniture    19th Settler's Handbook

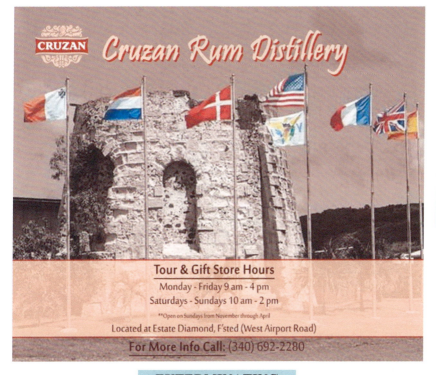

## EXTERMINATING

**Oliver Exterminating** - (340) 773-1630 (see display ad below)

## FINANCIAL SERVICES

**Merrill Lynch -** Walter Szturma (800) 937-0785 (see ad page 192)
**Schaffer Mortgage -** (340) 778-4444 (see display ad page 193)

## FURNITURE

**Ashley Furniture -** (800) 778-6440 (see ad page 185)
**Carlos Furniture -** (340) 778-6566 (see display ad page 193)
**Sweet Lime Furniture -** (340) 719-6360 (see display ad page 193)

# Financial Services

19th Settler's Handbook

## Our goal is to help you pursue yours. It's that simple.

At Merrill, we'll help you get ready for the future with a financial strategy that's just for you.

**Walter C. Szturma, CPFA**
First Vice President
Senior Financial Advisor
516.877.8293
walter_szturma@ml.com

**Merrill Lynch Wealth Management**
1325 Franklin Avenue
Suite 400
Garden City, NY 11530
800.937.0785
www.fa.ml.com/walter_szturma

Merrill Lynch, Pierce, Fenner & Smith Incorporated (also referred to as "MLPF&S" or "Merrill") makes available certain investment products sponsored, managed, distributed or provided by companies that are affiliates of Bank of America Corporation ("BofA Corp."). MLPF&S is a registered broker-dealer, Member SIPC and a wholly owned subsidiary of BofA Corp.

| Investment products | Are Not FDIC Insured | Are Not Bank Guaranteed | May Lose Value |
|---|---|---|---|

The Bull Symbol and Merrill Lynch are trademarks of Bank of America Corporation
© 2019 Bank of America Corporation. All rights reserved. | AR9PDGGT Vault-BA150C | MLWM-244-AD | 470948PM-0519 | 05/2019

Financial - Furniture - Ins     19th Settler's Handbook

**ST. CROIX**

## American Medical Plans of the VI

**Phone:** (340) 773-8658
**Fax:** (888) 977-3119

P.O. Box: 24389
Gallows Bay, C'sted
St. Croix, VI 00824-4389
amp@ampusvi.com

Insurance - Internet    19th Settler's Handbook

## INSURANCE PROVIDERS

**American Medical Plans of the VI** - (340) 773-8658 (see ad page 193)
**Elan Insurance** - (305) 890-1544 (see display ad page 195)
**Inter-Ocean Insurance** - (340) 773-4600 (see ad outside back cover)
**Marshall & Sterling Ins.** - (340) 773-2170/713-1101 (see ad above)
**Tradewinds Title Insurance** - (340) 719-0601 (see ad below)

## Tradewinds Title, LLC

"Serving All of Your Title Insurance Needs"

53A Company St. • Christiansted, VI 00820
Tel: 340 719 0601 • Fax: 340 719 0602

## INTERNET & INTERNET MARKETING

**Broadband VI** - (340) 719-2943 (see display ad page 196)
**Pink Elephant Promotions** - (see display ad page 196)
**VIYA** - (340) 777-8492 www.viya.vi (see display ad page 90)

Insurance     19th Settler's Handbook

**ST. CROIX**

# Looking for the best Group Health Insurance in USVI?
# GO FOR ELAN.

We offer what no other health insurance company in the USVI offers:

- ✓ Pick from a choice of insurance plans
- ✓ The only locally-owned health insurance company in the USVI
- ✓ Voted Best Health Insurance company in the USVI 2018/2019

**Contact Us, today!**
305-890-1544
Sales@elan.insure

**ST. CROIX**

### MORTGAGE SERVICES
**Schaffer Mortgage** - (340) 778-4444 (see display ad page 193)

### REAL ESTATE SERVICES
**Coldwell Banker** -Lorine Williams (340)690-9628 (see display ad pg 198)
**Frazier Premier Properties** - (340) 713-5547 (see display ad page 199)
**Island Life Realty** - (340) 626-6297 (see display ad page 198)
**Lignum Vitae Realty** - (340) 473-8934 (see display ad page 199)
**R&R Realty** - (340) 773-7740 (see display ad page 199)
**REMAX** - (340) 773-1048 (see display ad page 197)
**Team San Martin**- (340) 773-1048 (see display ad page 199)

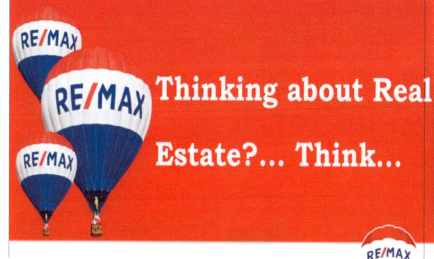

Real Estate 19th SETTLER'S HANDBOOK

## ST. CROIX

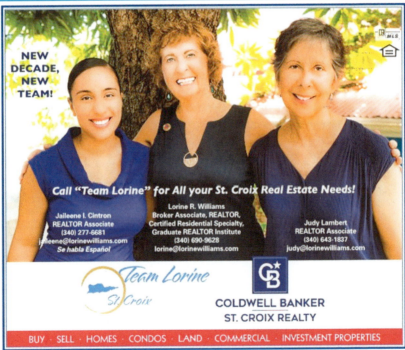

# Real Estate - Sales Land

**19th Settler's Handbook**

## REAL ESTATE APPRAISERS

Caribbean Engineering Associates - (340) 718-1936  fax: 718-3193

## REAL ESTATE HOME INSPECTIONS

St. Croix Home Inspections - (340) 201-4078  stxinspections@gmail.com

## SALES - LAND DEVELOPMENT

Jay-Ro-Mar Development, LLC - (340) 778-8747

Shippers - Surveyors       19th SETTLER'S HANDBOOK

## SHIPPERS, MOVERS & FREIGHT FORWARDERS (cont'd)

Bob Lynch Moving & Storage - (340) 774-5872  (see ad page 205)
Ferrol Trucking - (340) 778-9602
Fleming's Transport - (340) 778-9160 (see ad below)
O'Neale's Transport - (340) 778-1111
Paradise Freight - (340) 773-0033  (see ad inside front cover)
VI Cargo - (340) 778-6331
Water Spirit - (340) 773-0441

### FLEMINGS' TRANSPORT COMPANY, INC.
#### "FIRST IN FREIGHT"
Moving & Packing - Trucking - Air/Ocean Freight
Freight Forwarding - Customs Brokerage - Forklift Rental

Tel 340-778-9160
Fax 340-778-9003

ruby@flemingstransport.com
P.O. Box 4310
Kingshill, St. Croix VI 00851

## SHOPPING MALL / COMMERCIAL RENTAL SPACE

Sunny Isle Developers, LLC - (340) 778-5830 (see ad below)

## SUPERMARKET

Plaza Extra East - (800) 778-6240
Plaza Extra West - (340) 719-1870
Seaside Market & Deli -  (340) 719-9393 (see ad below)

## SURVEYORS - LAND

Survey Services Company - (340) 713-4555  Fax: (340) 692-0998

Shopping ~ Websites        19th Settler's Handbook

**ST. CROIX**

### TELECOMMUNICATIONS
VIYA - (340) 777-8492 www.viya.vi (see display ad page 90)

### TOURS

**Zefo's Limo Services**
(340) 277-8246

### WASTE
**VI Regulated Waste** - (340) 773-9121
**VI Waste Management Authority** - (340) 712-4962

### WEBSITES
**GoToStCroix.Com** - Locally grown, globally known!
**VisitStCroix.Com** - Home of the islands informational websites!

Accountants - Mortgage  19th Settler's Handbook

# Services Directory - St. John

## ACCOUNTANTS/CPA
Travel Tax - (866) 272-7871 (see display ad page 186)

## AIR AMBULANCE
Evac USA - 1-844-464-4277 (see display ad page 203)
SkyMed - • To St. Croix 866-349-1494 • St. Thomas 866-349-1494 (see display ad page 187)

## BANKS
Banco Popular - Cruz Bay (340) 693-2704
First Bank - (340) 776-6881
Merchants Commercial Bank - (340) 776-6881
Oriental Bank - The Marketplace (340) 776-6552

## COMMUNICATION SERVICES
Connections Communications - St. John (340) 776-6922
VIYA - (340) 777-8492 www.viya.vi (see display ad page 90)

## DRUGS/HEALTH
**Chelsea Drug Store**
(340) 776-4888
**Community Health Center**
(340) 693-8900
**Dept of Health**
(340) 776-6400, 779-4195
**Health Care Connection**
(340) 693-7444

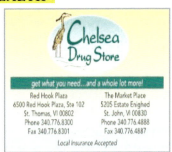

## FINANCIAL SERVICES
Merrill Lynch - Walter Szturma (800) 937-0785 (see ad page 192)

## INSURANCE PROVIDERS
Elan Insurance - (305) 890-1544 (see display ad page 203)
Inter-Ocean Insurance - (340) 773-4600 (see ad outside back cover)

## INTERNET
Broadband VI - (340) 774-5780 (see display ad page 196)
VIYA - (340) 777-8492 www.viya.vi (see display ad page 90)

## MORTGAGE SERVICES
Schaffer Mortgage - (340) 778-4444 (see display ad page 205)

Air Ambulance — 19th Settler's Handbook

# Are you or your family covered for life-threatening medical emergencies?

**ST. JOHN**

If No, get EVAC by Elan Insurance, a low-cost option for individuals & families in the USVI, with benefits like:

- ✓ 24/7 Emergency Air Transport
- ✓ $2M USD in insurance coverage for life-threating events
- ✓ 100% In-patient care coverage

## Get a quote in seconds!
Coverage is Guaranteed!*

**Contact us today:**
1-844.464.4277 | Sales@evac.insure | evac.insure

*90 day waiting period for enrollment

Private Schools - Websites    19th Settler's Handbook

## PRIVATE SCHOOLS
St. John Gifft Hill School - (340) 776-1730 (see display ad page 205)

## REAL ESTATE AGENTS
340 Real Estate -      (340) 690-9628 (see display ad page 205)
Blue Water Realty -   (340) 779-4600 (see display ad page 205)
Hang Your Hammock - (340) 775-1090 (see display ad page 205)
John Foster Real Estate - (340) 775-9000

## SHIPPERS, MOVERS & FREIGHT FORWARDERS
Blue Ocean Transport - (340) 690-1110 (see ad below)
Bob Lynch Moving & Storage - (340) 774-5872   (see ad page 208)
Norma H - 787-723-4114
St. Thomas Cargo - (340) 776-8660  (see ad page 209)
Water Spirit - (340) 773-0441

## SHOPPING
Starfish Market/Starfish Gourmet & Wines - (340) 779-4949
The Marketplace- Estate Enighed, (340) 776-6552

## TELEVISION
VIYA - (340) 777-8492 www.viya.vi (see display ad page 90)

## WASTE
VI Regulated Waste - (340) 643-4471
VI Waste Management Authority - (340) 712-4962

## WEBSITES
GoToStJohn.Com- Locally grown, globally known!
VisitStJohn.Com -Home of the islands informational websites!
VI Now - (340) 227-8121  www.vinow.com

Private School - Real Estate     19th Settler's Handbook

# Gifft Hill School
serves over 160 students from preschool to 12th-grade on our beautiful 14-acre campus on St. John.

Our mission is to educate, challenge, support, and empower students; igniting their passion for learning in preparation for college, careers, and their roles as stewards of our island and global community.

We are committed to academic rigor through experiential learning within a compassionate community, using the enriched environment of St. John as our classroom.

**ENROLLING NOW**

Gifft Hill School
5000 Estate Enighed, PMB # 336
St. John, VI 00830     call: 340-776-1730     e-mail: info@gifthillschool.org     visit: www.gifthillschool.org

## Serving the Virgin Islands for Over 30 Years

**Jackie Marin**, Broker/Owner
340-998-3057
www.JackieMarin.com

**Marsha Maynes**, Broker/Owner
340-690-0243
www.MarshaMaynes.com

4605 Tutu Park Mall
Suite 133, PMB 310
St. Thomas, US Virgin Islands 00802
340-779-4600

**ST. JOHN**

TAMMY DONNELLY
WWW.340REALESTATECO.COM
340REALESTATECO@GMAIL.COM
340-643-6068 / 340-779-4478

**Hang Your Hammock PROPERTIES**
VIRGIN ISLANDS REAL ESTATE
SALES & RENTALS
HRHS&THOMAS, Inc
www.HangYourHammock.com
Ken@HangYourHammock.com

**Kenneth Schulterbrandt**
Broker
340-690-2339
340-775-1090
Fax: 340-775-5206
P.O. Box 600103
St. Thomas, VI 00801

Accountants - Mortgage  19th Settler's Handbook

# Services Directory - St. Thomas

### ACCOUNTANTS/CPA
**Travel Tax** - (866) 272-7871 (see display ad page 186)

### AIR AMBULANCE
**Evac USA** - 1-844-464-4277 (see display ad page 203)
**SkyMed** - • To St. Croix  866-349-1494 • St. Thomas  866-349-1494

### BANKS
**Banco Popular** - All (340)  693-2777  • **First Bank** - (340) 775-7777
**Merchants Commercial Bank** - Tutu Park Mall (340) 779-2265
**Oriental Bank** - (340) 774-0037

### COMMUNICATION SERVICES
**VIYA** - (340) 777-8492 www.viya.vi (see display ad page 90)

### FINANCIAL SERVICES
**Merrill Lynch** - Walter Szturma (800) 937-0785 (see ad page 192)

### HEALTH
**Chelsea Drug Store** – (340) 776-4888 (see display ad page 207)

### INSURANCE PROVIDERS
**Elan Insurance** - (305) 890-1544 (see display ad page 203)
**Inter-Ocean Insurance** - (340) 773-4600 (see ad outside back cover)

### INTERNET
**VIYA** - (340) 777-8492 www.viya.vi (see display ad page 90)

### MORTGAGE SERVICES
**Schaffer Mortgage** - (340) 715-7744 (see display ad below)

## PHARMACY/PHYSICIANS

**Chelsea Drug Store** – (340) 776-4888 (see display ad page below)
**Paramount Medical** - (340) 776-9786 (see display ad page below)

## PRIVATE SCHOOLS

**Antilles School** - (340) 776-1600 x 1701/1702 (see ad inside back cover)

## REAL ESTATE AGENTS

**Blue Water Realty** - (340) 779-4600 (see ad page 205)
**Hang Your Hammock Properties** - (340) 775-1090 (see ad page 205)
**John Foster Real Estate** - (340) 775-9000

## SHIPPERS, MOVERS & FREIGHT FORWARDERS

**Blue Ocean Transport** - (340) 690-1110 (see ad page 204)
**Bob Lynch Moving & Storage** - (340) 774-5872 (see ad page 208)
**St. Thomas Cargo** - (340) 776-8660 (see ad page 209)
**Water Spirit** - (340) 773-0441

## SHOPPING/SUPERMARKET

**Moe's Fresh Market** - (340) 693-1910 (see display ad page 210)
**Plaza Extra** - Tutu Park Mall (340) 775-5646 (see display ad page 210)
**Tutu Park Mall** - Charlotte Amalie (340) 775-4658

## TELEVISION

**VIYA** - (340) 777-8492 www.viya.vi (see display ad page 90)

## WASTE

**VI Regulated Waste** - (340) 643-4471
**VI Waste Management Authority** - (340) 712-4962

## WEBSITES

**GoToStThomas.Com** - Locally grown, globally known!
**VisitStThomas.Com** - Home of the islands informational websites!
**VI Now** - (340) 227-8121 www.vinow.com

# Shippers

**WE MOVE YOU IN SO MANY WAYS.**

**Bob Lynch Moving & Storage**
St. Thomas, VI
340-774-5872

St. Croix, VI
340-778-1813
www.boblynchmovers.com

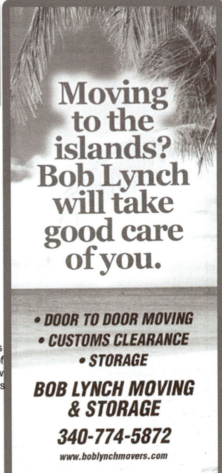

# Moving to the islands? Bob Lynch will take good care of you.

- DOOR TO DOOR MOVING
- CUSTOMS CLEARANCE
- STORAGE

**BOB LYNCH MOVING & STORAGE**
340-774-5872
www.boblynchmovers.com

Moving is one of life's great challenges and moving to a Caribbean island is a new venture for most of us. But is doesn't have to be a hassle if you do your homework and seek out the right company to handle your move.

What you need is a company with years of experience who will take good care of you from your old residence to your new home. You need a company who knows the island, the people, the regulations and systems.

Bob Lynch started his busines in St. Thomas in 1972. Now it's regarded as the "go-to" company to handle your move with professional efficiency, care and concern.

Bob Lynch and his team work with stateside and global professionals and are authorized agents for Allied & North American, United & Mayflower, Atlas & Redball, Belkins Worldwide, Graebel Movers International, Global World Wide and many more. Together they partner to ensure that your move is on schedule from start to final delivery.

They will handle customs clearance, arrange for delivery to the new location, and if necessary, hold your effects in storage. As Bob Lynch promises, "We will take good care of you, we know how to do it and we've been doing it for years."

Just ask the hundreds of satisfied customers.

Shopping 19th Settler's Handbook

# 19th Settler's Handbook

## Services Directory Index

| CATEGORY | Service | Page |
|---|---|---|
| **ACCOUNTANT** | Lil's Bookkeeping | 186 |
| | Theo Broodie | 186 |
| | Travel Tax | 186, 202, 206 |
| **AIR AMBULANCE** | Evac USA | 187, 202, 203, 206 |
| | SkyMed Virgin Islands | 187, 202, 206 |
| **ARCHITECTS** | Design Engineering, LLC | 187 |
| | Steve Crane/Create USVI | 187 |
| **ATTORNEYS** | McChain/Nissman, St. Croix | 188 |
| | Kiture Law Firm | 188 |
| **BANKS** | Banco Popular | 188, 202, 206 |
| | Bank of St. Croix | 188, 202, 206 |
| | First Bank | 188, 202, 206 |
| | Merchants Commercial Bank | 202, 206 |
| | Oriental | 188, 202, 206 |
| **BOWLING** | Tropical Ten Pins | 189 |
| **CAR RENTALS** | Budget Rental Car | 189 |
| **CHURCHES** | St. Croix Reformed Church | 189, 190 |
| **COMMUNICATIONS** | Connections Communications, St. John | 202 |
| | VIYA Communications | 90, 190, 202, 206 |
| **CONDO RENTAL** | Inter-Ocean Views | 190 |
| | Turquoise Properties | 190 |
| **CONSTRUCTION** | Castle Glassworks | 190 |
| | Zefo's Crane Rental | 190 |
| **DISTILLERIES** | Cruzan Rum | 190, 191 |
| | Leatherback Brewing Company | 190 |
| **DRUGS/HEALTH** | Chelsea Drug Store | 202, 206, 207 |
| | Community Health Center | 202 |
| | Department of Health | 202 |
| | Health Care Connection | 202 |
| **EXTERMINATING** | Oliver Exterminating | 191 |
| **FINANCIAL SVCS** | Merrill Lynch | 190, 192, 202 |
| | Schaffer Mortgage | 190, 193 |
| **FURNITURE** | Ashley Furniture Home Store | 185, 191 |
| | Carlos Furniture | 191, 193 |
| | Sweet Lime Furnishings | 191, 193 |
| **GLASS WINDOWS & DOORS** | | |
| | Castle Glassworks | 190 |

## Services Directory Index (continued)

| CATEGORY | Service | Page |
|---|---|---|
| **INSURANCE PROVIDERS** | | |
| | American Medical Plans of the V.I. | 193, 194 |
| | Elan Insurance | 194, 195, 202, 206 |
| | Inter-Ocean Insurance | 194, 202, 206 & Outside Back Cover |
| | Marshall & Sterling | 194 |
| | Tradewinds Title Insurance | 194 |
| **INTERNET SERVICE & INTERNET MARKETING** | | |
| | Broadband VI | 194, 196 |
| | Pink Elephant Promotions | 194, 196 |
| | VIYA Communications | 90, 194, 202, 206 |
| **LAND DEV/SALE** | Jay Ro Mar Development, LLC | 199 |
| **LAND SURVEYORS** | Survey Services Company LLC | 200 |
| **MORTGAGE SVCS** | Schaffer Mortgage | 193, 196, 202, 206 |
| **PHARMACY/PHYSICIANS** | | |
| | Chelsea Drug Store | 202, 206, 207 |
| | Paramount Medical | 207 |
| **PRIVATE SCHOOLS** | | |
| | Antilles School, St Thomas (Inside Back Cover) | 207 |
| | Gifft Hill School, St. John | 204, 205 |
| **REAL ESTATE** | 340 Real Estate | 204, 205 |
| | Blue Water Realty | 204, 207 |
| | Coldwell Bankers/Lorine Williams | 196, 198 |
| | Frazier Premier Properties | 196, 199 |
| | Hang Your Hammock | 204, 207 |
| | Island Life Realty | 196, 198 |
| | John Foster | 207 |
| | Lignum Vitae Realty | 196, 199 |
| | R & R Realty, St. Croix | 196, 199 |
| | ReMax - Gail Bourdon | 196, 197 |
| | Team San Martin | 196, 199 |

19th Settler's Handbook

## Services Directory Index (continued)

| CATEGORY | Service | Page |
|---|---|---|
| **SHIPPERS, MOVERS, FREIGHT FORWARDERS** | | |
| | Blue Ocean Transport | 204, 207 |
| | Bob Lynch Movers | 200, 204, 205, 207, 208 |
| | Ferrol Trucking | 200 |
| | Fleming's Transport Company, Inc. | 200 |
| | Norma H/Formel Shipping | 204 |
| | O'Neale's Transport | 200 |
| | Paradise Freight | (Inside Front Cover) 200 |
| | St. Thomas Cargo | 204, 207, 209 |
| | VI Cargo | 200 |
| | Water Spirit Freight Service | 200, 204, 207 |
| **REAL ESTATE APPRAISERS** | | |
| | Caribbean Engineering Assoc., St. Croix | 199 |
| **REAL ESTATE HOME INSPECTIONS** | | |
| | St. Croix Home Inspections | 199 |
| **SHOPPING MALL/COMMERCIAL RENTAL SPACE** | | |
| | Sunny Isle Developers, LLC | 200 |
| | Tutu Park Mall St. Thomas | 207 |
| **SUPERMARKET** | Marketplace, St. John | 204 |
| | Moe's Fresh Market | 207, 210 |
| | Plaza Extra, Tutu Park Mall, St. Thomas | 207, 210 |
| | Plaza Extra East, St. Croix | 200 |
| | Plaza Extra West, St. Croix | 200, 201 |
| | Seaside Market & Deli | 200 |
| | Starfish Market, St. John | 204 |
| **TELECOMMUNICATIONS/TELEVISION** | | |
| | VIYA | 90, 201, 204, 207 |
| **TOURS** | Zefo's Limo Services | 201 |
| **WASTE MGMT** | VI Waste Regulated Waste | 201, 204, 207 |
| | VI Waste Management Services | 201, 204, 207 |
| **WEBSITES** | GotoStCroix.com | 201 |
| | GotoStJohn.com | 204 |
| | GotoStThomas.com | 207 |
| | VisitStCroix.com | 201 |
| | VisitStJohn.com | 204 |
| | VisitStThomas.com | 207 |
| | VI NOW | 204, 207 |

# 19th Settler's Handbook

## Index by Subject

| | | | |
|---|---|---|---|
| **AGRICULTURE** | 160, 176 | Chamber of Commerce | 114, 170 |
| **AIR SERVICES** | | Charlotte Amalie | 2, 6, 7, 27-31 |
| Air Ambulance | 110, 187 | Charter Boats | 132 |
| Air Transportation | 82-84 | Christiansted | 1, 4, ,5, 6, 15-23 |
| Animal Welfare | 40, 111-115 | Churches/Synagogues | 20, 27, 118 |
| Annual Events | 128 | Cisterns | 12, 54, 93, 94 |
| Architecture | 6, 16, 17, 48, 126 | Climate/Weather | 6, 12, 41, 68, 69, 70 |
| Associations | 31 | Clothing | 63 |
| **AUTOMOBILES** | | Communications | 74 |
| Accidents | 45 | Condominiums | 36, 49 |
| Bringing Your Vehicle | 40 | Cooking | 64-66, 126 |
| Buying | 42 | Culture | 119 |
| Insurance | 42 | Dentists | 111 |
| Driver's License | 44, 45 | Diving | 135 |
| Titles | 42 | Drinks | 66, 67 |
| Vehicle Registration | 42, 43 | Duty Free | 21, 39, 156 |
| **BANKS** | 72-74 | Education | 99 |
| Banking & Insurance | 173 | Electricity | 91-93 |
| Mortgages | 55 | Water | 93-95 |
| Beaches | 139, 140 | Emergency #'s | 42, 54, 177, 182 |
| Birds | 112, 151 | Employment | 158-161 |
| Boating | 131 | Entertainment & Arts | 122 |
| Books | 125 | **FEDERAL GOVERNMENT** | |
| Botanical Gardens | 20 | U.S. Dept. of Agriculture | 163 |
| Buck Island National Park, | | District Court | 175, 176 |
| St. Croix | 15, 16, 60, 137, 138 | Dept. of Defense | 177 |
| Building Codes – VI | 5, 15, 51 | FBI | 178 |
| Building / Remodeling | 51 | General Services Admin. | 178 |
| Buses | 87 | Homeland Security | 178 |
| **BUSINESS** | | Immigration | 178 |
| Associations - All | 31, 114-117 | Health & Human Svc. | 179 |
| Offshore Companies | 161 | Justice | 179 |
| Property Taxes | 49, 56 | National Park Service | 180 |
| Taxes | 168 | Small Business Admin. | 182 |
| Services Directory | 184 | VI Delegate to Congress | 177 |
| Cable TV | 74 | US Postal Service | 38, 78, 79 |
| Cancer Center | 109 | Ferry Service | 85 |
| Cariso / Calypso | 119 | Film Industry | 163 |
| Carnivals | 120 | Fire Services | 178 |
| Cellular Phones | 77 | Fish Poisoning | 66 |
| | | Fire Arms | 16, 40, 148, 176 |

# 19th Settler's Handbook

## Index by Subject (continued)

| | | | | |
|---|---|---|---|---|
| Fishing | 16, 137 | | **INDUSTRY** | |
| Folk Arts | 119 | | Economic Development | |
| Folklife Festive (Carnival) | 121 | | Authority | 154, 159 |
| Frederiksted | 20 | | Offshore Companies | 153-161 |
| Furniture | 23, 39, 57 | | Insects | 61 |
| Gardening | 59 | | **INSURANCE** | |
| Hazardous Plants | 60 | | Automobile | 42 |
| Do-It-Yourselfers | 39, 52 | | Business | 167 |
| Geography | 1 | | Life & Health | 110 |
| Geology | 3 | | Property | 56 |
| Golf | 19, 142 | | Island Center for the Arts, | |
| Health Facilities | 105 | | St. Croix | 122 |
| **HOVENSA** | 9, 148 | | Labor/ Business Assoc | 170 |
| Hiking | 143 | | Landscaping | 47, 49, 53, 59, 60 |
| **HISTORY** | | | Libraries | 104 |
|   Columbus | 3 | | Locations | 1 |
|   Danish Era | 6 | | **MAPS** | |
|   U.S. Purchase | 7 | | Caribbean | vi, 218 |
| Holidays | 124 | | Marinas | 19, 133 |
| **HOME - CONDO - APT** | | | Marine Charts | 133 |
|   Architecture - Local | 48 | | Marine Industry | 162 |
|   Buying | 49 | | Mocko Jumbies | 120 |
|   Building | 51-54 | | Mortgages | 55 |
|   Carpeting | 57 | | **MOVERS / SHIPPING** | |
|   Construction | 53 | | Animals, Car | 40-42 |
|   Decor | 57 | | Household | 40-42 |
|   Financing | 55 | | Packing | 40-42 |
|   Furniture | 50, 56 | | **MUSEUMS** | |
|   Home Historical? | 50 | | Annaberg Est. Plantation, | |
|   Homesite | 51 | | St. John | 24 |
|   Maintenance | 58 | | Estate Whim Plantation, | |
|   Moving | 32-40 | | St. Croix | 18 |
|   Renting | 48 | | Fort Christian, St. Thomas | |
|   Property Insurance/Taxes | 56 | | | 27 |
|   Roof/Water Systems | 53 | | Fort Christiansvaern, | |
|   Security | 54 | | St. Croix | 16 |
| Horse Racing | 148 | | Fort Frederik, St. Croix | 20 |
| Hospitals | 105-110 | | National Guard | 180 |
| Hunting | 148 | | Sprauve Library, St. John | 105 |
| Hurricanes, Flood, Quake | 69-71 | | National Parks | 180 |
| Business/Income Taxes | 168, 171 | | Newspapers & Magazines | 124 |
| | | | Olympics | 145 |
| | | | Organic Act | 153, 171 |
| | | | Parks & Recreation | 182 |

# 19th Settler's Handbook
## Index by Subject (continued)

| | | | |
|---|---|---|---|
| Pets | 111 | Other Taxes | 168-171 |
| Physicians | 111 | Taxis/Bus | 88, 89 |
| Police | 181 | Telegrams | 81 |
| Population | 13 | Telephones | 75 |
| Public Transportation | 87 | Television | 75 |
| Radio | 77 | Tennis | 144 |
| **REAL ESTATE** (See HOMES) | | **TOURISM** | |
| Religion/Spirituality | 118 | Industry | 154 |
| **RENTALS** (See HOMES) | | Information Centers | 184 |
| Research & Tech Park | 103 | Publications | 124 |
| Rum Industry | 11, 17 | Traffic Hints | 46 |
| **ST. CROIX** | | U.S. Coast Guard | 176 |
|    Hotels | 16 | U.S. Customs | 183 |
|    Places to Visit | 15-21 | U.S. Postal | 78 |
|    Restaurants | 16, 21 | Vehicle Registration | 42 |
|    Schools | 99-102 | Veterinarians | 111-114 |
|    Shopping | 21, 23 | **V.I. GOVERNMENT** | |
|    University of the V.I. | 102 |    Admin Offices | 174, 177 |
| **ST. JOHN** | |    Board of Elections | 172 |
|    Hotels/Guest Houses | 23-26 |    Executive Branch | 173 |
|    Places to Visit | 23-26 |    Governor | 173 |
|    Restaurants | 23-26 |    Lt. Governor | 173 |
|    Schools | 101 |    Cadastral | 174 |
| **ST. THOMAS** | |    Coastal Zone Mgmt | 177 |
|    Hotels | 27-31 |    Council for the Arts | 176 |
|    Places to Visit | 27-31 |    Education | 177 |
|    Reichhold Ctr for the Arts | 122 |    Finance | 174 |
|    Restaurants | 27-31 |    Fish & Wildlife | 178 |
|    Shopping | 27-31 |    Health Dept. | 178 |
|    Schools | 99-102 |    Housing Authority | 178 |
| Shell Collecting | 141 |    Human Services | 178 |
| Snorkeling | 141 |    Justice, Courts, Tickets | 175 |
| Social Security | 166 |    Labor & Statistics | 153, 176 |
| Sports | 142-148 |    Licensing / Consumer Affairs | 168, 176 |
| Sports Associations | 149 |    Management / Budget | 176 |
| Sports Facilities - Gov't | 147 |    Medicare/Health Ins | 174 |
| Streets / Roads | 81 |    Motor Vehicles | 42-45, 182 |
| Swimming | 139 |    National Parks | 181 |
| University of the V.I. | 102 |    Personnel | 182 |
| **WATER ISLAND** | 36 |    Planning & Natural Resources | 182 |
| **TAXES** | | | |
| Employer Responsibilities | 166 |    Port Authority | 183 |
| Income Tax | 171 |    Property & Procurement | 183 |

# Index by Subject (continued)

**V.I. GOVERNMENT** (cont'd)
- Public Services Comm — 182
- Public Works — 181
- Recorder of Deeds — 174
- Small Business Admin — 182
- Small Business Dev Ctr — 182
- Social Security — 172
- Sports, Parks & Rec — 182
- Tax Assessor — 172
- V.I. Energy Office — 177
- VI Territorial Emergency Mgmt (VITEMA) — 182
- VI Dept of Tourism — 183
- Waste Management Authority (V.I.W.M.A.) — 95
- Water & Power (WAPA) — 91, 183
- Legislative Branch — 174
- Judicial Branch — 175

Voting — 172
Water Conservation — 51-54
Water Island — 36
Weather & Disaster Preparedness — 70

# 19th Settler's Handbook